ADVANCE PRAISE FOR

The Authority to Imagine

"The scholarly and practical imagination is likely the most valuable tool of educational researchers, and of educators generally. Garman, Piantanida, and colleagues offer ideas, inspiration, courage, and illustrations for aspiring educational researchers to write innovative, interpretive representations of educational experience. We need more dissertations that explore diverse ways of knowing and modes of expressing insights about education. I commend the authors of this book for showing how to do just that."

William H. Schubert, Professor of Education and Chair of Curriculum and Instruction, University of Illinois at Chicago

"Researchers seeking to gain expertise in this narrative interpretative approach may find, in reading these joyful accounts of collaborative search, discovery, and creation, an encouraging—even empowering—invitation to address their own research questions with similar concerns and energy, and, in turn, craft their own individual text in dialogue with critical readers on the way. This is an elegant and literary gold mine of narrative information for educational researchers, faculty, and students seeking real engagement with interpretative hermeneutic approaches to educational research."

Peter Willis, Senior Lecturer, Division of Education, Arts and Social Sciences, School of Education, University of South Australia

The Authority to Imagine

COMPLICATED CONVERSATION

A Book Series of Curriculum Studies

William F. Pinar
General Editor

VOLUME 11

PETER LANG
New York • Washington, D.C./Baltimore • Bern
Frankfurt am Main • Berlin • Brussels • Vienna • Oxford

The Authority to Imagine

The Struggle toward Representation in Dissertation Writing

Noreen B. Garman & Maria Piantanida, EDITORS

PETER LANG
New York • Washington, D.C./Baltimore • Bern
Frankfurt am Main • Berlin • Brussels • Vienna • Oxford

Library of Congress Cataloging-in-Publication Data

The authority to imagine: the struggle toward representation
in dissertation writing / edited by Noreen B. Garman, Maria Piantanida.
p. cm. — (Complicated conversation: a book series of curriculum studies; v. 11)
Includes bibliographical references and index.
1. Dissertations, Academic—Authorship. 2. Qualitative research.
I. Garman, Noreen B. II. Piantanida, Maria.
III. Series: Complicated conversation; v. 11.
LB2369.A885   808'.042—dc22   2004022763
ISBN 0-8204-7454-1
ISSN 1534-2816

Bibliographic information published by **Die Deutsche Bibliothek**.
Die Deutsche Bibliothek lists this publication in the "Deutsche
Nationalbibliografie"; detailed bibliographic data is available
on the Internet at http://dnb.ddb.de/.

Cover design by Lisa Barfield
Cover photo by TR Garman

The patchwork quilt, dated 1887, hangs on the wall directly behind the study group table
referred to in the book. Over the years the image has served to remind the writers
about how the imagination of women, stitched together in random, asymmetrical patterns,
has made a unique representation. Quilting represents a way in which women come together
to share their art, not unlike the authors of the book.

The paper in this book meets the guidelines for permanence and durability
of the Committee on Production Guidelines for Book Longevity
of the Council of Library Resources.

© 2006 Peter Lang Publishing, Inc., New York
29 Broadway, New York, NY 10006
www.peterlang.com

All rights reserved.
Reprint or reproduction, even partially, in all forms such as microfilm,
xerography, microfiche, microcard, and offset strictly prohibited.

Printed in the United States of America

Contents

Foreword. A Reaching Out for Meanings   vii
    Janet L. Miller
Preface   xvii
    Maria Piantanida and Noreen B. Garman

Chapter 1. Imagining an Interpretive Dissertation: Voice, Text, and Representation   1
    Noreen B. Garman

Part 1: Claiming a Stance for Self within Conflicting and Contentious Discourses

Chapter 2. Pictures in My Mind: Viewing Images of Dissertation Authorities through Process Drama and Narrative Inquiry   19
    Lynn Altman Richards
Chapter 3. Problematizing Educational Inclusion through Heuristic Inquiry   35
    Micheline Stabile
Chapter 4. Confronting Authority and *Self*: Social Cartography and Curriculum Theorizing for Uncertain Times   49
    JoVictoria Nicholson-Goodman

Part 2: Claiming a Language of Practice through the Logics of Inquiry

Chapter 5. A Search for Balance: Representing a Narrative Pedagogy   67
    Pamela Krakowski
Chapter 6. Reimagining Grounded Theory: Moving toward an Interpretive Stance   81
    Robin E. Grubs

Chapter 7. Embracing a Language of Spiritual Inquiry 97
    Marilyn Llewellyn

Part 3: Claiming a Way of Being in Practice through Inquiry

Chapter 8. Coming to Know through the Text of Talk: From Interviews to Inner Views Storied to Interpretation 113
    Kathleen M. Ceroni
Chapter 9. Imagining Reflective Artmaking: Claiming Self as Artist-Teacher-Researcher 127
    Wendy M. Milne
Chapter 10. Imagining in the Forest Dark: The Journey of an Epistemorph in the Land of Ologies 139
    Cynthia A. Tananis

Part 4: Claiming Self as Writer

Chapter 11. Writing Essays: Minding the Personal and Theoretic 155
    Marjorie Barrett Logsdon
Chapter 12. Speculations on the Personal Essay as a Mode of Curriculum Inquiry 167
    Maria Piantanida
Chapter 13. Narrative Yearnings: Reflecting in Time through the Art of Fictive Story 183
    Patricia L. McMahon

Afterword: Envisioning Complicated Conversation at the Table 201
    Maria Piantanida and Noreen B. Garman
Contributors 209
Index 211

Foreword: A Reaching Out for Meanings

Janet L. Miller

> We are interested in openings, in unexplored possibilities, not in the predictable or the quantifiable. . . . For us, education signifies an initiation into new ways of seeing, hearing, feeling, moving. It signifies the nurture of a special kind of reflectiveness and expressiveness, a reaching out for meanings, a learning to learn.
> Greene, *Variations on a Blue Guitar*, 2001, 7

To engage in any one kind of work for twenty-five consecutive years is a major achievement. But the shared intellectual labor of Noreen Garman and Maria Piantanida over twenty-five years has required not only a vast commitment of time but also exceptional vision, openness to new forms and versions of knowledge, and an exacting, passionate dedication. The collected essays in this book testify to the foresight and wide-ranging influence of these scholars' convictions about the generative effects of long-term collaborative deliberations and inquiries. The focus of their deliberations and inquiries—the challenges of qualitative dissertation research and representation—has remained constant throughout the remarkable twenty-five years that Noreen and Maria have met with graduate students in what is now known as the Dissertation/Writing Study Group.

All the authors in this collection have been members of this group that still gathers around Noreen's dining room table, and some continue as active participants well beyond the completion of their doctoral degrees. The theoretical and methodological connections among group members are evident in each chapter, even as authors' topics of inquiry differ. The emotional and intellectual ties among these authors, forged through a collaborative "reaching out for meanings," should inspire all doctoral students and faculty mentors who read this book to consider the possibilities—and meanings—that might be constructed in and through interactive and sustained deliberations among a group devoted to serious consideration of complexities associated with qualitative dissertation research and its representations.

The far-reaching benefits of such deliberations are evident in each of the chapters contained in this book. Because the authors all have participated in the study group across a range of years and dissertation topics, their writing reveals multiple and complex ways in which their group studies and relationships informed the conceptualizing and the writing of their dissertations. Moreover, each author gestures toward ways in which her involvement in the study group's discussions—whether completed or on-going—continues to enlighten her current work.

In particular, then, I want to call attention to the remarkable vision that the study group and this collection signify. Noreen Garman knew early on that students who wished to conduct qualitative dissertation research would need spaces where they could air their doubts, frustrations, and questions. For, in 1980, many of those in the American educational research community who maintained positivist and post-positivist worldviews regarded qualitative inquiry not only as fringe, but also as suspect. So Noreen knew, too, that in order for students to develop what Noreen and Maria support as a "self-conscious understanding of method" and to experiment with new forms of data representation, those forged spaces would have to be ones where they could engage with one another in "learning to learn."

Maria Piantanida was one of the five students who first answered Noreen's invitation to create such spaces. Along with the other originating members of the Dissertation/Writing Study Group, she attended meetings, not at Noreen's faculty office at the University of Pittsburgh, but rather at Noreen's dining table at home. Even in that unthreatening space, Maria knew that envisioning and writing her dissertation as a book would require the group's persistent attention and support. She knew, too, that group members also had to believe in possibilities of knowing and representing in ways that were considered, at that particular historical moment in American educational research, "alternative," at best.

I would argue that inquiries into complexities of qualitative research and writing conducted by Noreen, Maria, and numerous subsequent members of the group that Noreen founded in 1980 helped move qualitative research out of a lesser status that the term "alternative" often implies, and into the mainstream of American educational research. Indeed, the study group contributed to the still growing prominence of qualitative research in education (despite current "official" decrees about "what counts" as research) because the group itself enacts forms of "education" in ways Maxine Greene (2001) intends. The study group and its members' deliberations initially signified "an initiation into new ways of seeing, hearing, feeling, moving" (7) in dissertation research and writing. For twenty-five years now, group meetings have provided literal and figurative space for qualitative inquiry participation that requires a "special kind of reflectiveness and expressiveness" and a conceptualization of education and its inquiries as "a reaching out for meanings" (7)—meanings constructed, in this case, in and through the very processes of research.

Indeed, most qualitative researchers today must pursue, depict, and then question why and how they have constructed multiple meanings within their studies. Such an imperative derives from the now well-known "crisis of representation" wherein qualitative researchers had to acknowledge that they did *not* directly "capture" lived experience, but rather re-created that experience through the writing of a social text (Clifford 1988; Denzin and Lincoln 2000; Geertz 1988; Marcus and Fischer 1986). Grappling with this representational crisis necessarily involves attention to ethical, political, epistemological, and methodological issues that frame and influence all researchers' relationships to and portrayals of their participants and their constructions of meaning.

Members of the study group have supported as well as challenged one another by engaging in a special kind of reflectiveness that such issues demand. That reflectiveness involves what Noreen and Maria describe in their Preface as *the struggle* "toward representation of form, meaning, and way of knowing [that] is the essence of interpretive dissertation inquiry." That always in-process struggle has compelled these authors *not* to "reach out for meanings" as if those meanings were "out there," just waiting to be discovered, but rather *to question* how, for what purposes, in what forms, and by whom those meanings might and should get constructed and re-constructed in dissertation research and writing.

This collection, then, portrays various study group members' grapplings with questions of research method, with constructions of self as viable researcher, writer, and practitioner, and with forms and politics of representation in their own dissertation work. Read together, the essays in this collection also testify to the interwoven and far-reaching effects of their authors' recursive and elongated collaborative discussions and deliberations. Across a span of years and participants, Noreen and Maria have created a unique version of qualitative research and education as a "special kind of reflectiveness and expressiveness" within the context of a research and writing group devoted to constant examination of assumptions about qualitative inquiry as well as to a continuous "reaching out for meanings" that are constructed in the very act of mutual deliberation.

The chapters in this book thus do not stand in isolation from one another; each influences, frames, supports, and challenges the others through the very reiterative processes in which the authors have been engaged. For example, the contributors—who represent several generations of study group members and who work within an interpretive tradition of inquiry—articulate their research method as means by which to create an epistemologically rigorous and convincing portrayal of research data. Influenced by Smith and Heshusius (1986), they conceptualize the meaning of method not only as technique for managing data but also as logic of justification. This understanding of method reflects each researcher's rationale for why and how the truth-claims of her inquiry were generated and supported. Contributors also make connections among form, meaning, and ways of knowing through discussion of their choice of research genre(s) as well as their struggles toward what Noreen and Maria call "creative expression within the conventions of a particular form of inquiry."

So, here, as in other qualitative research edited collections, readers will find examples of various forms of inquiry, including case study, narrative, heuristic, grounded theory, personal essay and arts-based research, for example. But several features mark this book as unique. This collection vividly demonstrates for qualitative dissertation researchers/writers and faculty mentors the evocative, generative, and reciprocal benefits of participating in a dissertation writing/study group. Further, although not all chapters explore directly the notion of "blurred genres" in ways that Geertz suggested (1983, 1988), they do present self-reflexive analyses of each author's struggles within her chosen research genre to gain "the authority to imagine" herself creating a rigorous and provocative text. It is this direct attention to the difficulties most doctoral students face as they attempt to conceptualize themselves as researchers and scholarly writers that makes this collection so valuable to both novice and experienced qualitative researchers. And especially for those who consider themselves scholarly practitioners—or wish to develop "the authority to imagine" themselves as such—this collection provides thoughtful and detailed support for their particular commitments.

Foreword

Thus, each chapter in this collection may be read as offering both individually and collectively generated insights into the struggle to produce, represent, and justify particular "research knowledge" in a dissertation. The struggles detailed in each chapter also illuminate the importance and complexities of reflexivity in the research process. I believe that the collection as a whole illustrates that "reflexivity has to be both collective and contested because of the limits of individual visions and experiences. At least as an intention, reflexivity opens up possibilities for negotiation over what knowledge claims are made, for whom, why and within what frame of reference" (Ramazanoglu with Holland 2002, 119).

In broad terms, then, the essays here offer varied approaches to—and sometimes contested positions on—the multifaceted but necessary processes of reflexivity as one means of grappling with dilemmas of both participant and researcher representation. And the authors exemplify, through their interconnectedness, a collective emphasis on reflexivity—a "special kind of reflectiveness," if you will—as a way of analyzing overt motives and intentions as well as gaps, blind spots, and silences within their individual and joint negotiations over knowledge claims.

Olesen (2000) calls for such "unremitting reflexivity" (236) and at the same time notes:

> Kamela Visweswaran . . . makes a useful distinction between reflexive ethnography which questions its own authority, confronts the researcher's processes of interpretation, and emphasizes how the researcher thinks she knows, and deconstructive ethnography, which abandons authority, confronts power in the interpretive process, and emphasizes how we think we know what we know is not innocent. (240)

These distinctions gesture toward theoretical positions that differently conceptualize purposes, forms, and processes of self-reflexive work within qualitative research. As a qualitative researcher and dissertation mentor myself, what is most provocative to me is Britzman's (1995) charge to those of us attempting to work toward versions of "deconstructive ethnography":

> [E]thnographic narratives should trace how power circulates and surprises, theorize how subjects spring from the discourses that incite them, and question the belief in representation even as one must practice representation as a way to intervene critically in the constitutive constraints of discourses. (236)

The title of this book—*The Authority to Imagine*—threads as a reflexive theme through each of these selections and represents major aspects of the collective work and long-term negotiations of the study group. But further, I think that the phrase itself—*the authority to imagine*—serves not just as a goal for both authors and readers of this collection but also as a representation of how subjects—here, these particular authors—"spring from the discourses that incite them." What have been, what continue to be the constitutive constraints of academic research discourses for these authors? Might their collective and individual reflexive analyses of their dissertation research and representational practices have become one means of attempting to claim "the authority to imagine" as a way to intervene in those discourses and to re-position themselves as subjects with agency? Or should the concept and enactment of "authority" be something to abandon entirely as one confronts power and its circulations and surprises in the interpretive process?

I raise these questions because, for me, the title phrase of this collection indeed functions as laudable goal as well as sobering indicator of still-present constitutive constraints of particular academic research discourses in American institutions. Historically, those discourses have ignored how class, race, gender, and ethnicity, for example, have shaped the processes of inquiry and power circulations as well as representations of those processes. "The authority to imagine," as both goal and indicator, requests by implication not only that we consider the many different ways of writing the subject in research representations, for example, but also that we attempt to envision multiple subjectivities. The phrase further encourages us to imagine multiply determined subjectivities that are never unitary and complete, never able to simply escape the mediations of discourse, always located in particular times and places and yet occupying differing and often shifting positions in terms of gender, race, ethnicity, and sexuality, which "one cannot easily sever, separate out, or subsume under one another" (Smith and Watson 1992, xiv).

And so I wonder to what extent have ascribed and reified conceptions of gender, for example, played a part in the felt need for construction and maintenance of the study group over the years as well as in the development of this collection's major theme—*the authority to imagine*? In what ways might conceptions and experiences of women's voices as historically, socially and culturally "silenced," especially in college and university research contexts, have contributed to these authors' difficulties in claiming "the authority to imagine" themselves as researchers and writers whose dissertation work is viewed as "a contribution" that is "trustworthy"? Embedded within that question is another: how might these women researchers indicate that their research claims are "less false, less perverse, and less partial without falling back into positivist standards that measure acceptability of knowledge in terms of some ideal, unchanging body of knowledge" (Olesen 2000, 236)? How might these contributors examine such historically gendered constructions of "knowledge" and gendered enactments of "authority" within the contexts of the conundrum posed by Denzin and Lincoln (2000): "How can the researcher speak with authority in an age when there are no longer any firm rules concerning the text, including the author's place in it, its standards of evaluation, and its subject matter" (15)?

And in what ways might we who are committed to qualitative inquiry investigate such questions *without* conceptualizing these contributors from the study group as unified subjectivities easily located (and thus often dismissed) within essentialized categories of "woman" or "qualitative researcher" or "collaborator"?

Certainly, study group participants have engaged in collective deliberations that have challenged their conceptions of themselves as teachers, researchers, and scholars as well as their conceptions of themselves as gendered, raced, and classed human beings, for example. Indeed, because these authors' efforts are located within interpretive epistemologies, they necessarily acknowledge that their interactions have shaped one another as well as one another's scholarly work. I believe, in fact, that because those interactive and long-term deliberations characterize the interactions of the Dissertation/Writing Study Group, there is *no* chance that any participant feels as though she "knows already what she is, who exits the conversation the same as when she entered, who fails to put her own epistemological certainties at risk in the encounter with the other, and so stays in place, guards her place" (Butler 2001, 86).

But to what extent is the desire to claim *the authority to imagine* still an indication of research identities and research processes that have been produced and reiterated, for example, through gendered cultural norms taken to be fixed and permanent and thus regulatory, rather than provisional and unstable and thus able to be changed (Butler, 1993)?

I can imagine myself bringing a chair to the group at Noreen's dining table in order to discuss these questions and other responses evoked by the essays in this book. In raising such questions, I am certain that I would be welcomed into the group's deliberations, for I am involving myself in "a reaching out for meanings"—meanings that get constructed differently across varying theoretical frameworks and commitments. By asking questions as one means of engaging in the complex and intertwined work represented in this volume, I hope to honor the study group's contributions over the past twenty-five years and to highlight their conceptualization of educational processes and research as a "special kind of reflectiveness," open to multiple questions, challenges, and interpretations.

Ultimately, as a reader, a qualitative researcher and teacher, and a feminist scholar committed to collaborative forms of inquiry in education, I applaud not only the collective longevity of the Dissertation/Writing Study Group but also the conceptual, procedural, and methodological insights that its members offer here to all those who wish to conduct or mentor qualitative dissertation studies. This collection indeed signifies a remarkable achievement. It encourages both doctoral students and faculty members to constantly question what and how it means to do qualitative research and dissertation writing in a time when such work again is coming under scrutiny from those who demand certainty through "the predictable or the quantifiable." Most importantly, the authors of essays in this collection help us, in vivid and contextualized ways, to realize that somehow, in "a reaching out for meanings," there "is no end to it, that there is always more to see, to learn, to feel" (Greene 2001, 206).

References

Britzman, D. P. 1995. 'The question of belief': Writing poststructural ethnography. *Qualitative studies in education,* 8, no. 3: 229–38.

Butler, J. 1993. *Bodies that matter: On the discursive limits of "sex."* New York: Routledge.

———. 2001. Transformative encounters. In *Women and social transformation*, 81–98. Eds. E. Beck-Gernsheim, J. Butler, and L. Puigvert, New York: Peter Lang Publishing.

Clifford, J. 1988. *The predicament of culture: Twentieth-century ethnography, literature, and art.* Cambridge, MA: Harvard University Press.

Denzin, N. K., and Y. S. Lincoln, eds., 2000. *Handbook of qualitative research.* 2nd ed. Thousand Oaks, CA: Sage.

Geertz, C. 1983. *Local knowledge: Further essays in interpretive anthropology.* New York: Basic Books.

———.1988. *Works and lives: The anthropologist as author.* Stanford, CA: Stanford University Press.

Greene, M. 2001. *Variations on a blue guitar: The Lincoln Center Institute lectures on aesthetic education.* New York: Teachers College Press.

Marcus, G. E., and M. M. J. Fischer. 1986. *Anthropology as cultural critique: An experimental moment in the human sciences.* Chicago: University of Chicago Press.

Olesen, V. L. 2000. Feminisms and qualitative research at and into the millennium. In N. K. Denzin and Y. S. Lincoln, eds., *Handbook of qualitative research, 2nd edition,* 215–55. Thousand Oaks, CA: Sage.

Ramazanoglu, C. with J. Holland. 2002. *Feminist methodology: Challenges and choices.* Thousand Oaks, CA: Sage.

Smith, J. K., and L. Heshusius. 1986. Closing down the conversation: The end of the quantitative-qualitative debate among educational inquirers. *Educational Researcher* 15, no. 1: 4–12.

Smith, S., and J. Watson, eds. 1992. *De/colonizing the subject: The politics of gender in women's autobiography.* Minneapolis: University of Minnesota Press.

Preface

Maria Piantanida and Noreen B. Garman

Since the mid-1970s, a rich and robust discourse has evolved about the nature of legitimate research in education. Sometimes contentious, sometimes conciliatory, always evocative, this discourse has complicated conversations about the meanings of "qualitative research" and raised concerns about preparing a new generation of scholars (see, for example, Young 2001). In recommending strategies for preparing doctoral students in a time of epistemological diversity, Pallas (2001) advises, "Link discussions of epistemology to the practice of educational research," further noting, "This is particularly important for doctoral students destined for careers as educational researchers" (9). We (the editors and contributing authors of this book) wholeheartedly subscribe to Pallas's advice on linking the research of learning with its practice. We do not, however, accept the premise that understanding epistemological diversity need be the concern primarily of those preparing for careers in educational research. Rather, from our perspective as a community of academics and practitioners, we contend that understanding epistemology (as well as ontology and axiology) lies at the heart of both learning about and conducting educational research. In this regard, we resonate with Kilbourn's contention that:

> A doctoral thesis should demonstrate *self-conscious method*. It should betray the author's sensitivity to concerns of epistemology, to concerns about the connection between method and meaning. . . . The author should explicitly demonstrate an awareness of his or her role as a writer with a biography. The author should, in some way, make clear her or his sensitivity to the conceptual and methodological moves made during the conduct of the study and in the presentation of the study as a read-

able document. The author should show an awareness of the bearing of those moves on the overall integrity of the work, should be able to give *good reason* for making them. (Kilbourn 1999, 28, [italics in original])

The capacity to "demonstrate self-conscious method" does not come easily, nor in our experience, does it come in advance of conceptualizing and conducting a study. Elsewhere (Piantanida and Garman 1999), we have argued that this capacity evolves iteratively through cycles of deliberation as students move from early inklings of a study topic to a completed dissertation. This book speaks to the challenges that contributing authors faced as they engaged in this journey toward a self-conscious understanding of method.

We characterize this challenge as a struggle, but not in the sense of a contest or battle between self and others. Rather, the challenge lies in grappling with one's own preconceptions and assumptions about what counts as legitimate dissertation research. A willingness to enter into that struggle, in our collective experience, creates new possibilities for imagining one's self as dissertation author and as scholar.

Although this struggle occurs within individuals, it does not have to occur in isolation. Indeed, the editors and authors in this book are members of a dissertation/writing study group that offers a deliberative space for understanding what it means to ground one's dissertation within the context of professional practice. Newcomers to the group have found it helpful to hear the experiences of others who have engaged in the struggle and have successfully completed the dissertation process. Writing for this book has allowed us to distill some of our "lessons learned" for those outside our group and to share those lessons in a way that conveys a flavor of the complicated conversations[1] that comprise our study group's deliberations.

Complicated conversations have no beginnings or endings. Defining moments may appear to mark the start of a conversation, but even then, tendrils of thought twine into other conversations, past and current. Similarly, discursive exchanges continually open onto new horizons of conversational possibility. On occasion, however, a pause may occur, allowing participants to reflect on what has been said and what has been learned. Such quiet spaces afford opportunities for newcomers to enter a conversation.

This book represents a pause in a complicated conversation that coalesced in 1980 and has taken many twists and turns in the subsequent twenty-five years. The conversation began when five of Noreen Garman's advisees reached the dissertation phase of their doctoral work. Prompted by dissatisfaction with her own dissertation, Noreen extended an invitation, "Would you be interested in studying alternative methods for doing your dissertation? I did a traditional, quantitative study, and it wasn't very good," she explained to the five students gathered attentively around her dining room table.[2] "In fact," she admitted, "I was so embarrassed that I wanted to bind it on all four sides before it went to the library. I consoled myself with the thought that no one reads dissertations anyway. I was absolutely mortified when a few years later I started to see references to my dissertation in the literature on clinical supervision." Noreen's determination that her students would have an opportunity to do studies congruent with who they are as practitioners and scholars led to the formation of a dissertation study group devoted to conversations about methodological issues in dissertation research.

Maria Piantanida was one of the five students in the original study group. A practitioner at heart, Maria wanted to write a dissertation that would speak to her colleagues in the nascent field of hospital-based education. After two years of study and writing, she imagined her dissertation as a book. Today, that seems like such an innocuous departure from the traditional five-chapter dissertation format that had been privileged in our school of education at the time. Then, however, a major portion of her defense was devoted to a debate with one faculty member who kept insisting, "But a dissertation is a dissertation. It is not a book." In the end, the faculty member accepted the "dissertation as book" format, but the conversation had engendered questions that we would revisit for years to come. What makes a dissertation a dissertation? What is the rationale for imagining new dissertation formats? What authorial leeway, indeed responsibility, do doctoral candidates have in crafting their thinking into scholarly documents?

Gradually, almost imperceptibly, the five original study group members and the others who came to join them pushed the boundaries of what we could imagine as dissertation research.[3] Patricia Holland (1983) infused ideas from phenomenology and hermeneutics into the conversation. Susan Poe Goodwin's (1983) work pushed us to explore differences between description, explanation, and explication as modes of inquiry. Joan Leukhardt's (1983) use of literary figures as a heuristic ultimately led us to consider the difference between portraying results of an inquiry as contrasted to reporting findings. Barbara Knapp-Minick (1984) posed the concept of data accumulation as a counterpoint to the taken-for-granted notion of data collection. Her concept of "incredible tales" foreshadowed the interest in narrative and teacher stories that would blossom a few years after she completed her study. Helen Hazi (1980) and Kathryn Sanida (1987) used caches of legal documents as the data for their studies, helping us see beyond the simplistic notion that qualitative research equals fieldwork observations or interviewing.

The significance of these small imaginings came home to us one muggy summer evening when we hosted a gathering of first-generation study group members who had moved on after completing their dissertations and a new generation of study group members still in the throes of their dissertations. After hearing about the then-current dissertations underway, one of the "old timers" commented, "They really are standing on our shoulders." In that moment, we realized that we had entered a new conversational space.

There are many ways to characterize this new space. Most significant in terms of this book, however, was the freedom with which study group members were exploring alternative forms of representation in the dissertation.

Over the many years of study group meetings, our focus shifted. We no longer agonized over the acceptability of minor alterations in the traditional dissertation format modeled after the conventional science report and described by Duke and Beck (1999) as "a lengthy document (typically 200–400 pages) on a single topic, presented through separate chapters for the introduction, literature review, methodology, results and conclusions" (31). Although we resonate with Duke and Beck's contention that the traditional format is largely ineffectual as a means of contributing knowledge to the field of education, our concerns focused on another more fundamental issue—i.e., the relationship between form and meaning.

Arising from our sensibilities as authors was a growing conviction that the form of the dissertation needed to serve the meanings to be conveyed through the document. Further, the form of the dissertation often embodied the author's tacit way of making meaning (e.g., through narrative). At the same time, even incipient imaginings of form seemed to create spaces for the conceptual work of an inquiry. These inextricable connections among form, meaning, and ways of knowing led us to the notion of research genre.

"Genre" connotes a freedom for creative expression within the conventions of a particular form of inquiry (e.g., grounded theory, case study, heuristic, narrative, arts-based research). To give students a sense of how form and meaning interconnect, we offer a comparison to the more commonly understood notion of genre in literature. Writing a novel, for example, affords an author great latitude for shaping the themes, characters, symbolic meanings, imagery, and so on. Writing a play, short story, or poetry affords an author similar latitude. This creative latitude is expressed, however, within the conventions of what is commonly understood to be a novel, play, short story, or poem. In short, learning to create within any of these literary genres entails mastering the conventions and techniques of the craft, not applying a hard and fast set of rules. While this view of writing seems to make sense to many of our students in relation to works of literature, it engenders cognitive dissonance (and considerable anxiety) when we relate it back to writing an interpretive dissertation in education.

Over the years, we have come to believe that the dissonance stems in part from a nearly obsessive quest for a workable set of data-collection and management techniques. The rigorous application of proper techniques will, students often assume, legitimize their inquiry. Freeing oneself from this assumption is a struggle, for if technique does not imbue one's study with legitimacy, what does? This question lies at the heart of the struggle recounted in each contributing author's chapter. We do not presume that sharing our struggles will magically inoculate others from this struggle. Indeed, it is our belief that the struggle toward representation of form, meaning, and ways of knowing is the essence of interpretive dissertation inquiry. It is our hope that readers–both doctoral students and faculty—take from this book an appreciation for the struggle and a clearer sense of what the struggle entails.

No writing project is without its difficulties and challenges. But it is hard for us to imagine a project that could have been more fulfilling—and joyful—than the preparation of this book. For Noreen, in particular, it represents the fulfillment of a yearning to write collaboratively with the scholars who have matured from being her students to doctoral advisees and then to colleagues and friends. For all of us as contributing authors, the book has afforded an opportunity to continue deliberating with those whose thinking has contributed so much to our understanding of interpretive inquiry and ourselves as inquirers.

The chapters in this book have emerged from and evolved through our conversations around Noreen's table. The writing reflects this conversational milieu in several ways. Throughout the chapters, authors make reference to each other's work and thinking as well as to pivotal conversations they have had with various study group members. Rather than citing these within the stilted conventions of a style manual, we mention these exchanges more informally. In so doing, we hope to convey to readers a sense of the discursive nature of our deliberations.

In addition, complicated conversations comprise many individual voices, each with its own tone, inflection, cadence, and timbre. As editors of this book, our desire was not to homogenize the voices of our authors, but rather to provide a space for each unique voice to be heard. This represents more than a simple editorial decision. It is a manifestation of the worldview that underpins this book and the dissertations represented in the following pages, a worldview that values each individual's way of being in the world and respects each author's struggle toward representation of her thinking.

Finally, complicated conversations encompass many intertwining themes. Compartmentalizing the themes runs the risk of destroying the very essence of the conversation. Still, it is helpful for newcomers to have some orientation to the conversational themes so they can better choose where to turn their attention. For this reason, we have grouped the chapters into four sections. These groupings allow us to highlight issues that seem to be in the foreground of each chapter. But playing as leitmotifs in the background of all chapters are the recurring themes of our conversations.

In chapter 1, "Imagining an Interpretive Dissertation: Voice, Text and Representation," Noreen Garman situates the dissertations within an interpretive tradition of inquiry and introduces the conceptual issues that frame our conversations. In doing so, she explicates the key concepts in the title of the book, exploring what we mean by "the authority to imagine," "the struggle toward representation," and "the self in dissertation writing."

From there the book is divided into three sections, beginning with part 1, "Claiming a Stance within Conflicting and Contentious Discourse." In chapter 2, "Pictures in My Mind: Viewing Images of Dissertation Authorities through Process Drama and Narrative Inquiry," Lynn Richards recounts the disparate advice she received on how to approach her dissertation. Grappling with these conflicting messages might have been easier had she held any of the advisors in less esteem. By respecting their differences, however, and striving to reconcile them, Lynn comes to claim her own stance as dissertation author.

In chapter 3, "A Call to Conscience: Problematizing Educational Inclusion," Micheline Stabile describes how she engaged in cycles of heuristic inquiry to explore and ultimately portray the often contentious discourses surrounding the problematic movement of educational inclusion. Through the process, she was able to bridge her world of practice with the world of the academy and claim her stance as scholar-practitioner.

JoVictoria Nicholson-Goodman entered her dissertation journey in the dark days following the terrorist attacks on September 11. Deeply troubled by the contentious socio-political discourses in a time of public uncertainty, JoVictoria turned to social cartography as a method for portraying competing ideological positions and their implications for curriculum. Chapter 4, "Confronting Authority and Self: Social Cartography and Curriculum Theorizing for Uncertain Times," recounts her struggle to locate herself within this contested terrain and how she claimed her stance as artist-citizen-scholar.

Part 2, "Claiming a Language of Practice through the Logics of Dissertation Inquiry," begins with chapter 5, "A Search for Balance: Representing a Narrative Pedagogy," in which Pamela Krakowski describes how an aesthetic metaphor allowed her to craft a logic of justification for a narrative inquiry and, in so doing, to find a language for expressing her embodied knowledge of both the normative and narrative aspects of early childhood art education.

Chapter 6, "Re-imagining Grounded Theory: Moving toward an Interpretive Stance," is Robin Grubs's account of imagining a different way of being with clients who are referred for genetic counseling. Uncomfortable with an information-giving model of counseling, Robin wanted to better understand the experience of women and couples making decisions about genetic testing. Turning to the literature on grounded theory, Robin crafted an interpretive logic of justification for her research genre and through this process forged a language for expressing the existential angst that genetic counseling clients might experience.

Unlike Pam and Robin, who were working within research genre with an abundance of literature, Marilyn Llewellyn faced a different challenge—crafting a research genre congruent with her deeply held values of curriculum and pedagogy as spiritual praxis. Drawing upon theological and philosophical discourses, Marilyn conceptualized a logic of justification for a spiritual inquiry illuminated in chapter 7, "Embracing a Language of Spiritual Inquiry."

Next, we turn to part 3, "Claiming a Way of Being in Practice through Inquiry." In chapter 8, "Coming to Know through the Text of Talk: From Interviews to Inner Views Storied to Interpretation," Kathleen Ceroni revisits her dissertation, bringing a fresh perspective to her highly auditory and interpersonal way of knowing. Kathy draws from literary theory to warrant the "texts of talk" that she fashions from her conversations with others. Then, by claiming the stance of researcher as literary critic, she probes both the surface and submerged meanings of the texts for insights into her life as a teacher.

Wendy Milne, an elementary art teacher, had put aside her own artistic impulses, in part because of time limitations, in part because making art seemed at odds with the intellectual pursuits of the academy. In chapter 9, "Imagining Reflective Artmaking: Claiming Self as Artist-Teacher-Researcher," she weds visual images with verbal explications to depict her process of reclaiming an integrated stance of artist-teacher-researcher.

Cynthia Tananis brought to the dissertation process years of experience as an educational evaluator and a nagging sense that traditional models of evaluation practice no longer served her professional interests or those of her clients. Challenging her own epistemology, ontology, and axiology of practice propelled Cindy on a journey that she relates in chapter 10, "Imagining in the Forest Dark: The Journey of an Epistemorph in the Land of Ologies."

We conclude with part 4, "Claiming One's Stance as Writer." Written in the form of essays, chapters 11 and 12 portray Majorie Logsdon's and Maria Piantanida's growing interest in the personal essay as a mode of inquiry into curriculum and pedagogical practice. "Writing Essays: Minding the Personal and Theoretic" offers Marjorie's speculations on "giving voice to *mind*." In "Speculations on the Personal Essay as a Mode of Curriculum Inquiry," Maria explores the nature and value of knowledge generated through such an intimate genre.

In chapter 13, "Narrative Yearnings: Reflecting in Time through the Art of Fictive Story," Patricia L. McMahon theorizes about the nature and value of writing both mildly and wildly fictive narratives. Through authoring fictive representations, she frees herself from reflecting in chronological time and comes to see troubling events of the classroom more clearly.

Finally, in our afterword, "Envisioning Complicated Conversations at the Table," we offer some concluding thoughts in response to questions often posed to us at research conferences. In essence, the questions ask, "Are these dissertations an anomaly arising from the unique circumstances of your study group? In fact, isn't your study group itself somewhat of an anomaly?" Over the years, we have pondered these sobering questions and have no easy answer to them. Instead, we explore a set of counter questions. What might it take to engender such complicated conversations in other settings? What must students and faculty be willing to "bring to a table" in order to nurture such conversations?

Acknowledgments

We are deeply grateful for the opportunity to learn with so many students over the years—those who have participated in our introductory course on qualitative research and those who have chosen to deliberate for a while within our mini–discourse community. While it is impossible to mention all of these individuals, we do want to acknowledge past study group members who have contributed so much to our understanding of both the struggle and the power of imagining new forms of dissertation inquiry.

Gloria Barry	Patricia Mascaro
Donna Cellante	Patricia Mashburn
Rebecca Clothey	Marcy O'Shell Maloni
Cornelia Davis	Barbara Knapp-Minick
Kathy Gaberson	Angela Minnici
Susan Poe Goodwin	Monica Ondrusko
Mary Harris	Jane Partenan
Helen Hazi	Cindy Reed
Deanna Hill	Mona Rush
Patricia Holland	Kathryn Sanida
Nedra Kearney-Vakulich	Mary Sciulli
Jean Konzal	Mary Beth Spore
Mary Ann Lauffer	Barbara Stephens
Joan Leukhardt	Jo Welter

As much as we have learned from students who have spent at least some time around the table with us, we have also learned from other faculty members who have referred their advisees to us. Barbara Fredette, Eugenie Potter, and Jean Winsand showed great trust in the deliberations of our study group, and we are grateful for the faith they placed in us. We also owe a debt of gratitude to our colleagues Doug Conlan, Nelson Haggerson, Steve Koziol, John Smyth, and Peter Willis, who have enriched our conversations with perspectives from other academic institutions and countries.

Finally, we wish to acknowledge the dedication of our contributing authors and their willingness to engage in the complicated conversations that gave birth to this book.

Notes

1. We return to a more extended consideration of "complicated conversations" in the afterword, where we explore what it might take for others to envision and enact such a deliberative process in their own work.
2. Noreen's beat-up dining room table has become the space (literally and figuratively) for provocative dialogue as well as good food. Study group members often talk of bringing an idea or text "to the table." "Some time ago," Noreen recounts, "I arranged to get a new table. But at the last minute, I cancelled the order. I realized how much good energy had seeped into the old wood. It had taken on a mythic quality difficult to replace."
3. Over the span of twenty-five years, more than sixty students have entered the conversational space around Noreen's dining table. In all honesty, some did not find that space very comfortable and left to find other resources to support their dissertation work. Others participated until completing their dissertations and then were drawn away to more compelling conversations in their arenas of practice. All of the authors contributing chapters to this book, however, have remained in a conversation that has expanded to include post dissertation writing.

References

Duke, N. K., and S. W. Beck. 1999. Education should consider alternative formats for the dissertation. *Educational Researcher* 28, no. 3: 31–36.

Goodwin, S. P. 1983. *An explication of human resources supervision: A grounded theory study of a public alternative high school.* UMI Proquest Digital Dissertation #AAT 8327738.

Hazi, H. M. 1980. *Analysis of selected teacher collective negotiation agreements in Pennsylvania to determine the legal control placed on supervisory practice.* UMI ProQuest Digital Dissertation #AAT 8028105.

Holland, P. 1983. *A hermeneutic study of educational myth: Implications for clinical supervision.* UMI ProQuest Digital Dissertation #AAT 8411689.

Kilbourn, B. 1999. Fictional theses. *Educational Researcher* 28, no. 9: 27–32.

Knapp-Minick, B. 1984. *A study of dysfunctional stereotypes regarding women and promotion: Implications for educational remedy.* UMI ProQuest Digital Dissertation #ATT8511002.

Leukhardt, J. C. 1983. *Students in a special program for gifted female adolescents: A conceptual case study for planning curriculum.* UMI ProQuest Digital Dissertation #AAT 8327694.

Pallas, A. M. 2001. Preparing education doctoral students for epistemological diversity. *Educational Researcher* 30, no. 5: 6–11.

Piantanida, M., and N. B. Garman. 1999. *The qualitative dissertation: A guide for students and faculty.* Thousand Oaks, CA: Corwin Press.

Sanida, K. V. 1987. *The legal responsibilities of the school psychologist as determined by appeal opinions of hearing officers' decisions in the state of Pennsylvania.* UMI ProQuest Digital Dissertation #AAC 8719321.

Young, L. J. 2001. Border crossings and other journeys: Re-envisioning the doctoral preparation of educational researchers. *Educational Researcher* 30, no. 5: 3–5.

CHAPTER 1

Imagining an Interpretive Dissertation: Voice, Text, and Representation

Noreen B. Garman

This book is a representation of a major intellectual event. It is, for me, a culmination of the hopes I've had for several years to join my study group members in a book about the insights that have come as each one struggled to craft a dissertation. In the years since 1980, my colleague Maria Piantanida and I have been fortunate to be a part of a scholarly community of doctoral students committed to deliberative ways of understanding more about their own intellectual curiosity and work. Through our involvements, we've come to recognize the ways in which forms of understanding are related to forms of representation: this relationship between what one knows and how it is represented through voice and text lies at the center of our dissertation challenges.

Some of our group were at the 1996 American Educational Research Association (AERA) conference when Elliot Eisner and Howard Gardner debated whether a novel would be acceptable as a dissertation in education. It signaled to a wide research audience that there was national interest in debating issues related to legitimate doctoral research. In this era of unprecedented diversity, each study group member has faced the uncertainty about the basis of authority for portraying unique research, and most important, about what counts as an acceptable dissertation representation.

In this chapter I attempt to think out loud about some of the key ideas that were made complicated during our study group conversations. I mention key ideas and insights only briefly and it's important to read them, not as

absolutes, but rather as insights that have continued to guide and
_onversations. In the following chapters each author tells a part of
her[1] dissertation story and in so doing serves to situate and illuminate the
ideas with vivid detail.

An Interpretivist Orientation

As a study group we tend to think of ourselves as interpretivists.[2] A basic tenet of interpretivism suggests that as reflective human beings, we construct our realities, for the most part, in discourse communities. Our work grows out of a hermeneutic orientation based on notions of interpretation (Ricoeur 1974) and the search for deeper understandings. For the interpretivist, the world is constructed by each knower/observer according to both subjective and intersubjective dialogical exchanges (Putnam 1989). Interpretivists are concerned with symbolic meaning and various forms of representation that help the reader better understand the phenomenon under study. Thus interpretivists do not claim that their research portrayals *correspond* to a general reality, as do those postpositivists who strive for a logico-scientific truth claim (Bruner 1986). Rather, interpretivist portrayals strive for *coherence*, which provide the reader with a vivid picture and the meanings about the experience under study. We recognize that there are different genres of dissertation representations, which, by virtue of their theoretic orientations, espouse different truth claims.

Many of our dissertation writers have identified their research as qualitative-interpretive; however, as the literature about qualitative research began to proliferate, we noted with regret that the postpositivists had co-opted the term "qualitative." Postpositivists often espoused the use of "mixed method" as a way to continue claiming logico-scientific correspondence to their findings. It seemed to us that "mixed method" often meant using and treating qualitative data, primarily from interviews, as an add-on in order to enhance the findings—or as one faculty advisor said, "to spark up the report." (We avoid using the notion of "findings" in our dissertations since the studies are centered on enlarging understandings, not proving specifics.) Furthermore, the postpositivists seem to ignore issues of the theoretic or worldview orientation of the researcher, focusing primarily on method as a technique for legitimizing and analyzing data and generating findings.

We argue that one's epistemological and ontological perspectives are central to one's inquiry. In this regard we recognize two distinct meanings of method: method as *technique or procedure* and method as *logic of justification* (Smith and Heshusius 1986; Piantanida and Garman 1999). Postpositivist dissertations (even those claiming to be qualitative) tend to focus on the former, while interpretivist dissertations argue the two cannot be separated. One's worldview is reflected in the detailed procedures of the study; both, we believe, need to be made public.

The Authorial Voice

A few years ago a faculty member at one of our dissertation defenses announced that he was conflicted about the quality of Mary's document. "I loved it. It read like a compelling novel in places," he remarked, "but she used the first person all the way through it. I tell my student *never* to use 'I' in writing up their research." At that point Mary realized that she hadn't included in her logic of justification the discourses related to the authorial voice in qualitative texts. She had taken for granted that faculty understood that the traditional objective role of the scientific author was not appropriate for qualitative research. Instead, the voice of the storyteller reflected her authentic role. Polkinghorne (1997) suggests that when the author assumes such a role, the research act takes on an entirely different perspective. There are no longer *subjects*, but rather *participants* who become actors in a research narrative. Furthermore, as Tierney (1997) describes, "The author enters the text not simply to move the action along as a narrator, but also to present a human side to the discourse" (26). In his chapter, Tierney demonstrates how a particular author assimilates three different identities: narrator, interviewer, and participant. This complex understanding of authorship is especially significant to our work here, considering the interactive nature of the study group research.

All members of our group have focused on studying practice in one form or another, and in so doing, we recognize that we have an obligation to consider how one's authorial voice is present in the narrative. Madeline Grumet (1990) says of the practice of teaching, "If it is as a teacher that I engage in inquiry into teaching, then I do not deny or disguise my relation to the object of that inquiry but make that relation the object of the inquiry itself" (105). Eisner (1998) offers another perspective on the authorial stance as "the self as an instrument that engages the situation and makes sense of it" (34). In examining their respective work experiences, study group members have come to rich ontological understandings of the way in which dialogue is central for defining the core of one's practice. As a group we've come to better understand a simple yet profound assumption: to experience what it means to be human, we need to engage in dialogic relationships. Yet, to portray those experiences is not simple, and to name the insights with authentic voices, we hear the words of Sidorkin (1999): "The authentic self exists and manifests itself on the boundary of the self with the outside world" (71).

As we engage in our conversations around the table, we have also come to understand that we are, after all, studying ourselves in practice, and re-imagining our theoretic relationships with ourselves. Yet we have asked ourselves, Is this not narcissistic? What keeps our research from being solipsistic? It may be that we portray the fusion of the private and the public, the social and the subjective, even as we realize that these portrayals are, to an extent, illusory. Bill Pinar (2004) says it poignantly when he speaks of practitioners who are "dispersed along a jagged, crumbling social surface"; for them, "the embrace of the private . . . is a political, not a narcissistic act" (252). Stanley Fish (1980) also explored this idea. "The condition required for someone to be a solipsist or relativist, the conditions of being independent of institutional assumptions and free to originate one's own purposes and goals, could never be realized" (321). Fish believes that we all live, linguistically speaking, in *interpretive communities* that are *systems of intelligibility.* Our communication, he argues, "occurs only within such a system (or context, or situation, or interpretive community) and . . . the understanding achieved by two or more persons is specific to that system and determined only within its confines" (304). Interpretive communities share a common language that relies on the norms and possibilities embedded in the linguistic meanings of a community's history. As we discussed Fish's ideas, we were reminded of the faculty member on Mary's committee who questioned her use of the personal voice. It might be said that he was part of a different research tradition and therefore a different interpretive community from the one Mary represented.

The Texts of Inquiry

Several years ago at the AERA annual meeting, a session chaired by Jim Scheurich focused on a possible rapprochement between qualitative and quantitative inquiry. The major question of the session was, "Could disparate research traditions find similar research space?" During the session words such as "reliability," "validity," and "trustworthiness" became contested terms. After much debate, a member of the audience stood up and said firmly, "One term we all agree on and share is 'data'—we all base our truth claims on data." A few people shook their heads, and I found myself adding to the debate by saying, "Well, although we don't dismiss the notion of data, we don't find it particularly useful either. We tend to use 'text' to name the written responses and results of our various research activities."

This is the case in our group. Although some members would say that they create texts from the initial data they've collected, the notion of text is imperative, albeit complicated, in our interpretive research. Philosophers, literary theorists, and linguists deliberate about the meaning of text in relation to discourse (see Fish 1980; Ricoeur 1991; Foucault 1972). In "From Work to Text," Barthes (1989) attempts to explicate a theory of text and concludes that "a Theory of the Text cannot be satisfied with a metalinguistic exposition" (64). Barthes doesn't insist that text is only in written form (indeed, other scholars would say that text can be either spoken or written and can take many forms of representation). For *our* research purposes, we assume that text is primarily a written form with inherent meaning for the researcher—a chunk of related words or images that reflect an idea or ideas. Text may take the form of vignettes, profiles, stories, media excerpts, theoretic insights, images, pictures, and memos, to name only a few products of inquiry. The concern here is that these crafted texts are capable of hermeneutic interpretations and are not generally used for reductive purposes. In this way the researcher continues to create a repertoire of preliminary texts and, in so doing, deepens her understanding of the study, even if it hasn't come into full conceptual focus yet.

Three Essential Texts

Over the years of our group meetings, it became evident that we could identify three kinds of essential texts that occur, in various forms, in all of our interpretive dissertations. By using the repertoire of preliminary texts selectively, at some point authors realize that they are crafting three types of texts: *experiential*, *theoretic*, and *discursive*. Strands of these three texts are eventually woven into the final representation, the portrayal of the dissertation itself. For purposes of clarity, we refer to these as three essential texts, recognizing that they represent types of texts, rather than three individual portrayals.

iential text. In studying the situations of educational practice, we ated to let the reader into the context where the study is situated and where events happen. The experiential text is, in one sense, a description of "what happens when . . ." More importantly, however, it is based on stories that focus on the self in social context. It is here where we begin to pay close attention to language because it is language that makes thinking possible. How we think is influenced by what we think about and how we choose to represent our observations. Moreover, we see what we know how to say (Eisner 2002). The experiential text is the author's version of reality, which requires a *standing close* language full of evocative and persuasive sensibilities. A necessary characteristic of the experiential text is verisimilitude, to create the shared space where the author and the reader come together to experience the reality under study.

The multiplicity of lived experience challenges the author's literary ability to imagine powerfully crafted scenarios. As Maxine Greene (1995) tells us,

> People who lack access to the language of power, who are inarticulate even about their lived lives, are unlikely to "surmount the boundaries in which all customary views are confined, and to reach a more open territory" (heidegger, [sic] 1969, p. 13). Yes, becoming literate is also a matter of transcending the given, of entering a field of possibles. We are moved to do that, however, *only when we become aware of rifts, gaps in what we think of as reality* [emphasis added]. We have to be articulate enough and able to exert ourselves to *name* what we see around us—the hunger, the passivity, the homelessness, the "silences." (111)

Maxine Greene's notion of the "gap in what we think of as reality" is crucial. It points to a key feature of the experiential text, which is that the story of this text is not only about events under study, not a faithful description of "what happened," but rather an interpretation of "what happened *when*, *why* and/or *how*." These become a portrayal of the problematics inherent in the experience. These rifts require imagination to be conscious of them, "to find our own lived worlds lacking because of them" (Greene 1995, 111). Thus, we narrate an interpretive reality in order to allow us to contemplate the effects of our own and others' actions and to alter the direction of our educational lives.

Theoretic Text. In theoretic text, the author is expected to reflect on the experiential text and to resonate with the happenings at a distance. She can begin to interpret the conceptual meanings wrought through inferences and judgments that serve as her own meaning-making. The theoretic text represents the author's personal theories. Experiential text portrayals serve as warrants for the theoretic arguments of the study. Unlike researchers who claim specific relations of cause and effect or statistical correlations through analysis of data, interpretive researchers persuade by reason. Interpretation in educational research thus requires a rhetorical sensibility.

We are convinced that education is better understood as a rhetorical practice rather than a scientific one; teachers frame their actions hoping to *influence* students to learn from a planned curriculum. Likewise, the interpretive researcher assumes a stance of persuasion that might be said to *give one's self permission* to generate truth claims rendered from a rhetorical perspective (Cahn 1993). Rhetoric doesn't deal with abstract, logico-scientific truth, but with the truth that emerges in the context of distinctly complicated conversations. Eisner (1999) tells us,

> Qualitative inquiry . . . is ultimately a matter of persuasion, of seeing things in a way that satisfies, or is useful for the purpose we embrace. The evidence employed in qualitative studies comes from multiple sources. We are persuaded by its "weight," by the coherence of the case, by the cogency of the interpretation. . . . In qualitative research there is no statistical test of significance to determine if results "count"; in the end, what counts is a matter of judgment. (39)

By probing the experiential text rhetorically and generating conceptual explanations, we hope that a provocative and convincing theoretic text will begin to emerge.

Discursive Text. What we are calling the discursive text might be more commonly known as "Chapter 2: Review of Related Literature" in most traditional dissertations.[3] A common assumption is that novice researchers will explore bodies of literature to provide the rationale for the study as well as the method of inquiry. Some faculty suggest to students that they write the first three chapters of their dissertation (the introduction, review of literature, and methodology) as their research proposal, in the belief that this will give the dissertation writer a distinct advantage toward expeditiously completing their final documents. According to conventional wisdom (or perhaps, folklore), as the actual study proceeds, all that's left is to collect the data, do the analysis and write the final two chapters, typically identified as data analysis/display and findings/conclusion.

We find the concept of "the review of the literature" to be problematic. It suggests a dysfunctional notion that a one-chapter review of literature is a precursor to, rather than an integral part of the study. Furthermore, there may be a residue of linear thinking reflected in statements about *the* review of *the* literature, implying that there is a single body of literature, to be reviewed only once. We find the concept of "reviewing the discourses" to be more useful, or rather we refer to immersing ourselves in multiple discourses, including those related to the dissertation topic, the research tradition and techniques that can support a given genre.

As the poststructuralists use the concept of discourse, it "communicates the social relatedness of the human world, and more specific, our social relatedness as inscribed in and expressed through language" (Pinar et al. 1995, 49). In the academic sense, discourse has come to represent the language exchanges within a topic or field of study. Formal knowledge channels the flow of ideas into schools of thought, dialectics, perspective-taking—all lines of discourse. *Discourse* has come to mean a source of knowledge to be generated; it means socially constructed knowledge; it means communities of discourse; and in the academic sense, it means an institutional system for the production of knowledge in regulated language.

Constructing a discursive text is more extensive than doing a "Review of Literature" as a single chapter. As we refer to the discursive text here, it may also seem to represent a single portrayal, but this is not the case. Discursive text contains threads that are used throughout the dissertation to support various aspects of the study. One challenge is finding a way to transform the wealth of this scholarly text into insightful warrants for the experiential and theoretical texts. In doing so, the author gives the reader a sense that she is in a thoughtful *conversation* with scholars who influence her thinking. She is able to do more than what we often hear from students as "genuflecting to the literature gods." Our study group authors let the reader in on those conversations, and it becomes increasingly clear what the nature of the intellectual journey represents. The discursive text becomes part of the dissertation's intellectual map. As a result, the discursive text serves to enhance the author's persuasive ideas and to legitimize the insights of theoretic text. In addition, the discursive text provides the public space of intellectual dialogue and, as such, keeps the dangers of solipsism at bay.

Thus the author continues to struggle to get sufficient intellectual depth into the writing of the essential texts. At some point, it becomes apparent that there are at least two kinds of experiences going on in the research process.

One is the experience under study—the context and events being construed in what we are calling the experiential text. The other is the experience of the research process itself—planning the inquiry, crafting the essential texts, and finally, re-presenting the results in a form that portrays the major message (or messages) of the inquiry through the various threads of the essential texts.

The Darkness and Light: Getting to the Representation

Our interpretive dissertations have been influenced by Kant's notion that all knowledge of experience takes representational narrative form (Aquila 1983). We *see* when we look back on experience, and we can know reality only when we no longer experience, but rather represent experience to ourselves over time. Writing the dissertation is that final representation of the research experience and, as Eisner (1993) reminds us, "the act of representation is also an act of invention" (7). The researcher may have accumulated a wealth of rich texts, but only at the point of representation do the essence and quality of the dissertation emerge. Conceptual rigor and elegance are essential and yet extremely illusive. Some of our study group members have described this as a time of darkness, often pain and despair. Others thought it was an energizing, exciting time.

The many texts, however, can't provide an inherent, incremental way to organize the dissertation, no matter how rich the contents. At some point the writer faces a seemingly endless void, the tyranny of the blank page. Eventually, as we often say in our group, the writer has to put cursor to screen and begin with page one, line one—but with a vision of a particular representation in mind. To be in this dark space of ambiguity and frustration is common, if not frightening. Yet it is this darkness that also can serve to release the imagination (Greene 1995) and allow the writer to resonate with the texts while struggling toward the conceptual representation. It is through imaginative insight that the writer eventually sees the light in an "aha" moment when the conceptual point of the inquiry comes into focus. This moment of insight allows the writer to imagine what the dissertation might look like.

Stories about making a conceptual leap have become part of our dissertation folklore in the study group (see Piantanida and Garman 1999 for examples.) In one of these stories, Maria Piantanida tells about her experience in 1980 as she continued to accumulate data for her study (at that time we hadn't yet named our collections "texts"). At some point she realized that she had more data than she needed and began her analysis, searching for ways to make conceptual meanings from the data. She began by "sorting the piles," as she described, hoping that categories would emerge. Apparently they did, but she still found the results inadequate. Maria, in one of the study group meetings, used a vivid metaphor to describe her conceptual awareness:

> It was as if I had collected wonderful pebbles on beaches I visited. I sorted them endlessly fussing to pile them by size, then by color, by shape, by beach. I felt as if I needed to use *all* the stones (data) for the final representation. When I freed myself from that assumption, I realized that I was actually making a mosaic and that I had to *choose* just the appropriate stones to make it meaningful. Then I had to decide what the mosaic would look like, but at last I was free to create it.

We learned that it was when she could make complicated her single assumption about the use of data that she found a metaphor with enough power to help her imagine the form of representation for her dissertation.

The Authority to Imagine

Authoring a dissertation means that one takes the responsibility for a conceptual imperative—that is, the responsibility to undertake significant research activities and create an epistemologically rigorous and convincing representation of the results. The exciting part of writing an interpretive dissertation is the author's freedom to create forms of representation in harmony with her own ontological sensibilities. The fearful part, of course, is getting through the times of chaos when the author faces the uncertainties of crafting an innovative representation and writing a persuasive dissertation. "It is imagination," as Maxine Greene (1995) points out, "with its capacity to both make order out of chaos and open experience to the mysterious and strange—that moves us to go in quest, to journey where we have never been" (23). In releasing the imagination, however, authors are challenged to find internal as well as external resources to be assured that they are "on the right track." In other words, authors must work to claim the authority to imagine.

Like others, the members of our study group have learned to listen to many voices of authority. These voices—representing fields of study, inquiry methods, and professorial privilege—all serve to provide the academic and institutional legitimacy necessary for certifying what counts as dissertation knowledge.

In reviewing the discourses associated with the subject or issues under study, we've also realized how important it is to consider the history of one's field as well as the contemporary discourses. Pinar et al. (1995) emphasize "that all fields of study have histories, all evolve, all suffer 'paradigm' breaks, and all proceed in directions they might not have, had those who devoted their careers to these fields not existed" (849). These stewards who devoted their careers to their fields help us understand what the scholarship of a field sounds like and how a discursive text becomes our conversation with the scholars and the subject under study.

Research authority also resides in the method—or as we prefer, the logic of justification—that informs one's inquiry approach (Piantanida and Garman 1999). Crafting research procedures cannot be done in an epistemological and ontological vacuum. At first, the authorities representing a logic of justification begin to provide the rationale for how the results—the truth claims—are generated and supported. This rationale involves such basic questions as, What is the nature of the educational and social reality under study? By what norms will *truth* be defined? What is the relationship of the inquirer to that which is being studied? How are ethical principles and safeguards assured?

But at some point each of our study group members had to determine what Nelson Goodman (1978) calls "rightness to fit." Given the current contentious meanings of "knowledge" and "truth," Goodman offers a conception of rightness that transcends the modernist notion of truth, and in particular, scientific truth. Thus, we have become aware, in some cases, of the discrepancy between others' expectation of strict adherence to the scholars who espouse existing methods and the need for the dissertation author to adapt existing methods to one's unique situation. In other cases, our members found no clear methods and had to provide epistemological logics from their fields. Both of these approaches—balancing tradition with innovation and creating methodology from scratch—require knowledge of potential research logics, as well as confidence that one has the right to determine an appropriate *fit of method*.

Although dissertation researchers have the right to craft an inquiry to reflect a coherent fit of method, the research advisor and committee members have the dominant voices for authorizing the inquiry content and procedures. As Colin and Heaney (2001) describe, "It is the university's mission not only to disseminate knowledge, but also to legitimize those who acquire it and fail those who have not met dominant norms. The power to name what it is that constitutes knowledge and to stand in judgment over those who seek to attain it is the ground and substance of professorial privilege" (31). Since dissertation committees, through professorial privilege, are the educational gatekeepers and stewards of academic traditions, the choice of committee members is crucial for helping the candidate toward a legitimate representation of knowledge.

At our institution, however, interpretive research is relatively unknown. Over the years, we've had very few faculty members who claimed to understand interpretive inquiry enough to advise dissertation research. Recognizing this, each of our study group members has been challenged to address the issue directly. Authors have selected committee members as resources for various dimensions of the inquiry, such as the fields of study to which the dissertation has contributed and the discipline that underpins the content. In some cases, dissertation authors have taken the position of "educating" the committee about the research epistemological assumptions in the logic of justification section of the document. In other cases, faculty members have joined our study group sessions when their candidates were on our agenda. At the final defense, surprise is a common reaction of committee members toward these interpretive dissertations. They often say, "It doesn't read like a typical dissertation," or "I thoroughly enjoyed reading it," and sometimes even, "I could hardly put it down." When this happens, there is a special pleasure as we listen to these voices of authority.

Maxine Greene reminds us that imagination takes us to places where we've never been. Going to those "places" in the dissertation process, however, requires a special kind of power—the author's power to initiate, institute, and establish not only from the authority of academic discourse and the granting institution, but also from within one's self. Granting one's self permission to create is often more difficult than seeking assurance from faculty. Assuming authorial right means no longer "eavesdropping" on other scholars' discourses and relying on their ideas and concepts, but rather beginning to enter into those discourses by claiming authorship. Giving one's self permission to author means that one no longer needs ideas and concepts from what someone else says—one is free to name the world of one's research.

Thus there is a tension—a dance, between authority and representation. It is in the process of writing that one faces the need to claim the right of authorship and that, in turn, allows one to imagine the representation. Yet it is the need to imagine the representation that also pushes one to claim authority.

Each study group member experienced this rhythmic dance of the dissertation. Having immersed herself in multiple discourses and satisfied herself that she had gained internal and external authority, each author wrote many drafts of her dissertation until she could imagine the final, elegant representation and feel the harmony of her work. In the following chapters, these dissertation authors recount the results of their imaginings.

Notes

1. I use the feminine pronoun throughout this chapter since all of our study group members at the time of writing were women. The ideas in the chapter are situated within the study group's dialogue. As for the uses of the collective pronoun, I include myself as a member of the study group, but not as a dissertation writer.

    I also use the first and last names of certain scholars in the text citation because their work represents a significant part of our deliberations. We tend to think of them as discursive colleagues.

2. Although scholars such as Feinberg and Soltis (1992) have been useful to us in situating the interpretivist perspective in the social sciences, their work does not address epistemological and ontological concerns we continue to struggle with regarding the basic differences in truth claims.

    Eisner (1997) has been helpful in pointing out that during the past three decades, the concept of research was broadened in various fields of study, and therefore scientific research has been recognized as *one* among several of its species of knowledge generating. Eisner also introduced us to the distinction between coherence theory and correspondence theory (1979, 1998). We realized that these are distinctly different truth-claim perspectives which helped us to better understand the confusion between the qualitative-quantitative confusion. We tend to resonate with coherence theory.

3. Dissertation books such as Bryant (2004) assume that the conventional structure of a dissertation is a five-chapter document typically representing a science report: Chapter One, "Introduction"; Chapter Two, "Review of Literature"; Chapter Three, "The Research Design"; Chapter Four, "Report of Findings"; and Chapter Five, "Conclusion." For other examples see Roberts (2004) and Glatthorn (1998).

References

Aquila, R. E. 1983. *Representational mind: A study of Kant's theory of knowledge.* Bloomington: Indiana University Press.

Barthes, R. 1989. *The rustle of language.* Trans. R. Howard. Berkeley: University of California Press.

Bruner, J. 1986. *Actual minds, possible worlds.* Cambridge, MA: Harvard University Press.

Bryant, M. 2004. *The portable dissertation advisor.* Thousand Oaks, CA: Corwin Press.

Cahn, M. 1993. The rhetoric of rhetoric: Six tropes of disciplinary self-constitution. In *The recovery of rhetoric: Persuasive discourse and disciplinarity in the human sciences*, ed. R. H. Roberts and J. M. M. Good, 61–84. Charlottesville: University Press of Virginia.

Colin, S. A. J., and T. Heaney. 2001. Negotiating the democratic classroom. *New Directions for Adult and Continuing Education* 9, no. 1: 29–37.

Eisner, E. 1979. *The educational imagination.* New York: Macmillan.

———. 1991. *The enlightened eye.* New York: Macmillan.

———. 1997. The promise and perils of alternative forms of data representation. *Educational Researcher* 26, no. 6: 4–10.

———. 1993. Forms of understanding and the future of educational research. *Educational Researcher* 22, no. 7: 5–11.

———. 2002. *The arts and the creation of mind.* New Haven, CT: Yale University Press.

Feinberg, W., and J. F. Soltis. 1992. *School and society.* New York: Teachers College Press.

Fish, S. 1980. *Is there a text in this class? The authority of interpretive communities.* Cambridge, MA: Harvard University Press.

Foucault, M. 1972. *The archaeology of knowledge.* Trans. M. Sheridan Smith. New York: Pantheon.

Glatthorn, A. A. 1998. *Writing the winning dissertation: A step-by-step guide.* Thousand Oaks, CA: Corwin Press.

Goodman, N. 1978. *Ways of worldmaking.* Indianapolis: Hackett.

Greene, M. 1995. *Releasing the imagination: Essays on education, the arts, and social change.* San Francisco: Jossey-Bass.

Grumet, M. 1990. On daffodils that come before the swallow dares. In *Qualitative inquiry in education: The continuing debate*, ed. E. Eisner and A. Peshkin, 101–120. New York: Teachers College Press.

Piantanida, M., and N. Garman. 1999. *The qualitative dissertation: A guide for students and faculty.* Thousand Oaks, CA: Corwin Press.

Pinar, W. 2004. *What is curriculum theory?* Mahwah, NJ: Lawrence Erlbaum Associates, Publishers.

Pinar, W., W. Reynolds, P. Slattery, and P. Taubman. 1995. *Understanding curriculum.* New York: Peter Lang.

Polkinghorne, D. E. 1997. Reporting qualitative research as practice. In *Representation and the text: Reframing the narrative voice*, ed. W. G. Tierney and Y. Lincoln, 3–22. Albany: State University of New York Press.

Putnam, H. 1989. *Representation and reality.* Cambridge, MA: MIT Press.

Ricoeur, P. 1974. *The conflict of interpretations: Essays in hermeneutics.* Trans. D. Ide. Evanston, IL: Northwestern University Press.

———.1991. *From text to action: Essays in hermeneutics II.* Trans. K. Blamey and J. B. Thompson. Evanston, IL: Northwestern University Press.

Roberts, C. M. 2004. *The dissertation journey.* Thousand Oaks, CA: Corwin Press.

Sidorkin, A. 1999. *Beyond discourse: Education, the self and dialogue.* Albany: State University of New York Press.

Smith, J. K., and L. Heshusius. 1986. Closing down the conversation: The end of the quantitative-qualitative debate among educational inquirers. *Educational researcher* 15, no. 1: 4–12.

Tierney, W. G. 1997. Lost in translation: Time and voice in qualitative research. In *Representation and the text: Re-framing the narrative voice*, ed. W. G. Tierney and Y. Lincoln, 23–36.

PART 1

Claiming a Stance for Self within Conflicting and Contentious Discourses

CHAPTER 2

Pictures in My Mind: Viewing Images of Dissertation Authorities through Process Drama and Narrative Inquiry

Lynn Altman Richards

> Drama is creating meaning and visual mental models of our understanding together, in imaginative contexts and situations. It is not about performance, but exploration. And the teacher in drama becomes a learner among learners, a participant, and a guide.
>
> Wilhelm and Edmiston 1998, ix

Creating Textual Images and Narrative Framework

As the dramatist of this chapter, I depict a series of enlightening events that pointed me toward the conceptualization, writing, and completion of my doctoral dissertation. I spotlight in particular those people I characterized as dissertation experts and how I initially struggled to learn their research secrets, to become a participant in scholarly, deliberative conversations, and to be guided eventually by the dramaturgy of my own doctoral study process.

I illustrate how I struggled with my conceptions of "dissertation authorities" by presenting a series of flashbacks in the form of *textual images*. I then explore these images through narrative commentaries meant to depict the thoughts and emotions that propelled, sustained, and sometimes paralyzed me as I completed my dissertation research on creative dramatics as pedagogy in the elementary classroom. My hope is that through viewing these textual portraits in a narrative framework, the reader will be able to connect more fully with my experience of assuming the authority to imagine as I wrote my dramatic narrative inquiry.

Visualizing Dissertation Authorities—Initial Images

Years ago, as I stood contemplating my white bookshelves crammed full of university texts, I noticed that three of the painted wooden boards had sagged slightly. Was it the dampness of the basement or the weight of scholarly thoughts that made the shelves sag? I frowned as I scanned the rows of books and slid my fingers along their textured, rigid spines. Most felt cool to my touch—distant, lofty, tightly closed. Could I recall the contents, highlighted and notated, of so many pages? Perhaps—but not in depth and never with the full command that I was sure would be demanded of me as I pursued the title "Doctor of Education."

I imagined what a doctoral defense must be like: a courtroom setting—a juried committee of twelve professors dressed in black judges' robes—each judge sternly consulting a copy of my thin dissertation. I would stand before them alone, defenseless, with only my memory to aide me. "Now, Ms. Richards," they would question, "On page thirty-six, you state that the affective domain can help elementary school children to learn units of study. Please list all of the appropriate citations, including the page numbers, from Krathwohl's educational taxonomy that substantiate your findings. And then restate your dissertation paragraph verbatim to prove that it is indeed your own original thinking and writing."

Standing there in my basement, imagining the worst, I sighed. Thoughts of such a doctoral inquisition were frightening. How would I *ever* master these texts? I simply could not fathom it intellectually. But viscerally, I never doubted that I would attempt whatever was demanded of me by the scholarly authorities (whoever they might be) until I achieved that doctoral title. Even if I became the oldest doctoral student on university record. Even if I had to give up my elementary school teaching position and think scholarly thoughts full time. Even if it took so long that I died still trying.[1]

Images of Research Experts and Glimpses of Ontological Orientation

My initial impression of what I thought constituted a doctoral defense meeting was intimidating yet simultaneously inspiring; somehow I believed that the "dissertation authorities" would school me in what I needed "to do" to pass their test and to acquire such authoritative knowledge. But who *were* those robed dissertation experts? And how could I get them to reveal their scholarly secrets? What *did* I want to study? *How* should such a study be designed? Even after having completed my graduate coursework and proving myself to be "competent," I found myself unable to begin to adequately articulate any answers to these imagined doctoral questions.

Fortunately, I did have the glimmerings of an ontological orientation, though in those days I relied on relating examples of pedagogical activities to create images of my classroom for myself and others to exemplify my instructional thoughts. I offer the term "ontological orientation" retrospectively, as I never would have been able to name what I valued as a teacher as "ontology" decades ago. But I did have a firmly ingrained pedagogical philosophy—namely, that children learn best through active learning experiences and participation in meaningful classroom curriculum—which led me to believe that creative dramatics[2] and its connections to the prescribed school district curriculum could be a viable topic for my study. It was exciting to think of the intellectual opportunities writing a doctoral dissertation could provide in such an inquiry. However, as a fledgling researcher, I was completely uncertain about *how* such a study should be structured or what gave me the authority (as a primary classroom teacher) to become (or even imagine becoming) a contributing part of a scholarly university community.

In my search for *the* definitive dissertation format, I consulted four distinct authoritative sources: my academic advisor, who was well versed in the traditional university dissertation process as well as in creative dramatics; my father, a research psychologist, who had written his own doctoral dissertation at the same university over forty years earlier; a dissertation writing study group comprised of women in varying stages of their doctoral work; and several completed dissertations of other educators. All of these sources provided sage advice and introductory frameworks for authoring my inquiry, each originating in their own firmly held perspectives of what constituted "research." Often notes and ideas I had collected from one dissertation authority were contradicted when I expressed them during conversations with the others. Over a period of months I attempted to understand and prioritize those expert voices and to find a way to begin a study on creative dramatics. One possibility was revealed in the following recollection.

**Luncheon Lessons and Research Revelations—
Images of Possibilities**

One afternoon, during a National Council of Teachers' of English conference, I sat uncomfortably in a crowded downtown restaurant with two strangers who were conference presenters, picking at my meal and listening to their conversation about their latest research projects. Their discourse was fascinating, but I was unable to add to the conversation because of two overwhelming emotions: amazement at my intellectual inability to express a single coherent comment about their proposed research designs and acute embarrassment that my university advisor had saddled two experienced qualitative researchers with a beginning doctoral student like me while he hurried away to attend his conference coordination responsibilities—"Here," he'd said to me, "go to lunch with Mark and Mary. You can learn a lot from them." Perhaps I could surreptitiously signal for my check, I thought, and silently slink away to another conference session. But as they finished their deliberations and Mark clicked off the tape recorder, they turned toward me, and said, "Now—tell us about your study."

My study? What study? Why hadn't I gotten that waiter to bring the check while they were still busy? Trapped, I haltingly began to tell them of my interest in creative dramatics and its possible ties to content knowledge, experiential learning, emergent writing, classroom climate, and holistic teaching. Mary and Mark listened attentively to my jumble of thoughts and desires, and then Mary said the unimaginable: "Hmm. . . . You might want to consider doing a year-long study of your own classroom."

"Just study my classroom?" I asked. "But how would I make my results generalizable with such a small sample? Would my committee think my findings were valid if I only researched my own teaching and students?" Mark and Mary assured me that although qualitative research methodologies might not fit the conventional science-report model with which I was most familiar, it was quite possible for me to conduct a legitimate study of creative dramatics in my own school setting.

Imagining the Inquiry

Mark and Mary invoked a feeling of practitioner possibility and inquiry license in me that was an absolute (albeit frightening) revelation. In retrospect, I see that they granted me the authority to imagine a dissertation inquiry connected to my own ontological views. At that juncture on my dissertation journey, however, I was not sure I was capable of assuming that authority. When I shared our lunch conversation and my tentative beginning narrative writings with my advisor (a meticulous and careful researcher who believes that substantial data should support one's study), he cautioned,

"You know, you can't just write things down from recollection. You have to document your work thoroughly. And what's all this 'I' stuff? Perhaps you need to do more reading and think about your research questions more carefully."

When I talked with my father, a scholar from whom I most definitely had "inherited notions of authority" (Logsdon 2000, 23), Dad suggested that I could teach subject-area lessons both with and without the use of creative dramatics, code the lesson data, and see if blind observers could differentiate between the lessons, thus drawing conclusions about the impact that creative dramatics had on classroom instruction. I gave his suggestions a great deal of consideration but was perplexed as to how they "fit" with the affective, temporal nuances of the classroom drama process. As I pictured my schoolchildren enacting drama activities, I considered another image, from my own childhood.

Posing for an Imprinted Image of Authority

The photograph sits on my middle bookshelf. A small, square, black-and-white snapshot with a white decoratively ragged border, it's typical of most family pictures taken in the 1950s. In it a tall, bespectacled, handsome young man grasps a rolled diploma with both hands. The mortarboard of his graduation cap looks almost too small for his head, as though the photo itself were giving visual testimony to the tremendous amount of knowledge he had accumulated to earn his doctoral degree. Behind him, the stone wall of the main university building, its large blocks monumentally carved and assembled; beside him, two attractive young women in calf-length print dresses and pumps, his sisters, smile into the camera. In front of him, a small toddler in a white sundress and sunhat chews contemplatively on her thumb. The toddler is me.

Contemplating Authority and Ontology-ingrained and Emerging Images

My father completed his Ph.D. in 1954 in the field of research psychology. I was two years old at the time, but throughout my life, I have always pictured myself completing my own doctoral degree as well. I even attended the same university, although my study was focused in educational research/ instruction and learning.

This authoritative image created a dilemma forty years later: how to find a common language between father and daughter, between quantitative and qualitative researchers. For the most part, Dad and I carefully danced around our approaches to research, silently agreeing that different methods suit different inquiries. After talking with my dissertation advisor about my father's research suggestion, I quietly (and guiltily) decided to file away Dad's ideas about blind observers in my burgeoning data-collection folders—and turned to listen to other 'research authorities.'

Partaking of Intellectual Nourishment—An Image of Deliberation

At Noreen's on a typical study group night, a dozen women sit shoulder to shoulder around a large rectangular wooden dining table. The table is spread with an eclectic meal—platters of poached salmon and hoagies, baskets of muffins and brown corn chips, and take-out cartons from Boston Market and Chinese restaurants. Paper plates and forks teeter atop of piles of papers and books pushed aside to make room for the focus of the gathering: one of the group member's latest writings. The author distributes her stapled document and as the copies circulate around the table, she begins to speak. The other women read through the newly received document and start to discuss, debate, and deliberate its content, connections, and concepts.

Seeking an Authoritative Framework— Images of Advice and Abandonment

From the first, the study group gathered around the table consistently advised me, "Get *something* down on paper. You must write your way into the study. Talk about your experiences with creative dramatics, tell what brought you to this inquiry, and portray the different dimensions you are studying. Put yourself and your thinking into the document. Try to give a definite sense of your voice as the researcher and shape your guiding questions more succinctly." (I had generated a list of about two dozen research questions at the time!) I had also requested a copy of someone's overview document so that I could review the "proper" format prior to writing my own. Needless to say, the group advised me to write about my own thinking, not to pattern it after another's. I felt abandoned—if the group wouldn't provide me with an authoritative model to follow, where could I find the assistance I desperately felt I needed?

Images of Incompetence and Acknowledgment

Shortly after I had asked the study group for help structuring my overview proposal, I received a box in the mail from an anonymous sender. It was full of expensive books addressing qualitative research design. I was certain that the study group had taken up a collection in an attempt to educate such an unsophisticated, unscholarly elementary school teacher as myself. I was so disturbed by the image of my own academic incompetence that I sat on the floor of my bedroom closet and wept.

Days later during a phone conversation with my mother, I discovered that it was my father who had selected, ordered, paid for, and sent the qualitative research material. I was both relieved and surprised—it never occurred to me that my father would have the interest in or access to such detailed interpretative inquiry materials. After I hung up the phone, I ran up the two flights of stairs to our loft and eagerly opened my new intellectual treasures. With a revitalized sense of inquiry and confidence, I scanned the titles: Handbook of Qualitative Research (1994), filled with intellectual information; Research Design: Qualitative and Quantitative Approaches (Cresswell 994), symbolizing parental yet scholarly acknowledgment of my adult role as a beginning researcher; and Designing Qualitative Research (Marshall 1995), the back cover of which promised to "expand the scope of possible research strategies; (the) conceptualization of researchers' roles, and (the) possibilities for more collaborative ways of doing qualitative research." Now I couldn't wait to continue my discussions with experts who had designed their own research before me. Dad had chosen insightful gifts and with unspoken validation had pointed me toward the research authority within myself. I sat on the carpet of the loft floor, and as I read, I smiled.

Writing the Dissertation—Images of Propensity

This was, I believe, the beginning of my recognition that the doctoral authorities I looked to for guidance also looked to *me* as the author of the dissertation. They acknowledged my unique ontological landscape, even though at that time my research took the shape of "what felt right" rather than an articulated ontological statement.

Of the three completed doctoral dissertations that I consulted regularly as "finished experts," the one that energized my thinking and sparked possibilities for my own writing was a narrative inquiry of three levels of portfolio reflection authored by one of the members of the study group (McMahon 1993.) Earlier on, my advisor had suggested that I investigate narrative method as a possible dissertation avenue. Indeed, my own proclivity for constantly taking notes, writing down questions, and shaping my thoughts into written words (as I listened to others, read creative dramatics literature, or engaged in intellectual deliberation with the study group) evidenced how I made sense of and built upon my academic experiences through writing. And although I was deeply worried that I lacked the necessary writing skills to author a narrative dissertation with verisimilitude (Piantanida and Garman 1999), narrative inquiry seemed to be a logical extension of the innate and practiced processes through which I gathered intellectual information, shared pedagogic anecdotes, and perceived the educational world.

Exploring Narrative Inquiry—Textual Images

My feeling of comfort in having chosen narrative as the appropriate method to use in my inquiry was quickly replaced by a sense of bewilderment as how to begin collecting narrative data. It seemed to me that the structured style of narrative research was well suited to elaborate descriptions of the complex academic constructs, multiple social interactions, and evolving drama experiences encompassed within our elementary-school day. I also found that narrative inquiry in education focused on the development of personal and social accounts of school phenomena (Connelly and Clandinin 1988), which helped me to express most clearly how primary school children's content learning could be shaped by the classroom drama process. Once again I conferred with my dissertation authorities and began to systematically document our classroom drama process through my lesson plan books (one with the given district curriculum and the other outlining creative dramatics activities), field notes, a teacher journal (containing both descriptive and reflective notes), audiotapes (of adult, student, and peer interviews), classroom artifacts (learning logs, student writings/drawings, content area materials, and photographs) and videotapes of the creative drama activities themselves and of the children's debriefings after the drama experiences. By the end of that school year, I had collected a mountain of data and needed to find a way to explore, connect, and textually represent our dramatic experiences throughout an entire school year. My pathway into the data mountain was revealed through a gift of image, a photograph taken of us late that May.

Guided by a Gift of Image

On the last day of school, eight-year-old Alan brought a small framed photograph of our class to me as a goodbye gift. "My Mom says to tell you the good one is behind this picture," he said. As I looked at the image of our class, I laughed out loud. In the photo, the children are arranged in four tiers, with me standing behind them at the top of the human pyramid. We are each dressed in our royal blue Fun Day t-shirts and are making outrageous funny faces—tongues out, eyes crossed, heads askew.

Interpreting an Image through Narrative Writing

Initially, the photo seemed to be a reflection of the creative drama camaraderie and constructivist worldview that I had endeavored to build with the children during that school year—each of us improvising a response to the cue to "make a funny face for the camera." The picture both pleased the teacher in me and symbolized much of what we had experienced in our dramatic educational journey together—spontaneous, independent thinking intermixed with the sharing and scaffolding of one another's ideas as an entire classroom of learners. It was a reminder of the children's confidence in me as their teacher/facilitator/drama leader.

And yet several days after school ended, I discovered another aspect of the photograph. Six of the children, I realized, were not conjuring up funny faces for the camera or for their own engagement. Instead, they had turned towards the back row and were looking at me—their teacher. I was unsure what meaning to ascribe to their focused attention. Were they seeking my approval, looking to me as a funny-face model, seizing the opportunity to make a face at an adult, or choosing to perform to please their teacher rather than to create a photographic image for themselves? Where was the "good one" behind this picture, where was the hidden picture that would suit *my* images of creative dramatics as pedagogy and of drama leader as coach, not director?

Often during my study, I had had to look to the children as the dissertation authorities in providing answers to such questions. I relied on them to help me to peel away my adult overlays of skills and knowledge bases that had come to obscure my recollection of elementary-school students' perspectives on learning and life.[3] But school was over, and I could no longer gather our classroom community to deepen my understandings of primary school learning and revive forgotten childhood ways of being. Instead, I turned to my collected research and began to sort through my data fragments of videos, tape recordings and teacher/children's writings/drawings. I wanted to weave them into a connected wholeness by authoring the narratives of creative dramatics experiences in our elementary classroom, hoping to comprehend why—even at the very end of the school year—some children still looked to their drama leader for the "right answer" instead of creating their own unique response for the camera.

In retrospect, I see that I was engaged in a method of inquiry which Dorothy Smith (1999), a feminist essayist, refers to as "writing the social":

> The course of writing the social . . . is one of finding out how to make active, present, and observable the theoretical, conceptual, ideological, and other forms of thought. The text is a material object that brings into actual contexts of reading a standardized form of words or images that can be read/seen/heard in many other settings by many others at the same or other times. (7)

This view of temporal flexibility enabled through the flow of one's writing is a perspective that is also found in process drama—during enactments "as-if" one is experiencing the moment as another (Courtney 1995), and during drama debriefings as a conveyance of one's thinking through words expressed to others. Like Smith, I believed that "inquiry is in and of the same world as people live in" (Smith 1999, 8), and so I began to write about the dramatic world the children and I had experienced in our classroom contexts and curriculum.

As I wrote, I kept in mind the basic elements of narrative: character, plot, and setting. I also thought about the nuances and appeal of the dramatic, as well as the potential usefulness of my educational study to a reader who remained interested in what I had to say. I deliberately structured my narrations to capture the reader's attention, using different textual formats to delineate data sources (such as journals, learning logs, tapes, plan books, and so on). I gave myself permission to wander back and forth temporally through the years of data I had collected and to author the dissertation in a narrative style. I hoped to depict both the images of our elementary classroom interactions and of my ongoing thinking in a captivating and intellectual way. And as I wrote and rewrote, thought and rethought, discussed and deliberated, I began to see in myself the distinct image of an authorial dissertation writer.

Guiding the Images and Interpreting the Processes

During the writing of this book chapter (and through many discussions of its evolving drafts), I recognized that many of the images of authority I have portrayed are my own vivid impressions of scholarly characteristics I hoped to emulate. Because I found the images so compelling and so conceptually intimidating, I imbued them with an authority I could not imagine internalizing, at least initially. Yet as I continued my pursuit for the "magic formula" for writing a dissertation, I also engaged in recurrent conversations and shared experiences with others who were interested in what *I* thought and who wondered how *I* would structure my inquiry. Slowly, I came to realize that the authoritative images I looked to as "dissertation experts" were not specific external models of how to write a dissertation. Instead, they were interactive guides who inspired me intellectually to imagine and to craft my own doctoral study.

Just as important were the processes of classroom drama and of dissertation research. They provided "signposts along the way" or "markers" of my inquiry progress and "common referents" (Koziol and Pence, in Collins, 1991) through which I could focus my thoughts and share my classroom and inquiry experiences by portraying my unique ontological landscape.

The creative drama process not only helped me to explore my classroom pedagogy on many levels, but also provided a lens through which to imagine the possibilities for my dissertation research. One type of informal drama activity is called a "visualization" or an "imagery" exercise. In the elementary classroom, these exercises focus on activating and encouraging children to use their abilities to imagine both real and hypothetical events and experiences to support their learning (Koziol and Richards 1996). In retrospect, I see that I, too, prepared for and propelled myself through my inquiry journey by exploring both actual and imaginary representations of dissertation authorities, by connecting them with my previous experiences as well as new ideas and information. And in the writing of the dissertation, I "guided (myself) to form mental pictures of places and events through the use of narration" (Cottrell 1987) as I authored my narrative study and constructed an image of myself as a dissertation authority and scholar.

The recursive nature of writing the dissertation has also helped me authorize myself in a broader way as I look toward my future professional inquiries and writing. As Elliot Eisner (1991) says,

Images also generalize. . . . It is the generalizing capacity of the image that leads us to look for certain qualities in classroom life, features in teaching, or aspects of discussion, rather than others. Once we secure images of excellence in these realms, we apply them to other aspects of the world to which we believe them to be relevant. (199)

As I look toward the features of the classroom drama process and the imposed interconnections (revealed through my study) with external school district mandates and state and federal standards, I remind myself of aspects of narrative inquiry that can continue to authorize my pedagogical coexistence with those instructional impositions—as well as strengthen an individual resistance to intrusive demands. I can mentally formulate academic avenues and instructional images that help me to reconcile the civil servant and artistic teacher roles that are both an integral part of my professional being. And as I consider and am inspired by these aesthetic aspects of pedagogy, process drama, individual inquiry, and interpretive writing, an "excellent" dramatic pedagogical image replays in my mind.

Sharing a Pedagogical Image

We began that morning's lessons with a page from the district-purchased spelling book that contains the weekly unit words (chosen by the publishing company). That week's word list contained the consonant blends "sw," "sl," "sp," "st," and "sk." I noted that there were five word blends, exactly the number of small groups I had arranged in the classroom at the beginning of the school year. I distributed the phonics-blend magnet tiles to each small group, along with the instructions to find a word containing their given phonics blend.

Immediately, the children exploded into flurries of purposeful activity. Some referenced their spelling books, several stuck their magnet tiles to the side of their desks, others scrambled to the window shelves to retrieve copies of My First Dictionary, *a few others got chalkboards to write words on, and still other children consulted their sign language alphabet strips on their desks.*

When ready, the participant groups lined up to take turns displaying a sign language letter contained in a word with the assigned consonant blends, such as "s-w-e-e-t" or "s-l-i-p." As their little hands formed and fingerspelled the words, they often cued each other verbally, physically nudged one another to line up in the correct order, or used their own hands to correct a fellow group member's unclear finger spelling. This whole body enactment of the spelling words seemed to help them to internalize and memorize the word patterns of the spelling unit.

The children also followed my cues as drama leader: "First read your word in sign language, then think it in English. Then say it aloud. Next, spell your sign language letters together. Now say the word in English. Now show the sign for it." (Often they had to look up a word in their American Sign Language dictionaries, too.) "Okay, which group is next? Ready . . . begin!" I cued with my best drama leader's voice, tone, and pacing, while also maintaining my classroom manager's role as direction-giver and disciplinarian: "This group needs to look up another word." "Please open your dictionaries." "When you are finished demonstrating your word, please sit back down at your seat."

As always, I had to end that day's activity before the children were physically "spelled-out." A chorus of "Aww. . . . Can't we do two more?" ensued as I directed them to return to their desks and to complete—with pencil and paper—the spelling-book page the district required.

Narrating the Present—
Learning and Writing Drawn from the Images

The children's engagement in this spelling lesson exemplifies the active learning processes and informal drama frameworks that inspired the narrative writing of my dissertation. Through these writings, I could view the pedagogical nuances of the inclusion of the children's ideas and actions within the prescribed school district curriculum and fully consider such enacted learning opportunities.

In my years of narrative writing, I have experienced and expressed the challenges of capturing the ephemeral multilayered features of informal drama activities and of representing those experiential processes in both verbal and textual forms. I have come to believe that as I study the connections between creative dramatics and curriculum, I embody those processes in my classroom instruction.

During my varied inquiries, I have thought deeply about integrating drama processes with district mandates, and I have noticed a troubling intrusion into my pedagogical planning (although for a long while I mentally framed that intrusion as "acknowledging an already crowded elementary-school curriculum") and have continued to research ways that an integrated drama process can fit instructionally within those compulsory curricular frameworks. At times, I have been able to deflect the pressure of external impositions by perceiving drama as an integral part of teaching, learning, and knowing. Yet educational dictates—such as district benchmarks, the Pennsylvania State System of Assessment and its "proficiency" levels, and, of course, ESEA rhetoric (which I wish would translate as "Every Student Experientially Activated")—continually bombard the elementary classroom environment. Thus, I believe that it is more important than ever for me to make deliberate and consistent inquiries into my own teaching through narrative inquiry and process drama.

Participating in and Guiding Images of the Future

The "pictures in my mind" I've explored in this chapter are representative of the pedagogical images that consistently guide me toward and propel me through ongoing scholarly study (beyond the dissertation) and toward a continual reauthorization of myself as inquirer, writer, and interpreter of new classroom narrations and the dramatic ideas that underpin them. As Maxine Greene (1995) reminds us, "To learn and to teach, one must have an awareness of leaving something behind while reaching toward something new, and this kind of awareness must be linked to imagination" (20). As I leave behind the dissertation inquiry and my search for definitive academic authorities, I look ahead to individualized images of students and teachers in ongoing aesthetic activities, explored together through curricular experiences and classroom discussions. I imagine participating in a blend of artistic and academic conversations with many edified experts in varied, nonstandardized contexts, and I look forward to the opportunity to share our intellectual images as we individually author and collectively read the stages and settings of our dramatic educational explorations.

Notes

1. In actuality, both my overview and defense meetings were much more collaborative and collegial than my initial image of intellectual interrogation and intimidation. My committee suggested literary avenues for me to explore and raised questions that served me well as I worked through the inquiry process. Although I was still extremely nervous before both meetings and was asked to incorporate some minor rewrites at the final meeting, I truly cherish the memory of my doctoral defense, the memory of how I came to "own my study" and to engage in intellectual debate as a scholar rather than as a student.

2. At that time, "creative dramatics" was a term generally used in the field of theatre artists and drama educators. "Process drama" is a more recent term that has evolved from the principles and practices of creative dramatics. As Nelson and Moss (2003) describe it, "Process drama is a specifically designed theatrical experience where students/participants and teachers/facilitators co-create and explore an imagined world for the purpose of discovering new skills and levels of understanding. Its goal is to facilitate deeper learning in a specifically identified topic." (4)
3. In my dissertation, *Pictures in Our Minds: A Narrative Study of the Incorporation of Creative Dramatics as Pedagogy in Elementary Classroom Content Areas* (Richards 1996), I propose an analogy of "drama as synectics," as revealed through the data collection process. During group discussions and drama debriefings, the children and I shared our disparate perspectives of classroom roles, life stages, and ways of learning. We were able to synectically assume inclusive stances of teachers/learners, study participants, and co-constructors of classroom curriculum drawn from our mutual participation in creative drama processes and inquiry. Perhaps also of interest to the reader is that my father's research company was named Synectics Corporation. Dad is now a retired CEO but remains a continuing scholar and an ongoing contributor to my thinking.

References

Collins, J., ed. 1991. *Teaching and learning language collaboratively.* Portsmouth, NH: Heinemann.

Connelly, F., and D. Clandinin. 1988. *Teachers as curriculum planners.* New York: Teachers College Press.

Cottrell, J. 1987. *Creative drama in the classroom: Grades 1–3.* Lincolnwood, IL: National Textbook Company.

Courtney, R. 1995. *Drama and feeling: An aesthetic theory.* Montreal: McGill–Queen's University Press.

Cresswell, J. 1994. *Research design: Qualitative and quantitative approaches.* Thousand Oaks, CA: Sage.

Denzin, N., and Y. Lincoln, eds. 1992. *Handbook of qualitative research.* Thousand Oaks, CA: Sage.

Eisner, E. 1991. *The enlightened eye: Qualitative inquiry and the enhancement of educational practice.* New York: Macmillan.

Greene, M. 1999. *Releasing the imagination: Essays on education, the arts, and social change.* San Francisco: Jossey-Bass.

Koziol, S., and P. Pence. 1991. Collaborative opportunities through creative drama. In *Teaching and learning language collaboratively*, ed. J. Collins, 45–54. Portsmouth, NH: Heinemann Educational Books.

Koziol, S., and L. Richards. 1996. Informal drama as pedagogy. Unpublished manuscript adapted from materials from the Active Learning Project for Primary Education in Bosnia-Herzegovina. UNICEF.

Krathwohl D., B. Bloom, and B. Masia. 1964. *Affective domain.* Book 2 of *Taxonomy of educational objectives.* New York: Longman.

Logsdon, M. B. 2000. *A pedagogy of authority: Speculative essays by an English teacher*. UMI ProQuest Digital Dissertation #ATT 9998630.

Marshall, C. and G. Rossman. 1995. *Designing qualitative research*. Thousand Oaks, CA: Sage.

McMahon, P. 1993. *A narrative study of three levels of reflection in a college composition class: Teacher journal, student portfolios, teacher-student discourse*. UMI ProQuest Digital Dissertation #ATT 9329582.

Nelson, G., and E. Moss. 2003. Harnessing the winds. *Stage of the Art* 15, no. 3: 4–5.

Piantanida, M., and N. Garman. 1999. *The qualitative dissertation: A guide for students and faculty*. Thousand Oaks, CA: Corwin Press.

Richards, L. 1996. *Pictures in our minds: A narrative study of the incorporation of creative dramatics as pedagogy in elementary classroom content areas*. UMI ProQuest Digital Dissertation #ATT 9637875.

Smith, D. 1999. *Writing the social*. Ontario: University of Toronto Press.

Wilhelm, J., and B. Edmiston. 1998. *Imagining to learn: Inquiry, ethics, and integration through drama*. Portsmouth, NH: Heinemann.

CHAPTER 3

Problematizing Educational Inclusion through Heuristic Inquiry

Micheline Stabile

My dissertation, "A Call to Conscience: Problematizing Educational Inclusion," portrays understandings gleaned from my three-year practice-based study of educational inclusion (Stabile, 1999). The intent of my study was to problematize the concept of educational inclusion for the purpose of informing educational policy and practice. Through my practice, I'd become aware of the complexities inherent in applying educational inclusion policies—often discussed in overly simplistic and functional ways—and accordingly, I wanted my inquiry to be "practice-based." That is, I intended to gain deeper understandings of educational inclusion within the messy, unstable context of my practice rather than through the distanced stance I had assumed to be a prerequisite of research. In this chapter I describe my search for deeper understandings as I journeyed along research paths that spiraled into ever-deepening cycles of heuristic inquiry—the research genre that I adapted to fit an interpretive study of educational inclusion.

As I conceptualized my study of educational inclusion, I considered how an educational administrator with a desire to inform her own practice is uniquely positioned as a researcher and how such a position could be reflected in a research design. Inspired by the work of Douglass and Moustakas (1985), who work in the fields of humanities and psychology, I conceived a heuristic research process that would allow me to respond freely to the flow of events that occur naturally within my special education administrative practice.

In my doctoral studies, I noticed that the term "heuristic" often surfaced within the discourse of interpretive educators to indicate a conceptualization that is thought provoking but not prescriptive.[1] As I explored more fully the genre of heuristic inquiry, I was drawn to the idea of a research process designed "to awaken and inspire researchers to make contact with and respect their own questions and problems" and "to affirm imagination, intuition, self-reflection, and the tacit dimension as valid ways in the search for knowledge and understanding" (Douglas and Moustakas 1985, 40).

Douglass and Moustakas (1985) suggest a "natural series" of processes that come into play when one attempts to know a thing heuristically. In order to avoid the impression that heuristic "research phases" are experienced as discrete and linear, I imagined heuristic research processes to be embedded within iterative *cycles*. Thus my research path looped back upon itself many times, each iteration adding a new layer of complexity and understanding. Guided by reflection, deliberation, dialogue, narrative, interpretation, intuition and other processes that draw from the tacit dimension (Polanyi 1966), my heuristic research path led me through five cycles of inquiry that I used as a framework to describe the specifics of my study: engagement, immersion, acquisition, realization and creative synthesis (see figure 1).

Cycles of Engagement

Every so often, unsettling complexities that beg for reflective attention surface in the busy lives of educational practitioners like myself. As they linger in our awareness, waiting to be acknowledged and understood, these periodic ruptures threaten our complacency. There is usually little time to sort out these nagging inconsistencies and no simple answer to the underlying dilemmas. Gadamer (1975) in his philosophy of hermeneutics (interpretation), refers to these subtle yet jarring disruptions as a "break in the spell of one's own foremeaning" (268). These kinds of encounters are characterized as experiences that "surprise, question, challenge, resist, or refute what we take for granted" (268). According to Gadamer scholar Deborah Kerdeman (1998), encounters that challenge familiar assumptions force us to "come face to face with the strange" (p 275). In the language of the heuristic research genre, the unrest that is generated by such a confrontation represents an "initial engagement" that may be construed as an opportunity for growth—as an invitation to enter into a new cycle of inquiry that can yield deeper understanding. Though I did not know it at the time, the unrest generated by my search for a dissertation topic, a research method, and a resolution to the dilemmas of educational inclusion were inextricably intertwined. All converged to become a part of my initial engagement with the dissertation process.

Initial Engagement: Unrest at the Academy

When I reached the point in my doctoral program of selecting a topic for doctoral study, I resisted "contaminating" my academic respite with the messy uncertainties of "practical" problems. The idea of subjecting the complex dilemmas that characterized my administrative practice to the objective rigidity of a research process was equally distasteful.

Throughout my doctoral studies I had been content to maintain a comfortably schizophrenic existence between scholarship and practice. I took the helm of my dissertation process with lofty ambitions that my study would be a grand intellectual escape from the daily stresses of my administrative practice and from what I thought of as the confines of functionalist thought dominating my field. As an Ed.D. candidate, I understood that my contributions as a practitioner and scholar must be to the fields of special education and educational administration. I sensed with dismay that both of these fields embrace a strong tradition of functionalism and operate from research bases that place a high value upon the empirical. Each time I attempted to move toward what I considered to be higher intellectual places, I was confronted by hard realities. The more I attempted to free myself from the grasp of my functionalist roots, the more entangled I became. I was entrenched within the narrow intellectual confines of an educational practitioner.

Initial Engagement: Unrest in Practice

As I struggled at the academy to identify a topic for dissertation study that would be unhampered by reality, I became increasingly preoccupied by another disquieting struggle that threatened the hard-earned complacency and professional equilibrium of my thirty years of teaching and administrative practice. While the rhetoric of "educational inclusion," a popular movement to expand the scope of the general education system to serve more diverse populations of students, had a kind of intuitive seductive appeal, I was finding that the day-to-day realities posed by inclusion within the context of schooling held subtle problematics that were resistant to simple solutions. Called to action, I felt that I needed to commit to a pro or con position but instead teetered precariously on the fence of indecision—a sure sign of administrative weakness. I began to question the fence itself as arbitrary—a binary construction that typifies functionalist thinking.

And so just as I was pressed at the academy to choose a dissertation topic, dynamics of inclusion for students with disabilities played out around me in my practice, triggering yet another "rupture," ending my long sojourn in the schism between scholarship and practice. My two worlds converged, and the journey of my dissertation began.

Re-engagement

Throughout the inquiry process my engagement with the notion of educational inclusion deepened, marked by a persistent sense of unrest whenever I encountered troubling manifestations of the theory in practice. I grew to associate periodic times of intense re-engagement—triggered by a particularly poignant conversation, an emotional or puzzling encounter, or some incongruent piece of information—with the urgent need to "make sense" of something. These cycles jarred me into action, driving me to write a story, for example, or to engage with someone about some aspect of my study. I believe that my connection to the inquiry process was sustained throughout the course of my three-year study by these periodic awakenings.

Cycles of Immersion

During times of immersion I generated voluminous materials to use later in my portrayal and interpretation of various images of educational inclusion; I imagine heuristic cycles of immersion to roughly correspond to the idea of "data collection." In my study, these cycles were marked by my prolonged participation in discourses related to educational inclusion that I encountered in professional literature, tapes, movies, newspaper articles, fugitive documents, conference proceedings, and dialogue with other participants. In short, I immersed myself in anything I felt could deepen my understanding of the shapes educational inclusion could take.

My work as a doctoral student within a program of educational administration and my role as a special education supervisor put me into daily contact with many teachers, parents, students, university instructors, and educational administrators at local and state levels. E-mail correspondence and professional conferences expanded the boundaries of my world, offering seemingly unlimited opportunities for immersion. I refer to these dialogic interactions as "conversations," drawing on Gadamer's ideas:

> Every dialogue we have with the thinking of a thinker [that] we are seeking to understand remains an endless conversation. It is a real conversation, a conversation in which we seek to find "our" language—to grasp what we have in common. . . . In a conversation . . . one seeks to open oneself to him or her, which means holding fast to the common subject matter as the ground on which one stands together with one's partner. (quoted in Hahn 1997, 36)

Conversations

Assuming a stance of spontaneity and openness characteristic of heuristic inquiry, I took advantage of many unplanned encounters that occurred naturally within the daily course of my practice and my academic work. In addition, I deliberately planned experiences to inform my understanding of educational inclusion. During the course of one school year, I invited thirty-five participants—all from various school districts, including adult members of disability groups; university instructors; elementary, middle and secondary special education and general education teachers; principals; central office administrators; supervisors; parents; students; and policymakers—to engage in small group or one-to-one conversations about educational inclusion.

These planned interactions typically took place within informal settings over meals or snacks before school, during lunch or after work hours. My invitation was usually extended after some initial spontaneous interaction that led me to believe an individual had an interesting story or unique perspective to share. My interaction with these participants *prior* to our more focused conversation seemed to engender a comfortable climate that fostered open, trusting and often passionate dialogue. Almost without exception, I found participants willing and eager to engage in substantive conversations about educational inclusion.

Using a log of encounters, I documented pages of notes and reflections on hundreds of additional spontaneous interactions with teachers, administrators, parents and students. During the course of my study, I created an annotated database of over six hundred references from literature and fugitive documents. Continuous immersions in these formed the basis of my interpretations of these many encounters. Such was the "stuff" of my study.

I do not claim that the vast array of material generated by my research cloaks me with any degree of scientific objectivity or has earned me the right to claim scientific-like truths. Rather, I allude to this rich source of material to demonstrate the rigor of my strivings to grasp the complexities and problematics of educational inclusion and to capture these within portrayals of substance, authenticity and verisimilitude that are the hallmarks of "truth" in the interpretive sense of the word.

Cycles of Acquisition

The narratives, anecdotes, quotes, vignettes, and portrayals of my conversations are all products I created during heuristic cycles of acquisition. These cycles of acquisition and their resulting texts enabled me to draw forth and illuminate meanings embedded within my research encounters. I refer to my way of making meaning through narrative as "storying" and to the products of acquisition as "storied conversations."

Storied Conversations

Often my encounters prompted an almost immediate narrative urge to "story the conversation." Several scholars have explicated the use of narrative as a sense-making process.[2] In addition to drawing on the work of these scholars, I used Reason and Hawkins's (1988) "empirical topology" of four types of responses to an original tale to organize the various ways I tried to make sense of conversations through story. (I use narrative and story in this instance interchangeably).

Reason and Hawkins describe their typography in the following way:

1. A *reply* is 'my reaction to your story': an expressive way of giving shape to the feelings and ideas arising while listening to the story.
2. An *echo* or sharing response is 'your theme in my story': here the listeners tell their own stories on the same theme.
3. A *re-creation* is 'your story as re-created by me': here the listeners take the story and re-shape it into another form, finding their own way of telling the tale.
4. A *reflection* is 'my story about your story': essentially, the reflection involves standing further back, it is more 'about-ist', pondering the story. (90–92)

See figure 2 for an example of my storied conversation with Kate, a special education central office administrator. I see this storied conversation as an example of a reflection, according to the above empirical topology.

Cycles of Realization

Within iterative cycles of realization, I reached deeper and deeper levels of meaning-making through processes of reflection, deliberation, writing, interpreting, sifting, sorting and what Piantanida and Garman whimsically refer to as "slogging through the stuff" (1999, 166). Since understanding comes about through empathy and reflective probing, which I saw as hallmarks of the problematizing process, I attempted to portray and interpret various viewpoints of educational inclusion in such a way as to create an empathy for each while also making each debatable or topical for deliberation. Ultimately these multifaceted perspectives on inclusion were embedded in the texts of my storied conversations, where they revealed problematics within political, community, cultural, practical and moral/ethical frames (see figure 3).

Cycles of Creative Synthesis

During iterative cycles of creative synthesis, I stepped back from the ongoing details of my inquiry to grasp a bigger conceptual picture, getting a feel for which issues I would portray and how I might assemble and integrate isolated pieces of meaning from individual storied conversations to form a whole.

Often the products of this synthesis took the shape of heuristics that gave me opportunities to think aloud with others about meanings and helped me craft the portrayals that would ultimately represent the conceptual centerpiece of my work. Within the text of my dissertation, heuristics took the form of metaphor, story, anecdote, various portrayals of conversations in practice and in literature, quotations, charts and graphic displays. I imagined my document to be an assembly of many carefully crafted pieces of text interwoven to form an intricately designed pattern of meaning.

My dissertation text thus represents a synthesis of my understandings of educational inclusion. Written in the form of a nine-chapter book, its organization captures several levels of understandings that occured with each iteration of movement through heuristic research cycles. Gradually I came to see an interconnectedness between scholarship and practice. My quest for certainty gave way to an appreciation for uncertainty. My focus upon solving problems gave way to acknowledging problematics. I recognized, ultimately, that the complexities of educational inclusion lend themselves more to temporary resolution than to permanent solution and require a language other than that of technique. Hence, the language of technique that permeates my administrative world gave way to a discourse of ethics. Here I imagined conversation to occur on multiple levels—collectively through engagement in what I termed "deliberative discourse" and individually through self dialogue prompted by the "voices of conscience" described by Green (1985, 25) and referred to by Starratt (1994) as "callings" of sacrifice, membership, memory, craft and imagination (7–8).

In my qualitative/interpretive study of educational inclusion, two-dimensional metaphors ultimately give way to a creative synthesis that takes the form of an appeal. Practitioners, policymakers and others grappling with the painful trade-offs inherent in the notion of inclusion behind the closed doors of boardrooms, schools and classrooms are urged to heed their own calls to conscience as they exercise their freedom to decide and to act.

Epilogue

Through the dissertation process, I achieved my ambition to break away from the functionalist mindset that had constrained my thinking as a practitioner/scholar. I allowed my imagination to carry me far away to the lofty intellectual places of my dreams and was forever transformed.

After a year on sabbatical, I returned to my administrative position sporting the hard-earned title of "doctor" and guarding a new-found sense of authenticity deep within. Eisner (1991) charges the educational inquirer to reach beyond personal knowing, to be educative in a public way. Smyth (1989) maintains that to operate in an educative fashion implies "to make sense of things and to communicate that sense to others" (191). Accordingly, within a short time I accepted a new position in my school district as Special Education Coordinator of Curriculum, Instruction and Assessment. I continued my membership within the interpretive study group that embodies much of what I have come to believe about being a teacher and a learner. Perhaps most significantly, I was afforded the opportunity to engage with students as teacher once again. I accepted an invitation to teach a course on educational inclusion to general education pre-service teachers at a local university. I was scarcely able to contain my delight as students shared their final reflections at the close of the most recent term. One student wrote:

> I remember sitting in the first class thinking, "great, a class that is going to preach the necessity of inclusion," but I was mistaken. I have had teachers that made their beliefs the facts, instead of allowing the student to develop their own point of view. This course gave me experiences with inclusion. I was very impressed from the beginning. I soon realized that I would not be given an opinion, but the ability to form an opinion for myself based on my own experiences. (An undergraduate pre-service teacher, April 2004)

It has been suggested that teaching and learning situations need continually to give back a learner's narrative experience so that it may be reflected upon, valued and enriched (Connelly and Clandinin 1985, 197). How satisfying it is to have found a place within discourse communities of my profession where I myself can give back what I've come to know.

Figure 1. Cycles of Heuristic Inquiry

Resting in One's Own Experience
The practitioner is in a state of contented involvement feeling confident in her ability to meet the challenges of her practice.

Engagement Cycles
A type of rupture or awakening occurs creating a discontent and unrest in practice. The drive to gain a deeper understanding of educational inclusion sustains engagement throughout the inquiry process.

Creative Synthesis
The researcher crafts heuristic portrayals of understandings.

Immersion Cycles
The researcher continuously immerses herself in issues related to the content and processes of the inquiry. Raw material is gathered through dialogic encounters or conversations with various participants of educational inclusion, fugitive documents, newspaper clippings, audio and video tapes, artifacts of practice, educational conference proceedings, and literature.

Realization Cycles
The researcher takes a multiperspectival approach to interpret the text using various lenses in order to "illuminate" dilemmas, issues, concerns, and problematics that are embedded in the text. These lenses include: political, community, cultural, practical, and moral/ethical.

Acquisition Cycles
The researcher constructs text from notes, written correspondence, tapes, transcripts, and journal entries in an attempt to capture the essence of dilemmas, issues, concerns, and problematics related to educational inclusion. The text of the inquiry is constructed continuously throughout the research process through "storying" and the creation of portrayals.

Figure 2. An Example of a Storied Conversation with Interpretation

Kate is a central office special education administrator. Through story she discredits political or theoretic viewpoints of educational inclusion that she sees as based on principles rather than on important details of individual circumstances. Kate sees the move of her school district toward full inclusion as limiting her options to alleviate difficulties.

From a Distance

> We have a kindergarten kid that was in a special education pre-school program last year. Most folks agreed that he needed a full-time special education program for kindergarten, a self-contained class with a teacher, an aide and no more than twelve kids in a class. Because of an inclusion policy, we have disbanded self-contained special education classrooms, and we say that the kid is going to get a full-time program, but he's going to get it in a regular classroom. So the full-time program translates into someone coming in and saying to the regular education teacher, "You should make accommodations for this kid, and these are some ways you can do it."
>
> Normally the kindergarten classes have a class size limit of twenty-two kids, but this particular classroom has thirty-eight kids. The board should have assigned an aide to the class, but they aren't giving aides because they can't afford it. So now with the included kid, the class has thirty-nine kids and a teacher who is overwhelmed and feels unable to make all of the accommodations that this kid needs to help him with his learning.
>
> A philosophy that says, "This youngster deserves it, so he will get it," doesn't take into account the reality of limited budgets and people with limited skills. Through some of their own fault and sometimes just because of their position in life, their training, their age, life crises or whatever, they don't have that time or the skills. So we hoodwink ourselves into thinking that because we say a youngster deserves it, and we set a policy that says he is going to get it, that he actually gets it. There's no check on the reality of that. From a distance all looks well, but . . .

Kate's opinion about educational inclusion hinges upon the details of unique circumstances surrounding individual students within various school settings, rather than upon absolute values. Her viewpoint can be illuminated through the work of Diane Bricker and other interpretive researchers whose attention is drawn toward local irregularities rather than global generalities.

Bricker (1995), who has had a long-term professional involvement in developing integrated programs for young children with disabilities, describes the way in which she began to see that the "overriding value debate was diverting attention from careful analysis of what was happening to children in integrated sites" (183). Her description of educational inclusion, like Kate's, captures the essence of a viewpoint in which the value of inclusion is determined by its application, rather than by a wholesale advocacy.

Figure 3. Lenses That Reveal and Conceal Images of Educational Inclusion

POLITICAL	COMMUNITY	CULTURAL	PRACTICAL	MORAL/ETHICAL

While a political lens can reveal divergent interests and underlying dynamics of conflict and power, it can obscure ways in which actors reframe images of scarcity, conflict, mistrust, and competition in order to pursue authentic inclusive practices. Thus, a political lens:
 	
 • Illuminates complex dynamics that can prohibit a "rational" implementation of mandated inclusion policies.
 	
 • Conjures images of conflicting interests generated by policies of inclusion.
 	
 • Highlights ways that power within bureaucratic school organizations mediates such interests.
 	
 • Calls attention to gender, race, and class dynamics of educational inclusion as well as to disability issues.
	A lens of community conceals the way in which an emphasis upon sameness and "smoothing over differences" can exacerbate marginalization. Thus, a lens of community:
	
	 • Grants views of inclusion within the context of schools imagined as communities rather than as factories.
	
	 • Focuses attention upon such issues as:
	   – the collective good;
	   – caring;
	   – belonging;
	   – connectedness;
	   – interrelatedness;
	   – collaboration around shared values and human commonalities.
		A cultural lens conceals ways that oversimplification of the complexities of culture, identity, and community contribute to essentialist conceptions of difference, or can reinforce the instrumentalist notion that school cultures can be subject to manipulation. Thus, a cultural lens:
		
		 • Reveals responses to educational inclusion that are rooted in the shared norms, values, ideas, and beliefs that are a part of various cultures within groups.
		
		 • Allows different groups to be examined as sub-cultures, such as:
		   – disability groups;
		   – special and general education;
		   – elementary, middle, and secondary schools;
		   – policy levels, central office levels, and individual school levels.
			A practical lens focuses on functionalist images of efficiency, productivity, and accountability while obscuring more human aspects, subtleties and complexities. Thus, a practical lens:
			
			 • Emphasizes action over theory.
			
			 • Privileges contextual irregularities over global generalities.
			
			 • Makes visible the logistical challenges of inclusion policies such as:
			   – student scheduling;
			   – staff assignments;
			   – architectural redesigns;
			   – budgeting;
			   – curricular adaptations;
			   – school wide and classroom procedures like testing, grading, and instructional how to's.
				A moral/ethical lens calls attention to choices that reflect beliefs about the way the social world should be and the way one ought to live. This lens emphasizes reflection upon choices made in response to inclusive school policies and consideration of the consequences of action or nonaction upon others. Thus, a moral/ethical lens:
				
				 • Allows issues of power to be examined.
				
				 • Allows the self and other to be seen as belonging to the same consciousness.
				
				 • Elevates questions of "why" over technical questions of "how."
				
				 • Reveals dilemmas that emerge when moral rationality (based on what is believed to be good) clashes with technical rationality (based on what is seen to be effective and efficient).

Notes

1. As an adjective, the term "heuristic" is frequently used to describe an alternative to rational or technical ways of understanding. When used as a noun, "heuristic" often refers to a conceptual meaning or device constructed in such a way as to capture the essence of complex concepts. As a thought-provoking conceptualization a heuristic can take many forms, including graphic displays, charts, taxonomies, cartoons, metaphors and art forms including stories and other texts. For further discussion of the concept see Barone 1995, 1997; Eisner 1991, 1993; Garman 1994; Haggerson 1986, 1987, 1993; Haggerson and Bowman 1992; Janesick 1994; Piantanida and Garman 1999; Randall and Southgate 1981; Robinson and Hawpe 1986.
2. See Bruner 1985, 1987; Clandinin and Connelly, 1991, 1995; Polkinghorne 1988; Reason and Hawkins 1988; Richardson 1994.

References

Barone, T. 1995. The purposes of arts-based educational research. *International Journal of Educational Research* 23, no. 2: 169–80.

———. 1997. "Seen and heard": The place of the child in arts-based research on theatre education. *Youth Theater Journal* 11: 113–27.

Bricker, D. 1995. The challenge of inclusion. *Journal of Early Intervention* 19, no. 3: 179–94.

Bruner, J. 1985. Narrative and pardigmatic modes of thought. In *Learning and teaching the ways of knowing: Eighty-fourth yearbook of the National Society for the Study of Education*, ed. E. Eisner, 97–115. Chicago: University of Chicago Press.

———. 1987. Life as narrative. *Social Research* 54, no. 1: 11–32.

Clandinin, D. J., and F. M. Connelly. 1991. Narrative and story in practice and research. In *The reflective turn*, ed. D. Schon, 258–81. New York: Teachers College Press.

———. 1995. *Teachers' professional knowledge landscapes*. New York: Teachers College Press.

Connelly, F. M., and D. J. Clandinin. 1985. Personal practical knowledge and the modes of knowing: Relevance for teaching and learning. In *Learning and teaching the ways of knowing: Eighty-fourth yearbook of the National Society for the Study of Education*, ed. E. Eisner, 174–98. Chicago: University of Chicago Press.

———. 1990. Stories of experience and narrative inquiry. *Educational Researcher* 19 (June/July): 2–14.

Douglass, B. G., and C. Moustakas. 1985. Heuristic inquiry: The internal search to know. *Journal of Humanistic Psychology* 25, no. 3: 39–55.

Eisner, E. 1991. *The Enlightened eye: Qualitative inquiry and the enhancement of educational practice*. New York: Macmillan.

———. 1993. Forms of understanding and the future of educational research. *Educational Researcher* 22 (October): 5–11.

Gadamer, H. G. 1975. *Truth and method*. 2nd ed. New York: Continuum.

———. 1976. The universality of the hermeneutical problem. In *Philosophical hermeneutics*, ed. D. E. Linge, 3–17. Berkeley: University of California Press.

Garman, N. 1994. Beyond the reflective practitioner and toward discursive practice. *Teaching and Teachers' Work* 2, no. 4: 1–7.

Green, T. F. 1985. The formation of conscience in an age of technology. *American Journal of Education* 93: 1–38.

Haggerson, N. L. 1986. Reconceptualizing inquiry in curriculum: Using multiple research paradigms to enhance the study of curriculum. *Journal of Curriculum Theorizing* 8, no. 1: 81–102.

———. 1987. *Heuristic encounters with Ted Aoki: Six episodes in search of an author.* Paper presented at the Bergamo Conference, October 28–November 1, Dayton, OH.

———. 1993. Education for human rights: Demythologizing dysfunctional qualities of myths. *International Journal of Educational Reform* 2, no. 1: 49–55.

Haggerson, N. L., and A. C. Bowman, eds. 1992. *Informing educational policy and practice through interpretive inquiry.* Lancaster, Pennsylvania: Technomic.

Hahn, L. E., ed. 1997. *The philosophy of Hans-Georg Gadamer.* Chicago: Open Court.

Janesick, V. J. 1994. The dance of qualitative research design: Metaphor, methodolatry, and meaning. In *Handbook of qualitative research*, ed. N. K. Denzin and Y. S. Lincoln, 209–19. Thousand Oaks, CA: Sage.

Kerdeman, D. 1998. Between Interlochen and Idaho: Hermeneutics and education for understanding. In *Philosophy of education 1998*, ed. S. Tozer, (275). Urbana, IL: Philosophy of Education Society.

Moustakas, C. 1990. *Heuristic research.* Newbury Park, CA: Sage.

———. 1981. Heuristic research. In *Human inquiry: A sourcebook of new paradigm research*, ed. P. Reason and J. Rowan, 207–17. New York: John Wiley & Sons.

———. 1994. *Phenomenological research methods.* Thousand Oaks, CA: Sage.

Piantanida, M., and N. B. Garman. 1999. *The qualitative dissertation: A guide for students and faculty.* Thousand Oaks, CA: Corwin Press.

Polanyi, M. 1967. *The tacit dimension.* Garden City, NY: Doubleday.

Polkinghorne, D. 1988. *Narrative knowing and the human sciences.* Albany: State University of New York Press.

Randall, R., and J. Southgate. 1981. Doing dialogical research. In *Human inquiry: A sourcebook of new paradigm research*, ed. P. Reason and J. Rowan, 349–61. New York: John Wiley & Sons.

Reason, P., and P. Hawkins. 1988. Storytelling as inquiry. In *Human inquiry in action: Developments in new paradigm research*, ed. P. Reason, 79–101. Newbury Park, CA: Sage.

Richardson, L. 1994. Writing: A method of inquiry. In *Handbook of qualitative research*, ed. N. K. Denzin and Y. S. Lincoln, 517–27. Thousand Oaks, CA: Sage.

Robinson, J. A., and L. Hawpe. 1986. Narrative thinking as a heuristic process. In *Narrative psychology*, ed. T. R. Sarbin, 111–25. New York: Praeger.

Smyth, J. 1989. A "pedagogical" and "educative" view of leadership. In *Critical perspectives on educational leadership*, ed. J. Smyth, 179–204. New York: Falmer Press.

Stabile, M. 1999. *A call to conscience: Problematizing educational inclusion.* UMI ProQuest Digital Dissertation # AAT 9928088.

Starratt, R. J. 1994. *Building an ethical school.* Washington, DC: Falmer Press.

CHAPTER 4

Confronting Authority and *Self*: Social Cartography and Curriculum Theorizing for Uncertain Times

JoVictoria Nicholson-Goodman

I write here about struggling with/in space: the theoretical space within which my dissertation was forged (Goodman 2003) and the spatial relations[1] of discourse about "America" and being "American" following September 11th, 2001. I frame it here as a confrontation, a confrontation first with authority writ large,[2] which in that moment was laying claim to the entire space of the nation, and second with self, that is, with my own spatial relations both to the work and to the moment under study. This chapter is therefore a narrative of my authority to imagine as it was shaped and constrained by confrontation. I begin by setting the scene, looking first at confronting authority and then at confronting self. I then turn to my visual portrayal of this moment, because the visual is the embodiment of the struggle and also of its tentative, temporal resolution.

I elected to map discourse about America and being American as cultural phenomena under reconstruction in deeply troubled times. I was, of course, caught up in that turmoil myself. Kemmis's (1986) notion of curriculum theorizing as "ideology-critique"[3] was instructive. He depicts this in terms of mapping "contemporary historical and social circumstances . . . not only to identify the key landmarks and symbols in the social territory 'out there' . . . but also to identify the key landmarks and symbols in the way we understand the world" (71–72).

I was also guided by Pinar's (1994) thoughts on *currere* as a research method "whose aspiration is not only contribution to a 'body of knowledge' but a contribution to the biographic-intellectual and thus political emancipation of those who employ it" (61). In Pinar, what seems essential to me is "the experience of knowledge creation," which "represents movement, release from our arrest" (1994, 61)—this, too, is a part of my narrative here. I worked to confront authority, challenging the exclusivity of its claim to space, acknowledging that my lived experience had everything to do with this desire on my part. At the same time, I worked to distance my study from self and find balance to perform the mapping, exercising what Kincheloe (1993) calls "post-formal thinking"[4] in the process. This, then, is my narrative of imagining my authority to portray difference and imagination in a cultural moment characterized by intense fear and extreme uncertainty.

In this cultural moment, a prescriptive enunciation (Foucault 1972) of "what *should* be" emerged abruptly as the defining discourse for the nation and its citizens. The moment I speak of was a stretch of time following September 11th, 2001, during which some strands of discourse spoke repeatedly of "silence" and "silencing," and in which the pervasive notion of "unity as defense" usurped the space of civic debate. Apprehending difference in this moment would require a confrontation with this enunciation. Nevertheless, in order to map the discourses with integrity, I would have to afford this dominant narrative its space while also working to see and show the spaces of competing and conflicting narratives. My opposition to the dominant narrative was self-evident, and I acknowledge that here to make my dilemma clear.

I wanted to portray a multiplicity of "social imaginaries" (constructs emerging from the work of imagination as social and cultural practice) (Appadurai 1996), to explore the space and potential contributions of social imagination. I focused on interrelations between competing narratives of the nation and of citizenship, and I did so because the surreal spectacle of attack burst upon us as though in a dream, shattering prior illusions/delusions of grandeur and invincibility, thus constituting a psychosocial rupture of national identity. This spectacle, further, was delivered to us in living color through the medium of television, over and over again in a sort of searing unreality, in that space normally reserved for our public amusement, jarring our sensibilities and putting us, I suspect, into what I would characterize as a condition of collective public trauma.

My aim was to draw a more inclusive picture of meanings of "America" and "American" than what was being proffered at the time by our public officials. I wanted to find a *way to see* that could dispel my shock. Thus, my dissertation had its beginnings in a space of tension, tension between a dominant prescriptive enunciation and my own determination to search out alternative visions and to find new meaning(s) in an otherwise devastating moment.

This meant that as a researcher, I would have to integrate interpretive work, whose interest is illumination, with critical discourse, whose interest is emancipation (Kemmis 1986, 71–72).[5] Thus would I lay hold of my prerogative as artist/citizen/scholar to re-present reality, mapping a cultural moment to recast it in new light (Paulston and Liebman 2000).[6] Through the heuristic of my map (see figure 1), I sought to portray how the "agonistics" of language (Lyotard 1984)—the contest of battling narratives—played out in a uniquely American moment to determine what America would become/create as we responded to terrorism. My purpose was to map linkages between what was said and what insights the discourses might bring to curriculum theorizing for a post-September 11th world.

Following September 11th, some of our citizens questioned the meaning(s) of "America" and "American" as the powerful used these terms to constrain and castigate difference amongst our people. Their questioning evoked a multiplicity of ways of seeing these constructs, creating diverse narratives of nation and of citizenship. Many of our citizens sought answers to this question of becoming/creating, a question that constitutes both a reconsideration and a reconstruction of our national identity and of corresponding meanings of citizenship. The visions of America that I encountered in the sometimes heated discourse of that moment lay at the center of our agonistics as we sought to make sense of where fear and uncertainty were propelling us.

These visions or "imaginaries" also pointed the way to seeing diverse possibilities for the nation's *currere* (the Latin infinitive of *curriculum*, meaning "to run the course"), which lies at the heart of curriculum theorizing (Pinar 1975). Pinar saw autobiography—the working out of what makes us who we are as an influence on how we see—as an essential element of *currere*. It seemed to me, therefore, that the imaginaries interacting at that time with this new narrative of the nation should play out in various ways as we thought about how to educate our young for a post-September 11th world.

As noted, we weren't lacking a prescription for how to view or experience the nation or the meaning of citizenship. In fact, one prescriptive enunciation of our national experience and the meaning of citizenship within that experience seemed to engulf us. The narrative clearly enunciated by President George W. Bush placed America center stage in a mythic battle between good and evil, a battle in which we were on the winning side, the side of "good," and therefore blessed by the Almighty in all of our pursuits. It was a triumphal narrative grounded in a doctrine of faith, the kind of narrative to be expected in a moment of such national trauma, grief, and fear. Right-wing pundits—on radio, in print, on the Internet, and on national television "newstalk" shows—elaborated on this enunciation with unmatched fervor. They honed that narrative, however, into something new, drawing the boundaries for the circle of belonging in America ever more tightly within the narrow confines of their own convictions. They were thus able to advance a particular narrative of American character and belief and, more importantly, to advance a hypernational narrative of its limits.

These limits circumscribed other narratives of what it meant to be American in this moment and amounted to one espoused worldview maneuvering to claim *all* of America as its space. This is what Bourdieu (1992) describes as the logic (or epistemology) of resentment, within which those who have new ideas, or perhaps just unconventional ideas, are made culpable for having them. Bourdieu elaborates:

> Many epistemological conflicts are wars of religion. What for me is disastrous, is that all these strategies are self-mutilating. People struggle against each other, but for their own satisfaction, to pander to their own limits. This is the epistemology of resentment. (1992, 48–49)

Under such circumstances, the narrative pushed to the fore by authority loomed large, and civic courage was required not just to stand up for alternative narratives, but even to make space for genuine inquiry. It was a moment where America as some of us knew it seemed to disappear, and the President, armed with his bastion of support from the New Right, seemed to be enunciating a new American way. Most alarming was the link between the triumphal narrative and its hypernational counterpart, which muddied our ability to see what direction the nation was actually taking. The result appeared to be that one political faction in our American culture was attempting to lay claim to the whole of the nation's discursive space. Apparently, difference and imagination were to be forfeited.

My struggle for conceptualizing my dissertation took place within this context, and so the shape it took was at least partially constrained by confrontation with authority. As an interpretivist, however, my conceptualization was forged as well in the emboldening fires of self-knowledge and of lived experience. Where confrontation seemed to back me into a critical negativism, my own desire for understanding, framed in terms of the active practice of social imagination, moved me forward toward a new way of linking multiple narratives in the heated terrain of the moment. And thus it was that I came to assert my artist's claim to space, my citizen's right to my own imaginary of the nation and of citizenship, and my scholar's perspective of the nation's *currere*. This is reflected in my cultural portrait of the moment.

Social Cartography: Cognitive Art for Curriculum Theorizing

I also struggled for aesthetic cognitive space from which I might explore these social imaginaries. Under Eisner's (2002) influence, I began the mapping project by thinking of it as a work in the process of becoming, and I therefore focused less on discovery and more on exploration itself[7] (hence it is a "working map"). The story of the map, then, is framed here in terms of its value as a cognitive art form that may transcend resentment, and at the same time, as a vehicle for curriculum theorizing.[8]

Freedom to explore meant that I needed to conduct my work without engaging in my own epistemology of resentment. As noted, this is a way of being in the world that always reflects a formal enunciation of right and wrong views or ideas, usually via some variation of a "with us or against us" mentality, the result of which is the production of some form of orthodoxy. This way of being cannot help but stifle both difference and imagination; it knows no other way, because it is always focused on reinforcing limits.

Illuminative scholarship cannot broach such orthodoxies, but must always consider a diversity of perspectives, arrangements, interpretations, and so forth, and present them with scholarly integrity. However, avoiding the pitfalls of resentment was a tall order since I viewed the triumphal hegemonic narrative as inherently dangerous and had a healthy aversion to the elaboration and extension of that narrative into a hypernational telling of the "American way." The former struck me as leading us into denial of our present difficulties as a nation, the latter as leading us down the path of coercion toward a new brand of domestic cultural repression and oppression.

I wrestled simultaneously, then, with the prescriptive terrain I was confronting, with the larger backdrop of my own lived experience and my own sensibilities about the agonistics of the moment, and with the contested discursive terrain surrounding America and American as social imaginaries. Confronting authority within this scenario required imagining my own authority as artist/citizen/scholar on three levels. First, I had to assume authority to explore the contested terrain of the discourse, despite this prescriptive enunciation censuring difference. Second, I had to find within myself the authority to take and defend an authentic stand within a terrain so clouded by fear and uncertainty that vertigo seemed to be the order of the day. Finally, I had to exercise my authority to imagine a portrayal of the terrain and to perform that portrayal in a scholarly manner, while still evoking some resonance in my reader.

The work of Rolland G. Paulston, who spent more than a decade cultivating a comparative method called social cartography,[9] came to my aid. This approach would serve me well in my endeavor to provide a portrait of this stormy moment in American discursive history as it reflected the diverse narratives of citizens struggling to make sense in the midst of anxiety and uncertainty. However, the experience was one of performing the work of mapping as though from a tightrope, where positioning from some distance would be crucial to not losing balance.

Social cartography may be useful for interpreting bewildering and/or contested "social scapes" (some aspect of our social milieu impacted by a phenomenon that generates debate or produces disorientation) to orient ourselves to the discursive terrain surrounding a conflict or tension (Paulston and Liebman 2000). This may be accomplished by portraying truth- and/or value-claims inherent in each of multiple ways of seeing a phenomenon and arranging them in relation to one another in a visual image (a "social map"). In this form of inquiry, the researcher maps the intertextual field formed by some set of discourses and discloses self by indicating her own position in/on the map. The researcher must assume the aesthetic authority to imagine the interrelations of alternative claims to space (including the dominant narrative) and to portray the terrain they form, while also alerting the reader to the stance from which the map is drawn.

The discursive terrain of "America" and "American" emerged in these discourses as fragile, changing, uncertain social constructs following September 11th. I provided an in-depth analysis of "oppositional" discourses from three venues: *Qualitative Inquiry* (a special 9/11 edition); op-ed commentary from the *New York Times*; and op-ed commentary from tompaine.com. I also included both the triumphal narrative enunciated by President Bush and its hypernational version espoused by the New Right.

I chose *Qualitative Inquiry* because it was the work of scholar-practitioners sharing their most intimate reflections on their personal and professional thoughts and experiences in this moment. My decision to use the *New York Times* was partly geopolitical, since New York City bore the brunt of the attacks. I also felt that in the moment under study, New York embodied the heart of the nation. Finally, I chose tompaine.com because it radically differed from the other two venues in its strong critique of the role of the media and its broad range of advocacy voices. All of these represented potential sources for alternatives to the dominant narrative. For balance and contrast, I included President George W. Bush's State of the Union address (2003)[10] and the public discourse of a New Right advocacy group, Americans for Victory over Terrorism (AVOT), a group that proclaimed that it would pursue liberal "dissidents," exposing them in the courts of public opinion. I drew the contours and the interrelations of the map from these discourses (silencing none), and positioned each text within these contours according to my reading of their language.[11]

Social cartography, then, is a cognitive art form that thrives on alternatives, a "play of figuration" (Paulston 1993, 3) in which the cartographer performs an exegesis of texts to decipher interrelations of meanings within and between them. The artist-scholar then portrays the resulting intertextual field through a figure. I would ask my reader to bear in mind Paulston and Liebman's (2000) caveat that while "maps can shape the system of objects, . . . rather than carve out a truth, they portray the mapper's perceptions of the social world, locating in it multiple and diverse intellectual communities, leaving to the reader not a truth, but a cognitive art, the artist's scholarship resulting in a cultural portrait" (14).

The working map I present here, then, reflects an autobiographical approach to the nation drawn from these discourses, and it is indeed a "cultural portrait."

56   *The Authority to Imagine*

Social Cartography: An Exhibit

My portrayal of the discursive moment may be seen in figure 1. I invite my reader to look closely at how interrelations within the broad intertextual field appear. I highlight particular features of the terrain. I introduce *cultures of citizenship* that emerge as "perceptual codes" (Huff 2000, 161) within the convergences of these interrelations. I also disclose my own position with a star. My working map portrays how truth- and value-claims shape our sense(s) of citizenship, what "America" means to us, and how we perceive our relationship with the world, which I think of as a *currere* of national identity.

Figure 1. A conceptual mapping of cultures of citizenship derived from subdialogues of civic debate post-September 11th, 2001 (Goodman, J. (2003), *Mapping civic debate following September 11th, 2001: Civic Courage, Social Cartography & Curriculum Theorizing*, Pittsburgh, PA: University of Pittsburgh Theses (Ph.D.).

In Figure 1, I conceptualized the range of constructs of nation and citizenship as forming a porous whole (indicated by broken lines), using two organizers to depict their differences. The first is represented by a horizontal axis, which indicates an epistemology of foundation for citizenship (seeing the nation from a space of orthodoxy, of reason, or of perspective). The second is represented by a vertical axis, which indicates an axiology of civic engagement (values that support control, representation, or activism). I begin my discussion with the horizontal axis.

Orthodoxy lies at one end of this continuum and denotes a nationalistic end of the pole, one that is anchored to symbols and narratives that coincide with the state as the repository of national identity, legitimacy, and power as defined and represented by authority. Authority may be construed as the power of government, of hegemonic belief, or as providential authority (God). Texts located in this space reflect being socialized to defend the character of the nation as defined or construed by authority, in which case the nation and the state are conflated. Here, the voice of authority is understood to *be* the voice of the nation. The discursive mode is *consensus* and the primary feature is *doctrine*.

Where *reason* is the framework for citizenship, texts reflect being socialized to question and seek information in order to support the good of the nation as defined by foundational principles, civic debate, and civic conscience. In this case, the nation represents a diverse public. The discursive mode here is *debate/dissent*. In this space, the debate itself forms the voice of the nation, and contestation within a principle-based or local knowledge terrain serves to legitimate both the project of democratic governance and divisions/diversity within the culture of the nation through its primary feature, which is *accommodation*.

In a space where *perspective* is the framework for citizenship, texts reflect being socialized to consider broader gestalts of belonging and to act in good faith toward a more global sense of community. In this case the nation itself may be seen as a global citizen. The discursive mode here is *dialogue*. In this space, the project of governance is impacted by a multiplicity of perspectives that may be immutable, eroding a sense of the nation as a discrete entity that can contain all of its parts. This space is holistic in terms of the world within which the nation is positioned, opening out to global or nodal senses of the nation/world connection, and therefore its primary feature is *diversity*. I turn now to a discussion of the vertical axis.

The vertical axis, an axiology of *modes of civic engagement*, is intended in part to problematize the horizontal—in other words, to look at how we engage as citizens from within any of the frameworks above. Here I see three modes represented in the discourse: *control*, *representation* and *activism*.

The *control* mode involves texts whose central focus is government *for* the people, and its operative feature is *sanction*. Texts positioned here put their trust in the government to "do the right thing," so that tacit support is granted to the government to do its best without concern for major civic debate or consideration of difference. The engagement of citizens in this location is centered on support for authority, leaving the government in control of the nation.

The *representation* mode involves texts whose central focus is government *of* the people, and its operative feature is *legitimacy*. Texts located here exhibit the expectation that the system will work as representatives respond to the needs of all, in other words, that citizen engagement will result in a negotiation of legitimacy that works to serve all. There is a trust here not only in the system itself, but also in civic conscience as enacted through the citizenry of the nation.

The mode of *activism* involves texts whose central focus is government *by* the people, and its operative feature is *empowerment*. Texts that speak from this end of the continuum hold the people accountable for change through citizen participation and response (which may include resistance) to government policy and practice, and activists work to transform both.

As I thought about the interrelations of these discourses, it occurred to me that I was seeing cultures of citizenship corresponding to convergences within the larger surround. I have identified four convergences that open out to eight cultures of citizenship that seem worthy of consideration, and I briefly elaborate on each.

At the convergence of *orthodoxy* and *control*, where the state and the nation are seen as one and the operative feature is *sanction*, civic passivity may play out in one of two ways, forming either a triumphal or voyeurist culture of citizenship. The *triumphal* culture proclaims that America has already actualized its destiny, that it is exceptional and blessed by God. Not acknowledging debate, dissent, or difference, the state may set the tone and the agenda for civic engagement. Since our experience of the nation is largely media-controlled, a culture of citizenship may also emerge in this space whose essential nature is *voyeurist*. That is to say, it involves a passive watching of national events as portrayed by media (or by the state *through* the media), along with a tacit acceptance of this media replication of the triumphal enunciation.

At the convergence of *orthodoxy* and *activism*, which embraces *empowerment* as its operative feature, another pairing of cultures of citizenship appears to emerge: *hypernational* and *communitarian*. The *hypernational* is not only aligned with *orthodoxy*, but also with *activism*, and therefore it is a space where *coercive* consensus may emerge. Where hypernationalists actually occupy seats of power, support is magnified to create the appearance that these three cultures of citizenship—voyeurist, triumphal, and hypernational—are one. Here is the space of the "silent majority." However, texts expressing "faith" in America, situated close to *activism*, may see the nation in terms of devotion to *reason* and to *representation*. The culture of citizenship here is *communitarian*. That is, this space may exhibit the solidarity of the triumphal and the hypernational cultures, but its interests are more aligned with an activism that attends to the unmet needs of community and with consensual thinking about those needs.

At the convergence of *control* and *perspective*, a third pairing of cultures of citizenship emerges: *vigilant* and *pluralist*. In the *vigilant* culture, *sanction* is still the operative feature. There is a different kind of watchfulness here, however, than in the voyeurist culture. While authority still sets the standard and pace for change, the effects of *reason* may lead to an awareness of civic responsibility, and legitimacy may be an issue because of the proximity of this culture to *representation* as well. In this space the citizen is still sovereign, responsibilities accompany privileges, and government is not mythic (as in the triumphal or hypernational cultures), but rather answerable to the people. Proximity to *perspective* in this convergence may also produce a *pluralist* culture, where *diversity* plays a more central role, and citizens may perceive themselves as "nodal," living both as members of the nation and also of some other *imagined community*,[12] usually of a particular racial or ethnic group. Texts in this space focus on both difference and privileging within the nation.

At the convergence of *perspective* and *activism*, a fourth pairing of cultures of citizenship emerges: *globalist* and *reparationist*. Since *perspective* is a space where citizens consider broader gestalts of community, and *activism* embraces *empowerment* as its operative feature, the resulting cultures in this convergence are highly dynamic. The *globalist* culture of citizenship may be manifested in global or nodal engagement, i.e., with a global perspective that embraces world as community, or with nodal causes and communities within the nation connected or related to out-of-country linkages. Also found within this convergence is the *reparationist* culture. Like the pluralist culture of citizenship, the reparationist culture is deeply influenced by *perspective* and demonstrates serious concern for issues of difference and privilege. However, its clear connection with *activism* may be reflected as it works to repair or undo historical legacies of social injustice. Texts located in this space speak of helping our own underprivileged so that we might become the "beacon of light" that triumphal texts proclaim we are.

Conclusion

I hope that I have managed to convey my confrontation with authority and its accompanying struggle with self, resisting my own natural impulses toward an epistemology of resentment. I hope that my reader has seen that it *is* possible to overcome the "us or them," "with us or against us" mentality. I have tried in good faith, despite my reservations about some cultures of citizenship, to keep the map open to *all* ways of seeing the terrain. I have tried to imagine what our differences are about and to draw from them a new vision of the many social imaginaries that come together to form our understandings of what "America" and "American" mean. Finally, I hope that my work might prove insightful for curriculum theorizing about preparing young citizens for a post-September 11th world. It is my hope that we would do so in such a way as to grant our young space to dream, to imagine, and to create a better world for themselves, for their children, and for ages to come.

Notes

1. I am referring here to the interrelations of different ways of seeing as they compete for legitimacy. The notion derives from Nietzsche's (1956) critique of the *progressus*, a force that constrains the possibilities of alternative moves gaining ground against a dominant stronghold. Nietzsche claims "the fitting of a hitherto unrestrained and shapeless populace into a tight mold . . . had to be brought to conclusion by a series of violent acts," so that "the earliest commonwealth constituted . . . oppressive machinery . . . fiercely dominating a population perhaps vastly superior in numbers yet amorphous and nomadic" (219). This domination may be contained in or advanced by a particular narrative that puts *progress* forward as the rationale for repression of alternatives. Spatial relations, therefore, refers both to our relations with power and also to the relations between competing ways of seeing that vie for power within a social context or surround. I suggest that exploring spatial relations of discourse may reveal multiple meanings, some of which might otherwise be obscured by the dominant narrative.
2. I use "authority" here to indicate power that manifests in ownership of social space through discursive enunciation.
3. In Kemmis, curriculum theorizing as "ideology-critique" derives from Habermas's (1972, 1971) work in this area.

4. In Kincheloe, "post-formal cognition" is a conceptual model for tolerating ambiguity in a postmodern world framed by uncertainty.
5. Kemmis analyzes approaches to curriculum theory using Habermas's (1972) "theory of knowledge-constitutive interests" to derive his typology.
6. In Paulston and Liebman (2000), the aim is to communicate "how we see the social changes developing in the world around us," (14).
7. Eisner (2002) calls for "an educational culture that has a greater focus on becoming . . . assigns greater priority to valuing . . . and regards the quality of the journey as more educationally significant than the speed at which the destination is reached" (16).
8. Thanks to Dr. Noreen Garman for this formulation.
9. Rolland G. Paulston's work spans more than a decade; the most definitive of these is *Social Cartography: Ways of Seeing Social and Educational Change*, ed. R. G. Paulston, New York: Garland (2000).
10. I felt that the 2003 address embodied what Mr. Bush had been saying consistently since September 11th, 2001.
11. The texts appear on the figure under their authors' last names and are listed under references. For elaboration of texts, see Goodman 2003, chapters 4–6. These chapters are "readers" intended to preserve a cultural record of the moment under study and to serve as warrants for the map.
12. In Appadurai, Benedict Anderson's work (1991) on the nation as imagined community is extended to consider non-territorial groups (e.g., terrorists) operating transnationally as communities of sentiment and simulating the nation as an imagined community.

References

AVOT (Americans for Victory over Terrorism). 2002. Advertisement. *New York Times*. March 10.
Appadurai, A. 1996. *Modernity at large: Cultural dimensions of globalization*. Minneapolis: University of Minnesota Press.
Bochner, A. P. 2002. Love survives. *Qualitative Inquiry* 8, no. 2 (April): 161–69.
Bourdieu, P. 1992. Trans. R. Boyne. Thinking about limits. In *Cultural theory and cultural change*, ed. M. Featherstone, 37–49. London: Sage.
Brady, I. 2002. Show me a sign. *Qualitative Inquiry* 8, no. 2 (April): 176–80.
Bumiller, E. 2002. America as reflected in its leader. *New York Times*. January 6.
Burleigh, N. 2001. Op-Ed pages trot out the white hawks. September 12. http://www.tompaine.com/feature.cfm/ID/4523.
Charmaz, K. 2002. Tenets of terror. *Qualitative Inquiry* 8, no. 2 (April):189–90.
Corn, D. 2001. The loyal opposition: Far from normal. October 5. http://www.tompaine.com/feature.cfm/ID/4586.
Danner, M. 2001. The battlefield in the American mind. *New York Times*. October 16.
Denzin, N. K. 2002. Week four. *Qualitative Inquiry* 8, no. 2 (April): 199–202.
Dowd, M. 2001a. Going really postal. *New York Times*. October 24.
———. 2001b. These spooky times. *New York Times*. October 31.
———. 2001c. Uncivil liberties? *New York Times*. November 25.

Eisner, E. 2002. What can education learn from the arts about the practice of education? *Journal of Curriculum and Supervision* 18, no. 1 (Fall): 4–16.

Ellis, C. 2002. Take no chances. *Qualitative Inquiry* 8, no. 2 (April): 170–75.

Faux, J. 2001. Three things we learned: On workers, the public sector, and American exceptionalism. September 20. http://www.tompaine.com/feature.cfm/ID/4548.

Fine, M. 2002. The mourning after. *Qualitative Inquiry* 8, no. 2 (April): 137–45.

Fish, S. 2001. Condemnation without absolutes. *New York Times*. October 15.

Ford, R. 2001. The worry trap. *New York Times*. November 1.

Foucault, M. 1972. Trans. A. Sheridan. *The archaeology of knowledge*. New York: Pantheon.

Friedman, T. 2002. Let's roll. *New York Times*. January 2.

Gergen, K. J. 2002. September 11 and the global implications of interpretive inquiry. *Qualitative Inquiry* 8, no. 2 (April): 186–88.

Gergen, M. 2002. Changing the ways of the world. *Qualitative Inquiry* 8, no. 2 (April): 150–52.

Goodall, H. L. 2002. Fieldnotes from the war zone: Living in America during the aftermath of September eleventh. *Qualitative Inquiry* 8, no. 2 (April): 203–18.

Goodman, J. 2003. *Mapping Civic Debate following September 11th, 2001: Civic courage, social cartography and curriculum theorizing*. University of Pittsburgh: UMI ProQuest Digital Dissertation. AAT 3104731.

Greenwood, D. J. 2002. Alone and together: A reflection for *Qualitative Inquiry* on the terror attack. *Qualitative Inquiry* 8, no. 2 (April): 191–93.

Guzy, M. W. 2001. The end of the world as we knew it. October 24. http://www.tompaine.com/feature.cfm/ID/4634.

Habermas, J. 1971. Trans. J. J. Shapiro. *Toward a rational society*. London: Heinemann.

———. 1972. J. Trans. J. J. Shapiro. *Knowledge and human interests*. London: Heinemann.

Hagler, Rev. G. S. 2001a. A worldview on peace and restraint. October 25. http://www.tompaine.com/feature.cfm/ID/4637.

———. 2001b. Selfish, arrogant, blind and deaf: A pastoral letter. December 19. http://www.tompaine.com/feature.cfm/ID/4775.

Helvarg, D. 2001. Consume for victory: Support the war—buy! buy! buy! October 29. http://www.tompaine.com/feature.cfm/ID/4643.

Huff, A. S. 2000. Ways of mapping strategic thought. In *Social cartography: Ways of seeing social and educational change*, ed. R. G. Paulston, 161–90. New York: Garland.

Kemmis, S. 1986. *Curriculum theorising: Beyond reproduction theory*. Victoria, Australia: Deakins University.

Kincheloe, J. 1993. The questions we ask, the stories we tell about education. Introduction to *Thirteen questions: Reframing education's conversation*, ed. J. L. Kincheloe and S. R. Steinberg, 1–19. New York: Peter Lang.

Klein, N. 2001. Legends in our own minds: Ideology makes Christmas shopping so much fun! December 19. http://www.tompaine.com/feature.cfm/ID/4782.

Krugman, P. 2001. An alternate reality. *New York Times*. November 25.

Lincoln, B. 2001. The new crusade: New rounds in an endless string of reprisals. September 28. http://www.tompaine.com/feature.cfm/ID/4567.

Lopez, G. R. 2002. From sea to shining sea: Stories, counterstories, and the discourse of patriotism. *Qualitative Inquiry* 8, no. 2 (April):196–98.

Lyotard, J. F. 1972. Trans. G. Bennington and B. Massumi. *The postmodern condition: A report on knowledge*. Minneapolis: University of Minnesota Press.

McGovern, G. 2002. The healing in helping the world's poor. *New York Times*. January 1.

Miller, W. L. 2002. A time for butterflies and salmon. *Qualitative Inquiry* 8, no. 2 (April): 156–57.

Nietzsche, F. 1969. Trans. F. Golffing. *The birth of tragedy and the geneology of morals*. Garden City, NY: Doubleday.

Oates, J. C. 2001. Words fail, memory blurs, life wins. *New York Times*. December 31.

Olesen, V. 2002. Working it through: Interpretive sociology after 9/11/01. *Qualitative Inquiry* 8, no. 2 (April): 181–82.

Palermo, J. A. 2001. A new deal for our era: America's leaders are failing the leadership test in the current crisis. October 30. http://www.tompaine.com/feature.cfm/ID/4649.

Paulston, R. G. 1993. Mapping discourses in comparative education texts. *Compare* 23, no. 2:101–14.

Paulston, R. G., and M. Liebman. 2000. Social cartography: A new metaphor/tool for comparative studies. In *Social cartography: Ways of seeing social and educational change*, ed. R. G. Paulston, 7–28. New York: Garland.

Pinar, W. F., ed. 1975. *Curriculum theorizing: The reconceptualists*. Berkeley, CA: McCutcheon Publishing Corporation.

———. 1994. *Autobiography, politics and sexuality: Essays in curriculum theory, 1972–1992*. New York: Peter Lang.

Pitts, L. 2001. The barbarians will learn what America is all about. September 13. http://www.tompaine.com/feature.cfm/ID/4528.

Rich, F. 2001a. No news is good news. *New York Times*. October 13.

———. 2001b. Wait until dark. *New York Times*. November 24.

———. 2002. Patriotism on the cheap. *New York Times*. January 5.

Rieger, J. 2001. What does retaliation mean in a media war? September 12. http://www.tompaine.com/feature.cfm/ID/4524.

Ryan, M. 2001. Outrage, not rage. September 15. http://www.tompaine.com/feature.cfm/ID/4534.

Safire, W. 2001. Seizing dictatorial power. *New York Times*. November 15.

Segev, T. 2001. Learning from Israel and its mistakes. *New York Times*. November 25.

Taylor, B. 2001. Heed not the calls of the consumers-in-chief. October 24. http://www.tompaine.com/feature.cfm/ID/4636.

Teodosijevic-Ryan, J. 2001. A gift from the ashes of war: Rediscovering simple beauties and lasting values. October 11. http://www.tompaine.com/feature.cfm/ID/4602.

Tierney, W. G. 2002. A walk in the olive grove. *Qualitative Inquiry* 8, no. 2 (April): 183–85.

Vellenga, T. 2001. Now, engage the world: Uncovering the value of multilateralism. October 1. http://www.tompaine.com/feature.cfm/ID/4570.

Weis, L. 2002. Thoughts beyond fear. *Qualitative Inquiry* 8, no. 2 (April): 153–55.

Zinn, H. 2001. Not vengeance, but compassion. September 13. http://www.tompaine.com/feature.cfm/ID/4529.

PART 2

Claiming a Language of Practice through the Logics of Inquiry

CHAPTER 5

A Search for Balance: Representing a Narrative Pedagogy

Pamela Krakowski

Until the second night of a qualitative research course, I had never read a dissertation. I imagined those foreboding black-bound books were boring, full of hard-to-decipher statistics, with little relevance to classroom practice. I picked up one of the dissertations at the end of class and read the title: "Pictures in Our Minds: A Narrative Study of Creative Dramatics as Pedagogy in Elementary Classroom Content Areas" (Richards 1996). It intrigued me, and so I borrowed it.

That night, instead of watching television, I sat down to read the dissertation. I found that I could not put it down. It read like a story and was full of accounts I could relate to as a teacher. I kept asking, "Are you really allowed to do this?" I couldn't believe that a teacher was allowed to write about her own teaching, in her own context, much less in a narrative form.

The night that I read Lynn Richards' narrative inquiry of her practice was the beginning of my interest in engaging in a scholarly study of my own pedagogy. It was also the beginning of my biggest struggle in dissertation writing—giving myself permission to imagine what shape my study would take. I would later name my own practice a "narrative pedagogy" and study it within the context of my early childhood art classes (Krakowski 2004), using narrative inquiry as my research genre as Lynn had done.

When it came time to craft my overview proposal, I had read both Lynn's and Pat McMahon's (1993) narrative inquiries very closely. I envisioned that my approach would take a similar path. Because their work resonated so much with me, the images of their dissertations guided what I thought a good narrative inquiry should look like. Art educator Harry Broudy (1987) refers to the images that we gather in our memories as our "imagic store" (18). Eisner (1991) explains how Broudy's concept of the imagic store operates in evaluating what we view as good teaching. He writes:

> Refined sensibilities allow us to make fine-grained discriminations from which concepts may be formed. These concepts are images that are construed from our experience with qualities. For example, we have an auditory image of Baroque music that allows us to distinguish it from Romantic music. We have an image of Gothic architecture that allows us to distinguish it from Georgian architecture. . . . Similarly, we have forms of teaching, kinds of classroom life, and types of student activity that allow us to distinguish between degrees of excellence in each. (Eisner 1991, 69–70)

Lynn's and Pat's dissertations became part of my own "research imagic store," guiding my notion of what constituted an exemplary narrative inquiry. I did not know it at the time, but the strength of those images kept me from seeing how my own version of narrative inquiry would unfold.

To make a long story short, for four summers I struggled to find my own research voice in the writing process and my own images in representing a narrative pedagogy. Eventually I arrived at my own conceptual leap, what Piantanida and Garman (1999) describe as the "aha" moment in which "the researcher sees the essence of the study and how the pieces fit into a larger, coherent portrayal of the phenomenon under study" (172).

My Conceptual Leap

> When everything goes right, a mobile is a piece of poetry that dances with the joy of life. (Sartre's description of a Calder mobile, quoted in Lipman 1976, 261)

Early in my study, I had defined narrative pedagogy as a pedagogy that listened to the children's narrative and welcomed it into the teaching-learning space. The children's narrative was what I referred to as the "is"—what *is* happening in the children's lives at that moment. It included the children's interests, ideas, stories, experiences, emotional concerns, backgrounds, ways of coming to know, and ways of being in the world.

A narrative pedagogy, I maintained, invited the narrative to inform the normative. The normative was what I referred to as the "ought"—what I thought *ought* to be happening in the classroom. It represented my notion of curriculum, my aims, objectives, specific lesson plans, expectations, and values. It stood for what I believed was "true, beautiful, good, and just" (May 1995, 59) and what I believed was worth teaching (Schubert 1986).

My study's intent was to better understand the relationship between the narrative and the normative as well as the sensibilities that I embodied when I listened to the narrative—when I responded in a narrative frame of mind. I resonated with the writings of Max van Manen (1991), who maintains that pedagogical sensibilities cannot be learned as behavioral principles, techniques, or methods. Pedagogical sensibilities, he argues, are *embodied knowledge*, not a body of knowledge.

In the early years of my dissertation, I experimented with writing vignettes that captured some tension between the narrative and the normative. I then reflected on these situations to better understand what happened in the teaching-learning space when I responded or didn't respond to the children's interests. I further reflected on what sensibilities were present or missing in these situations, connecting my own conclusions with what I was reading in the theoretical discourses.

During this time, as I discussed my vignettes with the study group, it became apparent to me that I was failing to capture the complexity of the relationship between the narrative and normative; I was bordering on presenting the two as a false dichotomy. Our conversations also revealed to me that I lacked an overall conceptual organization for my study.

In moments of insecurity, I returned to Lynn's and Pat's dissertations, and since many more dissertations had been written by study group members over my four years of struggle, I read those as well. I found myself mentally "trying on" others' dissertations. This was not necessarily a bad idea, but the more I looked to what others in the group had written, the less I relied on my own ability to author and imagine my overall conceptualization.

Aware that I needed to experience a conceptual leap, I pressed on. I returned to my teaching journals, in which I had captured the events of my classroom, and continued to search for patterns. I also went ahead and wrote a rough draft of my core portrayal to the best of my ability. Piantanida and Garman (1999) state that it is "through the act of writing that researchers find their way out of the conceptual morass. Writing seems to engage researchers in a level of deliberation and sets the stage for an 'aha' moment" (172)—and so it happened for me. One afternoon I met with an early childhood colleague to discuss one of my drafts, and as we talked about how difficult it was to negotiate the tensions between the narrative and the normative in certain classroom situations, the notion of balance stood out significantly. Images of two-sided scales and mobiles began to float through my mind.

Dance educator Susan Stinson (1991) suggests that metaphor in dissertation writing can help the researcher portray the phenomenon under study. Eisner (1979) also states that the "metaphors and images of schooling and teaching that we acquire have profound consequences for our educational values and for our views of how schooling should occur" (261). I began to consider different images of literal balance that might help me articulate my understanding of the intangible balance between the narrative and normative to other art teachers. First I focused my attention on the two-sided scale, similar to the kind I used in eleventh-grade chemistry class. After some reflection, I dismissed this image because it lent itself to the notion of either/or thinking and did not capture the complexity of the balance I encountered in my teaching. I then turned my attention to the mobile.

I had always been fascinated with the mobiles created by the American artist Alexander Calder, and the image of the mobile resonated with me as both an artist and art teacher. Maxine Greene (1997) states that "metaphor enables us to understand one thing better by likening it to what it is not" (391); by comparing the scale with the mobile, I saw that balancing on a scale does not require any aesthetic sensibilities, but mathematical precision and accuracy instead. The mobiles created by Calder, on the other hand, required skill, experience, and above all, the sensibilities of an artist: intuition, an embodied understanding of materials, a feeling for coherence, an eye for color, a playfulness with form. Balancing a scale reminded me of the teacher as technician; balancing a mobile reminded me of the teacher as artist.

I went to the library and took out books on Calder and his art. As I poured over photographs of his work and deliberated with my colleagues over the next few months, I confirmed the mobile as my central metaphor for my narrative pedagogy. As I explained in the introduction to my study, a mobile is a balanced hanging sculpture with shapes that move, especially in the flow of air. In my metaphor, those shapes represent the narrative and normative elements in any class, in any situation, at any moment. The narrative elements include the children and their ideas; the normative elements include my aims, objectives, lesson plans, expectations, and values. As in a mobile, all of the shapes are gently suspended in a state of tension.

In making a mobile, the artist must rely on her sensibilities to balance all the elements. Placing the delicate vertical wires at just the right point requires her to use both her senses and her body. Typically she balances wires on her finger to find and test the center of balance; if one side is heavier, she must make adjustments. This is similar to adjusting or balancing the narrative or normative in an art classroom. If there is too much of the art teacher's normative agenda, the sensibilities of the teacher must guide her in adjusting the center of balance to give more weight to the children's narrative agenda. Sometimes she must bend the edges of the normative shape or even pare it down. When an art teacher senses a subtle shift in the children's level of engagement, or reads a lack of interest in their facial expressions and body language, she can respond and adjust her lesson to accommodate their interests.

The very essence of a mobile is motion, so it is always in a state of flux, just as nothing in a classroom is fixed or predictable. Children and teachers daily encounter new experiences, acquire new interests, and develop new understandings of art, self, and others. Attesting to this reality in classroom life, Maxine Greene (1978) writes, "From a human perspective, that of a teacher beginning a school year, a writer beginning a book, a child beginning the first grade, nothing is fully predictable or determined. All kinds of things are possible, although none can be guaranteed" (56).

This motion, in the case of a mobile, is triggered by wind or air currents; whenever one shape moves, the others move as well. In my pedagogical analogy, those currents are the unexpected pressures that affect teaching and classroom life at every moment: large class sizes, limited budgets, inadequate space, and insufficient time. The "wind" could be an administrator who unilaterally decides that the art teacher must follow a certain curriculum. It could be the premiere of a Harry Potter movie, sickness or family trauma in a child's home situation, or simple timing: the first day of school or the last. In unpredictable or pressured situations, the art teacher must rely heavily on her sensibilities so that the normative is not lost entirely. The stronger the winds that shift the elements of her lesson plans, goals, and so on, the more finely tuned, flexible, and agile her sensibilities must be to retain balance. In the classroom, the narrative and normative, like shapes in a mobile, exist in a dynamic state striving toward equilibrium.

Guided by this new image of the mobile, I was now able to see every chapter of the whole dissertation through the lens of balance. The title of my dissertation became *Balancing the Narrative and the Normative: Pedagogical Implications for Early Childhood Art Education* (Krakowski 2004). My selected review of relevant discourses in chapter two became "A

Call for Balance." My procedures and rationale for narrative inquiry as my research genre in chapter three became "A Search for Balance." In chapter four, the core portrayal, I created narratives that explored the tensions between the narrative and normative in five early childhood art classroom contexts. I explored the sensibilities of a narrative frame of mind in each, always concluding with "Balancing Lessons." In my fifth chapter, I explicated the aesthetic dimension of the sensibilities of a narrative frame of mind, using the lenses of aesthetic knowing and teacher-as-artist. I concluded with "A Delicate Balance: Cultivating Aesthetic Sensibilities," implications for teaching derived from cultivating these sensibilities. The notion of balance provided a coherent framework for the overall dissertation that had been missing in my earlier drafts.

Crafting the Core Portrayal

Piantanida and Garman (1999) state that the core portrayal creates "a 'picture' that allows others to experience vicariously the phenomenon and context under study" (133). In a sense, it brings the classroom to the reader, and therefore, it must be richly descriptive and believable. My core portrayal consisted of five separate art classroom portrayals: "Art Classroom as Museum Gallery," "Art Classroom as Studio," "Art Classroom as Haven," "Art Classroom as Stage," and "Art Classroom as Laboratory." Each portrayal offered me space to explore the relationship or tension between the narrative and the normative in that specific context. For example, in "Art Classroom as Haven," I explored the tension between the normative expectations of my preplanned art lesson for the first day of school and the kindergarten children's real emotional concerns—their need to feel welcomed and safe. Each classroom context also revealed pressures specific to that context, so in "Art Classroom as Haven," I had to negotiate the kindergartener's emotional concerns within the context of a multi-age, K–1–2 classroom configuration of twenty-four children.

For each portrayal I wrote one to two vignettes that best portrayed the narrative and normative tension. I found that vignettes expressing trouble— what Jerome Bruner (1996) calls the "the engine of narrative" (142)— expressed the tensions better than others. Often I paired two vignettes that portrayed contrasting situations. In "Art Classroom as Haven," my first vignette described my difficulty listening to the emotional concerns of my new kindergarten students. About one student in particular, I narrated:

Paula was having trouble adjusting to school. Not only did she cry in art class, she cried all day long in her other classes. She began to miss school, and I saw her only a couple of times during the first month. One day her mother phoned and said that Paula was afraid to come to art class. "You have to be kidding," I thought. "How could anyone be afraid of coming to my class?" I redirected the conversation back to Paula having difficulty adjusting to "all" of her classes. I discussed possible reasons why Paula may be having trouble with the separation (from mom!) and with transitioning to kindergarten.

After I hung up the phone, I thought about what Paula's mother had said. I had a very challenging class that year. A number of first grade children behaved aggressively toward each other and constantly tested the boundaries. I had to be very firm with them the first week—and many weeks after—to make sure that they understood my expectations and the classroom rules. If I did not address it now, I rationalized, it would only get worse. I could not deny that Paula was having difficulty adjusting to school in general, but in relation to art class, had I been too firm? Had I come across as scary—or even mean? (Krakowski 2004, 95–96)

At the end of each vignette I reflected on what sensibilities were present or missing. In the case of Paula, I came to see that I lacked what Maxine Greene (1978) called "wide-awakeness" (42). When my school had changed the self-contained kindergarten classroom into two multi-age K–1–2 classrooms, the developmental range of the class left me mentally and emotionally exhausted. I had begun to lose touch with the experience of the kindergarten child. According to van Manen (1991), I lacked sympathetic understanding—the ability to stay caringly attuned "to the inner life of the child" (97).

This first vignette and its reflections I followed with a second vignette, "The First Day of School." Taking to heart my need to be attuned to the child's emotional concerns, I planned with "heightened awareness" a first-day-of-school art lesson with the theme of feeling safe and welcomed. I decided to use two puppets, a Talking Art Box and a komodo dragon named Felix, to help ease the transition and create an atmosphere of play and imagination. The vignette began like this:

The First Day of School
The kindergarten children arrived at the art studio—many for the first time—and I invited them in. They walked in quietly, tiptoeing as if the floor were made of glass. They looked, without touching, and spoke in whispers. It was the kind of quietness that only a first visit could inspire. I found myself also speaking softly, mirroring their inquisitive and shy mood.

> Ben broke the quietness. He asked excitedly, "You have a dinosaur in here?" He pointed to the stegosaurus on the ledge next to the Stegovolkasaurus art print. His question seemed to combine "Why is there a dinosaur in an art room?" and "How did you know that I liked dinosaurs?" Little did Ben know that I was thinking about children just like him when I placed the dinosaur on the entranceway ledge.
>
> I acknowledged Ben's interest in dinosaurs and then welcomed the children to sit down at the table that I had prepared for them. I introduced myself and began sharing some ideas of what would be happening in our time together. Giving an overview, I believed, helped to give the children a sense of security. I then said that I wanted them to meet my art room friends.
>
> Immediately, pointing to the Talking Art Box, Ben asked, "What's that?"
>
> The perfect segue, I thought. "That's my friend, the Talking Art Box. He lives in the art studio. Would you like to meet him?"
>
> Immediately I sensed a shift in their mood and attention. They slipped easily into a world of fantasy, and the Talking Art Box had cast his spell. (Krakowski 2004, 102–3)

After the children listened to the tape recorded voice of the Talking Art Box, I brought out the komodo dragon puppet. The vignette continued:

> I placed Felix on my hand and brought him out. He immediately buried his head on my shoulder, trying to hide from the children. "This is Felix. He's feeling a little shy today." Felix kept his head buried. "Felix, I have some children that I'd like you to meet." Felix slowly turned his head around to take a peek and then immediately buried it again on my shoulder. His quick movements made the children laugh. "Felix, it's okay to feel shy. These children are new, too. This is their first day of school also." He peeked again and then quickly hid his head. The children laughed again.
>
> Sean, one of the youngest boys, asked curiously, "Why is he so shy?"
>
> Felix, who at this time only talked to me, whispered in my ear. I replied. "Felix says that he's a little sad because he misses his mom and dad." The children gave a look of compassion.
>
> I turned to Felix and said, "Felix, it's okay to feel a little sad." And then, I turned my attention to the children and said, as if I had this thought for the first time, "I know, maybe you could say something to make Felix feel better."
>
> Immediately they all had a suggestion. Marta, who seemed to be feeling very comfortable with school, said, "Tell him that's he's going to make lots of friends. You know, have some fun, make some friends, and then go home and be with your mom and dad."
>
> I turned to Felix, "Did you hear that Felix? You're going to make lots of friends. Does that make you feel better?" Felix felt a little braver, looked at the children out of the corner of one pink eye, and nodded his head "yes." (Krakowski 2004, 104)

The children continued to share their suggestions, all the while growing more comfortable and more endeared to Felix. The vignette closed with the children creating self-portraits with their own beloved soft toys—what child psychoanalyst Donald Winnicott (1971) refers to as "transitional objects." The Talking Art Box returned to say good-bye. As the children left, they either shook Felix's hand or gave him a hug and rubbed his favorite spot on top of his head.

When I reflected on this vignette, I discussed the sensibilities of being present to mood and the emotional atmosphere (Bollnow 1989) and being in touch with one's childlike-ness (Ayers 1989). I also explored what possibilities opened up in the teaching-learning space. I wrote that I generated a greater possibility of creating what Winnicott (1971) calls a "holding environment," a place where children would sense that the art classroom was a safe, friendly, and fulfilling place.

As I mentioned earlier, at the conclusion of each art classroom portrayal, I wrote a section called "Balancing Lessons" where I discussed what I had learned about balancing the narrative and normative in that specific context. In "Art Classroom as Haven," I shared how I saw more clearly that children's emotions were the basis for all learning (Greenspan 1997). If I wanted children to be meaningfully engaged in arts learning, I needed to be finely attuned to their emotional concerns. In balancing the narrative and normative, I saw that "caregiving, expression of feeling, and resolving problems and interpersonal conflicts are not interruptions to the curriculum; they are the basic curriculum" (Jones and Reynolds 1992, 90). I also realized that as much as it was possible for children to have positive art experiences, it was equally possible for them to have what John Dewey (1934) calls a "non-esthetic experience" (49). He writes, "There is an element of passion in all esthetic perception. Yet when we are overwhelmed by passion, as in extreme rage, fear, jealousy, the experience is definitely non-esthetic" (49).

Because the art experience has the potential for a wide range of powerful emotions, I concluded that when balancing the mobile, I needed to be attuned to the subtlest shifts in children's moods and rely on my intuitive sensibilities to make adjustments at the slightest indication of disequilibrium.

Crafting the Interpretive Portrayal and the Implications

Before I arrived at the metaphor of balance for my study, my interpretive portrayal consisted of explicating further what it meant to listen to the narrative in the five art classroom contexts. Without that filter of balance, I struggled to see the patterns and deeper meanings embedded in my core portrayal.

I immersed myself in the discourses on aesthetic knowing, the art of teaching, and the teacher as artist (Barrell 1991; Eisner 2002; Sullivan, 2000). I also continued to read texts on the life and art of Calder. As I revisited my insights from the art classroom portrayals, I saw that I could cluster them according to related qualities. Viewing their similarities through an aesthetic lens, I arrived at six groupings: "Aesthetic Vision," "The Rightness of Fit," "Improvising the Dance of Shapes," "Holding the Tension of Opposites," "Imagining and Playing with Possibilities," and "Experiencing Aesthetic Satisfaction."

The lessons that I learned, then, in cultivating these aesthetic sensibilities became my implications for the study. For instance, one implication I discussed was the importance of listening. I learned that I needed to make "the art of listening to what the children say and trying to figure out what they mean" the impassioned focus of my teaching/research (Paley 1986, 82). I came to understand more deeply that I did not "see with [my] eyes or hear through [my] ears, but through [my] beliefs" (Delpit 1995, 46). I needed to reflect thoughtfully on my beliefs about children, because if my theories about children were incomplete, I could "limit the possibilities for educating, caring for, and simply being with them" (Matthews 1984, 29).

Crafting My Version of Narrative Inquiry

Writing the dissertation was an iterative, not linear, process. I kept cycling back to previous chapters after I drafted a new chapter. My narrative inquiry evolved as I wrote. Throughout this time I remained immersed in the discourses on narrative, and eventually I was able to clearly articulate the discourses that formed my rationale for narrative inquiry as my research genre. The metaphor of balancing the mobile set me free to imagine my own version of narrative inquiry. I drew from Lyons and LaBoskey (2002) on teachers' use of narrative, Connelly and Clandinin (1988) on personal practical knowledge, Bruner (1986) on narrative as a way of knowing, ordering experience, and constructing reality, and Barone and Eisner (1997) on the presence of certain features or design elements in aesthetic forms of representation.

I saw the tensions that I encountered between the narrative and normative as puzzles. Lyons and LaBoskey (2002) maintain that narrative inquiry is "especially useful to capture the situated complexities of teachers' work and classroom practice, often messy, uncertain, and unpredictable" (15). Through narrative, they suggest, teachers can construct meaning, understand how they think, and even rethink their craft. Narrative is "a way of making teacher's knowledge conscious and public, and open to scrutiny" (Lyons and LaBoskey 2002, 12), a way to think through the "puzzles" that teachers encounter in their practice and gain new insight.

Connelly and Clandinin (1988) maintain that teachers' personal narratives help them reflect on their pedagogy in relation to specific contexts. This inquiry process then deepens what they refer to as "personal practical knowledge," a knowledge that embraces a language of practice that permits teachers to talk about themselves in situations and tell stories of experience (59). This language of practice makes visible the images, metaphors, personal philosophy (the normative), and narrative unity in one's teaching—a language that became useful to me in talking about my pedagogy.

Bruner (1986) writes that narrative emphasizes ambiguity, the metaphorical, and "sense"—how a situation feels. It prizes believability or lifelikeness, what he calls "verisimilitude." Similarly, Barone and Eisner (1997) write that aesthetic forms of representation such as narrative have the capacity to promote empathetic understanding, call attention to the particular, use a language which is expressive, and rely on the vernacular. These qualities were all essential for crafting richly descriptive art classroom portrayals. Daily I encountered situations in my teaching art to young children that were "never without affect" (Eisner 1988, 17). Narrative as a language allowed me to create images of feeling (Langer 1942) and capture the sentient qualities of pedagogical life.

As a whole, then, writing my dissertation was in many ways also like balancing a mobile. The normative pieces were the academic expectations of the university; the writing group's expectations of what constitutes a rigorous, scholarly, coherent study of one's pedagogy; the professional expectations of my field of art education; and the individual expectations of committee members. Many of these expectations became images I carried in my head of what I thought a dissertation *should* look like. The narrative pieces were my experience of my practice; my fleeting images of my imagined dissertation; my teaching journal; my interpretation of the events in my classroom; my ability as a writer; and everything that occurred in my teaching and personal life. The pressures—or the air currents—that I encountered were the limitations of my teaching schedule; requirements of teaching full time; available time to write; impending deadlines; and unexpected life circumstances such as family illness or 9/11.

To balance all of these narrative and normative pieces, I needed to listen with an open mind to the different voices of authorities—the academy, my study group, the discourses of my research rationale—while at the same time staying attuned to my own voice, intuition, and guiding images. When I floundered, I placed more emphasis on the ideas and images of the authorities and listened less to myself, and my composition became unbalanced.

Earlier in this chapter and at the beginning of my dissertation, I included a quote by Jean-Paul Sartre: "When everything goes right, a mobile is a piece of poetry that dances with the joy of life" (quoted in Lipman 1976, 261). I found in my study of narrative pedagogy that when I valued, listened to, and welcomed the children's narrative into the teaching-learning space, and when I created a space for the children's narrative to inform the normative, the art classroom became a place of wonder, respect, dialogue, passion, stories, imagination, possibility, and *joy*.

When I eventually made the conceptual leap to use the mobile as a metaphor for my pedagogy, I reached the place where I could rely on my own authority. I could balance the voices of the experts with my own voice. I could position all of the individual pieces of my writing and create a coherent whole. I had the feeling of all of the pieces falling into place—or rather, into balance. I experienced what Nelson Goodman (1978) refers to as a "rightness of fit" (138), the frame of mind that Csikszenmihalyi (1990) calls "flow." Although the process continued to have struggles—and I can't say that I experienced a rush of joy until the day of my defense—ultimately, there *was* an element of joy, a genuine fulfillment and satisfaction.

References

Ayers, W. 1989. *The good preschool teacher*. New York: Teachers College Press.

Barone, T., and E. Eisner. 1997. Arts-based educational research. In *Complimentary methods for research in education*, ed. R. M. Jaeger, 71–98. Washington, DC: American Education Research Association.

Barrell, B. 1991. Classroom artistry. *Educational Forum* 55, no. 4: 333–42.

Bollnow, O. F. 1989. The pedagogical atmosphere: The perspective of the child. *Phenomenology + Pedagogy* 7: 12–36.

Broudy, H. S. 1987. *The role of imagery in learning.* Los Angeles: The Getty Center for Education in the Arts.

Bruner, J. 1996. *The culture of education.* Cambridge, MA: Harvard University Press.

Connelly, F. M., and D. J. Clandinin. 1988. *Teachers as curriculum planners: Narratives of experience.* New York: Teachers College Press.

Csikszentmihalyi, M. 1990. *Flow: The psychology of optimal experience.* New York: Harper Collins.

Delpit, L. 1995. *Other people's children: Cultural conflict in the classroom.* New York: New Press.

Dewey, J. 1934. *Art as experience.* New York: Putnam.

Eisner, E. 1979. *The educational imagination.* New York: Macmillan.

———. 1988. The primacy of experience and the politics of method. *Educational Researcher* 17, no. 5: 15–20.

———. 1991. *The enlightened eye: Qualitative inquiry and the enhancement of educational practice.* New York: Macmillan.

———. 2002. What can education learn from the arts about the practice of education? *Journal of Curriculum and Supervision* 18, no. 1: 4–16.

Goodman, N. 1978. *Ways of worldmaking.* Indianapolis, IN: Hackett Publishing Co.

Greene, M. 1978. *Landscapes of learning.* New York: Teachers College Press.

———. 1997. Metaphors and multiples: Representation, the arts, and history. *Phi Delta Kappan* 78, no. 5: 387–94.

Greenspan, S. I. 1997. *The growth of the mind.* New York: Addison-Wesley.

Jones, E., and G. Reynolds. 1992. *The play's the thing: Teachers' roles in children's play.* New York: Teachers College Press.

Krakowski, P. G. 2004. *Balancing the narrative and the normative: Pedagogical implications for early childhood art education.* UMI ProQuest Digital Dissertation #AAT 3139692.

Langer, S. 1942. *Philosophy in a new key.* Cambridge, MA: Harvard University Press.

Lipman, J. 1976. *Calder's universe.* Philadelphia, PA: Running Press Book Publishers.

Lyons, N., and V. K. LaBoskey, eds. 2002. *Narrative inquiry in practice.* New York: Teachers College Press.

Matthews, G. B. 1984. *The philosophy of childhood.* Cambridge, MA: Harvard University Press.

May, W. T. 1995. Teachers as curriculum developers. In *Context, content, and community in art education: Beyond postmodernism.* ed. R. W. Neperud, 53–86. New York: Teachers College Press.

McMahon, P. 1993. *A narrative study of three levels of reflection in a college composition class: Teacher journal, student portfolios, teacher-student discourse.* UMI ProQuest Digital Dissertation #ATT 9329582.

Paley, V. G. 1986. On listening to what children say. *Harvard Educational Review* 56, no. 2: 122–31.

Piantanida, M., and N. B. Garman. 1999. *The qualitative dissertation: A guide for students and faculty.* Thousand Oaks, CA: Corwin Press.

Richards, L. 1996. *Pictures in our minds: A narrative study of the incorporation of creative dramatics as pedagogy in elementary classroom content areas.* UMI ProQuest Digital Dissertation #ATT 9637875.

Schubert, W. 1986. *Curriculum: Perspective, paradigm, and possibility.* New York: Macmillan.

Stinson, S. W. 1991. Dance as curriculum, curriculum as dance. In *Reflections from the heart of educational inquiry: Understanding curriculum and teaching through the arts*, ed. G. Willis and W. H. Schubert, 190–96. Albany: State University of New York Press.

Sullivan, A. 2000. Notes from a marine biologist's daughter: On the art and science of attention. *Harvard Educational Review* 70, no. 2: 211–27.

van Manen, M. 1991. *The tact of teaching: The meaning of pedagogical thoughtfulness.* Albany: State University of New York Press.

Winnicott, D. 1971. *Playing and reality.* London: Tavistock Publications.

CHAPTER 6

Reimagining Grounded Theory: Moving toward an Interpretive Stance

Robin E. Grubs

In this chapter I describe how dissatisfaction with my professional stance led me to enter a doctoral program in genetic counseling. Choosing grounded theory for my dissertation research (Grubs 2002) at first appeared to be congruent with my functionalist roots, and I turned to the grounded theory literature to find the "right" method for generating a grounded theory. I explicate here how after examining the grounded theory discourses and deliberating with several colleagues about this research genre, I realized the futility of searching for the "right" grounded theory method and instead focused attention on crafting an interpretative logic of justification for my grounded theory. An interpretative logic of justification provided a rationale for creating narrative vignettes and a narrative typology that allowed me to portray the emotional richness of participants' stories and depict my empathetic sense of the different ways they experienced and responded to the existential nature of being at-risk and making a decision about prenatal testing. Lastly, I discuss how my grounded theory study allowed me to imagine a professional stance that acknowledges the importance of being attuned in an "empathetic moment" to the variations of angst genetic counseling clients might experience when confronting genetic-related decisions.

Background to the Study

During my career as a genetic counselor[1] I worked in busy prenatal clinics where pregnant women and their partners received genetic counseling immediately prior to a prenatal genetic test such as amniocentesis or chorionic villi sampling.[2] This arrangement is common in clinics that offer prenatal genetic testing to women and couples at-risk for having a child with a birth defect or genetic condition. The fast-paced nature of prenatal genetic clinics frequently results in counselors and clients having limited time together, usually thirty to forty-five minutes. During the typical counseling session, counselors have the responsibility of explaining available prenatal tests—including the procedures, risks, and benefits—as well as ascertaining a detailed pregnancy and family history. The decision whether to have prenatal testing is an important part of counseling, and therefore the counselor needs to obtain informed consent.

In my early working environments, the efficient worker able to see many patients in a short period of time was valued, and so I adapted accordingly and focused my efforts on providing clients with the most up-to-date genetic information. I felt comfortable and confident providing information to my clients, and often they appeared appreciative of someone taking the time to explain complex genetic concepts. Some of my encounters with clients, however, caused me to recognize the limitations of my information provision and to appreciate the complicated nature of clients' decisions. I could no longer rely on my naïve assumption that information alone would allow people to make and cope with difficult decisions. As my discomfort with my role of information provider grew, I decided to enter a doctoral program in genetic counseling.

When planning my doctoral research, I chose a dissertation topic that would allow me to speak with individuals who had been offered genetic counseling and prenatal genetic testing because of the mother's age. The participants in my study represented the types of clients I encountered during my career as a genetic counselor. In contrast to the fast-paced setting in which I had worked, however, my study afforded me the luxury of time. I was no longer in a setting in which I had only thirty minutes to meet with an individual and to address my checklist of genetic and prenatal testing items. Rather, I could focus my attention in an extended time frame on the experiences of my participants without the burden of having to convey complex genetic and medical information. My aim was to study the experiences of individuals who were offered prenatal genetic testing because the mother's age created a risk factor for having a child with a chromosome condition. However, I was uncertain as to how I should approach such an inquiry.

My exposure to research first began within the fields of biology and human genetics. Not surprisingly, the post-positivist perspective dominates research within those disciplines. Consequently, I knew little of other research traditions, and the post-positivist perspective influenced my ideas about how research should be performed and the types of meanings ascribed to the results. As I grappled with the uncertainties and complexities that permeated my interactions with clients, I began to sense that my research and the findings I was hoping to generate would not be best addressed by a post-positivist approach.

In search of an alternative to a post-positivist, scientific frame, I decided to enroll in an introductory course on qualitative research, which ultimately led me to grounded theory for my dissertation study. I was initially drawn to grounded theory because my functionalist side was comforted by the detailed, systematic procedures often described in the literature (Strauss and Corbin 1990, 1994, 1998; Strauss 1987). My dissertation was the first qualitative study within my department, and I was fearful that a qualitative inquiry would be perceived as "soft" research (Labaree 1998). The clear-cut procedures and steps of grounded theory offered reassurance that my approach would be perceived as rigorous. However, my feelings of reassurance engendered by the systematic procedures of grounded theory—which I outlined in detail in my dissertation proposal—began to waver after receiving a review for a grant proposal I submitted and attending a conference on qualitative research.

Encountering Dissonance

After completing and defending my dissertation proposal, I had the opportunity to attend a conference on qualitative methods. At the conference I enrolled in a workshop on grounded theory conducted by Dr. Juliet Corbin (1999) and listened to several grounded theory research presentations. Comments made by both presenters and attendees during the conference increased my awareness that there was disagreement regarding the "appropriate" way to conduct a grounded theory inquiry. For example, when one well-known researcher was discussing grounded theory in her presentation, one of the participants declared, "She is the *real* grounded theorist!" Listening to such remarks, I became confused.

Uncertainty with the way I outlined the grounded theory methods section in my proposal increased after receiving a review for a grant proposal I had submitted to obtain funding for my dissertation study. Although my grant submission received positive reviews and I was selected as a finalist, I was not funded. One of the reviewers, who identified herself as a grounded theorist, commented that the grounded theory procedures described in the proposal were not representative of "true" grounded theory and would fail to generate a substantive grounded theory. To help make sense of these dissonant responses, I began to delve more deeply into the discourses on grounded theory.

Turning to Grounded Theory Discourses

The method of theory development Glaser and Strauss first described in *The Discovery of Grounded Theory* (1967) grew from their collaborative work on terminally ill patients within hospitals. As the popularity of grounded theory grew, Glaser and Strauss continued to write, albeit separately, to further clarify the grounded theory method. When Strauss, in collaboration with Juliet Corbin, published *Basics of Qualitative Research: Grounded Theory Procedures and Techniques* (1990), Glaser responded with a derisive critique in his book *Basics of Grounded Theory Analysis: Emergence vs. Forcing* (1992), which argued that Strauss and Corbin's method would lead not to theory development but to "forced, full, conceptual description" (5). It became clear in these and subsequent publications (Charmaz 2000; Corbin 1998; Glaser 1994, 1998; Stern 1994) that Glaser's conception of grounded theory differed from Strauss's view.

The debate between Glaser and Strauss has created a contentious thread within grounded theory discourses, as some authors argue that those following the "Glaserian school" of grounded theory are producing a more "pure version" of grounded theory than those adhering to the "Straussian school" (Charmaz 2000; Stern 1994). The contentious nature of this debate created some considerable anxiety; I feared that choosing the "wrong" method of grounded theory would call the legitimacy of my dissertation into question.

As I continued my quest for the "one" article that would place this dissonance into some coherent perspective allowing me to decide which approach to choose, I began to meet regularly with three members of the study group. Maria Piantanida, a member of my dissertation committee, had used grounded theory in her dissertation on hospital-wide education (Piantanida 1982) and Cindy Tananis had embarked on a grounded theory inquiry of her work as an educational evaluator (Tananis 2000). Van Manen (1977) contends that "underlying every orientation is a definite epistemology, axiology and ontology, i.e., a person's orientation is composed of what he believes to be true, to be valuable, and to be real" (211). Using the term Cindy had whimsically coined, we called ourselves the "epistemorphs" because we shared the common experience of grappling with "our assumptions about . . . what we take to be true (epistemology), what we take to be real (ontology), and what we take to be of value (axiology)" (Piantanida, Tananis, and Grubs 2004, 2).

"Morphing" became our metaphor to describe the shift in epistemological, ontological, and axiological assumptions we experienced while engaging in our grounded theory inquiries and our professional endeavors. Although all three of us worked in fields where the post-positivist perspective dominates research, we recognized that some of the complexities within our professional practices might be better understood from an interpretative perspective. We found ourselves "morphing" from a post-positivist stance to a more interpretative worldview. Noreen Garman, also a member of my dissertation committee, joined our meetings. Because Noreen is more rooted in an interpretative perspective, we joking labeled her the "plus one" member of our group and soon called ourselves the "epistemorphs-plus-one."

When we first began to meet, I had hoped our epistemorphs-plus-one discussions would help me choose the "right" grounded theory method. We spent considerable time reading various articles, and as we examined the grounded theory discourses, we began to see the futility of searching for the "right" method. Instead, the work of several researchers (Annells 1996; Charmaz 1994, 2000; Miller and Fredericks 1999; Rennie 1998a, 1998b) highlights the importance of crafting a logic of justification for the theorizing process. Annells (1996) suggests that the "grounded theory method has traditionally been sited in a postpositivist inquiry paradigm but is evolving and moving toward the constructivist inquiry paradigm" (379). She further writes:

> The researcher is encouraged to consider philosophical and paradigmatic aspects . . . prior to selecting grounded theory method for a research project. However, it is vital to recognize the method is subject to evolutionary change with differing modes resultant and is therefore not static in regard to philosophical perspective, fit with a paradigm of inquiry, and research process. (Annells 1996, 391)

Charmaz (2000) agrees, further arguing that the description of grounded theory in Glaser and Strauss's *Discovery of Grounded Theory* (1967), Strauss and Corbin's *Basics of Qualitative Research: Grounded Theory Procedures and Techniques* (1990), and Glaser's critique of *Basics* (1992) appear "untouched by either epistemological debates of the 1960s . . . or postmodern critiques" and appear to be situated within "a realist ontology and positivist epistemology" (513). However, Charmaz does not believe a grounded theorist needs to be objectivist or positivist: "Grounded theory can provide a path for researchers who want to continue to develop qualitative traditions without adopting the positivistic trappings of objectivism and universality" (2000, 523). She also suggests that since "grounded theory methods evolve in different ways depending on the perspectives and proclivities of their adherents," researchers should examine their ontological and epistemological assumptions; by recognizing our assumptions, "we can acknowledge the limits of our studies and the ways we shape them" (Charmaz 2000, 528).

The work of these researchers led us to recognize the importance of crafting a logic of justification for grounded theory rather than simply choosing one version of grounded theory as authoritative. Viewing method as logic of justification instead of as techniques for data collection allows for an "elaboration of logical issues and, ultimately, on the justifications that inform practice" (Smith and Heshusius 1986, 8). Piantanida, Tananis, and Grubs (2004) note, "By approaching method as logic of justification, the grounded theory researcher makes explicit the connections among research paradigm, strategies and techniques" (10). Letting go of my preoccupation with finding the right method and my fear that the grounded theory "authorities" (whoever they may be) would question the rigor of my study, I began to focus my energies more productively on crafting an interpretive logic of justification for my study. It was not the grounded theory procedures outlined in the literature but an interpretive logic of justification that allowed me to imagine a way to portray the powerful emotions and stories participants shared when telling me about their experiences of making genetic-related decisions. For my study, an interpretive logic of justification provided a rationale for constructing narrative vignettes and a typology.

The Struggle to Create a Theoretic Portrayal

The grounded theory procedures of coding, constant comparative analysis, and memoing have been extensively described in the literature (Charmaz 2000; Corbin and Strauss 1990; Glaser 1978, 1992, 1994, 1998; Glaser and Strauss 1967; Strauss and Corbin 1990, 1994, 1998; Strauss 1987). Using these procedures helped me come to deeper understandings about the participants' experiences, but they did not allow me to create a theoretical construct or portrayal. When I tried to separate the codes from the participants' experiences, the concepts I generated did not convey the richness and complexity that I began to appreciate in participants' stories. I struggled to find a way to portray the emotional richness of participants' experiences and after some deliberation I decided to write narrative vignettes.

When participants shared their experiences with me during our conversations, they did so in a narrative fashion. Thus, creating narrative vignettes afforded me a form of portrayal consistent with the ways in which participants described their experiences, as well as providing another text for interpretation. As Richardson (1990), a social scientist, writes:

> Narrative is the primary way through which humans organize their experiences into temporally meaningful episodes. . . . People link events narratively. . . . People can apprehend the world narratively and people can tell about the world narratively. (21)

"Narrative," Richardson argues, "is the best way to understand the human experience, because it is the way humans understand their own lives" (1990, 65).

In creating my narrative vignettes, I pulled excerpts from conversations with participants and interwove them with commentary. The concepts I had generated in my coding, comparative analysis, and memoing allowed me to select excerpts that appeared to be significant. Working within an interpretive paradigm, I did not claim that these vignettes corresponded directly to some objective external reality of my participants' experiences (a claim more compatible with a post-positivist perspective). Instead, the vignettes represented my understanding of what seemed to be meaningful aspects of participants' experiences.

When discussing the issue of writing to portray a social phenomenon, Richardson (1990) raises the following point: "Language is not simply 'transparent,' reflecting a social reality that is objectively out there. Rather, language is a constitutive force creating a particular view of reality" (12). As I worked to craft the vignettes, this comment became increasingly significant to me. The very process of writing and interpreting the vignettes allowed me to portray participants' experiences and to probe more fully the meanings of concepts I had generated through the processes of coding, comparative analysis, and memoing. I was also able to share the vignettes with others, allowing me to receive critical feedback during my nascent conceptualization. Through this writing, interpreting, and sharing I began to identify relationships between various concepts and to develop a core concept or the conceptual centerpiece of a substantive grounded theory. In the case of my own study—contextualizing the existential experience of being at-risk and reaching a decision about prenatal testing—was the core concept that began to emerge.

As an example, I offer the following excerpt from a vignette in which I attempted to portray the fear Sean, a participant, described as he and his wife, Dana, considered prenatal testing for their fourth pregnancy. When Sean shared this poignant account of the events surrounding the death of his son, tears welled in his eyes:

> One of our friends said, "Well, you know . . . somebody had the test one time and it broke their water at the time and they lost the baby because of that." And I'm thinking, well here we go again cause she had miscarried. I don't know how many years ago it's been now three years, a little over three years, and I'm like, man I don't know if I can deal with that emotional thing again, cause that ripped me up because number one it was a boy and it was like five months into it. . . . I just wasn't ready for that emotional roller coaster again . . . whenever we had the miscarriage, I remembered when I called off work, my boss said "Well, how many days do you need off?" and I'm like, "I don't know". . . . it was like a birth of a dead baby, I mean how many days do you really need off to get your emotions back in order to do certain things? "I don't know," I said, "I'll call you in the next day or two to let you know when I'll be back," but emotionally, I was ripped up, I had to go out, bawling my eyes out for a good couple days, I mean I was ripped up and, um, I don't know, I could cry now.

In my dissertation, I interwove his statements with my own analysis:

> Sean feared experiencing another miscarriage and was troubled by the risk associated with amniocentesis but when he and Dana discussed the option of testing, Sean told her, "Whatever you want to do I'll support you either way."

When I asked this participant to explain why he believed the decision should be "entirely up" to his wife, he responded:

> I was only part of it, the conception. Everything else is going through her body. She has to watch what she eats, drinks, whatever and anything that goes into her mouth affects the baby. Anything that's pronged, poked, or anything affects the baby, any

drug, whatever. And it's her decision. I can give her my view on it, on how I feel about certain procedures or whatever, but ultimately I think it should be her choice because it's her body that's being affected, no matter if they're checking for the baby, they're also checking her. Something could happen to her; it's going to affect the baby and vice versa and I just want her to, no matter what she has to do, she has to take care of her body first because we can always have another baby, but she's first. I mean I'm attached to her, I'm not attached to the baby yet, I am, but she's more important to me at this moment in time . . . I don't know what I'd do if something happened to her right there, I don't know. Oh, I'd be a basket case. (Grubs 2002, 189–191)

Although Sean feared experiencing another pregnancy loss, his major worry appeared to be related to Dana's well being. Reducing my interpretation of Sean's story to a single code or a cluster of codes did not allow me to convey the emotional tenor in Sean's story. By creating vignettes, however, I was able to represent emotions embedded in participants' stories and to portray my narrative reconstruction of their experiences as well as the core concept of contextualizing the existential experiences.

To further explicate this core concept, I created a narrative typology to depict my empathetic sense of the different ways individuals experienced and responded to the existential nature of being at-risk and making a decision about prenatal testing. The typology helped me move from idiosyncratic details to theoretic understanding by portraying exemplars of how participants appeared to experience and cope with existential angst.

I have included a brief description for each of the types that comprised the typology in Appendix 1. There is no hierarchical order, and for the sake of ease, they are listed alphabetically; a more detailed narrative accompanied each type in my dissertation. The following is an excerpt from the narrative description for the type "Evading the Angst" and was drawn from my interpretation of Dana and Sean's story:

> While participants shared their stories, it appeared that by reflecting upon past experiences they were able to imagine their reactions to future possibilities created by prenatal testing. For example, their comments suggested that they often considered how they would cope with a test-related miscarriage, how they would react to facing the option of selective abortion, and how they would feel about having a child with a chromosome condition. Examining past experiences allowed participants to project into the future to assess their ability to cope with these different outcomes and to arrive at a decision about prenatal testing. After listening to Dana describe her difficulty in trying to reach a prenatal testing decision, my impression was that unlike most of the other participants, she was not able to determine what

Sean and she would do if they received an abnormal test result or to predict if they would be able to cope with another miscarriage. Dana told me, "if I did go through with it [prenatal testing] and something was wrong, I don't know what I would have done." Considering prenatal testing appeared to bring forth painful memories of Dana and Sean's previous pregnancy loss. When Sean recounted the story of their miscarriage, he became tearful and said that he did not think he could "deal with that emotional thing again." My sense was that thinking about the possible outcomes of prenatal testing such as having an amniocentesis-related miscarriage or being confronted with the option of abortion for a genetic diagnosis created unfaceable angst for Dana and Sean. Women and couples who revisit the painful memories of a previous loss might find the prospect of experiencing another pregnancy loss related to prenatal diagnosis overwhelming and difficult to face.

Dana spoke with her friends, family members, as well as an obstetrician about prenatal testing and had hoped someone, particularly her obstetrician, would ease the burden of making the decision by telling her what to do. (I describe Dana as the individual making the decision since Sean deferred to her). At one point in the pregnancy Dana decided she would have maternal serum screening, and then if the results were abnormal, she would proceed with an amniocentesis. However, after learning that maternal serum screening could not detect all chromosome abnormalities she became uncertain again. She told me, "Then it came time [to have maternal serum screening], I think time just passed and I never got the test done either." So, Dana did not appear to commit to a particular decision. Trying to give the responsibility of making a decision to her physician did not work, but letting time pass so that testing was no longer an option seemed to allow Dana to evade the angst of having to make a decision.

In their study Lippman-Hand and Fraser (1979b) found that some women who could not make a decision about whether to attempt a future pregnancy engaged in "reproductive roulette" or "inefficient contraceptive practices" [81]. In describing reproductive roulette Lippman-Hand and Fraser (1979b) write:

> [It] is a choice not to decide, a choice of "fatalism" made when one does not want to exert control. . . . A woman who knows she is taking a chance of getting pregnant and clearly chooses to take this chance is not behaving in an undecided fashion, but is selecting a course of action that for her may best neutralize the dilemma. [81]

Allowing time to pass so that prenatal testing was no longer an option may have permitted Dana to relinquish control and to help "neutralize" her dilemma by evading the existential angst generated by being at-risk and confronting a decision about prenatal testing. (Grubs 2002, 222–24)

When discussing the use of typologies (classification systems) in qualitative research, Richardson (1990) writes, "Typologies are excellent rhetorical devices for framing qualitative work, for they can be written with an open-endedness" (51). The typology I crafted did not represent "an exhaustive classificatory scheme" (Richardson 1990, 50) that could be generalized to all women and couples at-risk for having a baby with a health problem due to the age of the mother. Rather, it offered exemplars of a range of responses women and couples may have to the profound existential experience of being at-risk and facing difficult genetic-related decisions. In creating a typology, I offered an interpretation of the different ways in which I came to think of the existential angst the participants in my study may have been experiencing as they attempted to contextualize their decisions within the framework of their lives. It was and still is my hope that my typology might help genetic counselors become more attuned, in an "empathetic moment," to the variations of angst their clients might experience as they face difficult genetic-related decisions.

I do not want to give the mistaken impression that the processes of coding, comparative analysis, memoing, writing vignettes, and creating a typology were discrete and linear steps in my inquiry. These processes were interrelated. Through successive iterations of writing and interpretation, I moved from specific details in individual interviews to an empathetic gestalt of how I resonated with the stories. Through the narrative vignettes and typology I was able to construct and portray an interpretive grounded theory. In contrast to a more post-positivist perspective of grounded theory, an interpretive grounded theory is not meant to be predictive. Instead, it serves as a heuristic, putting a complex phenomenon into a coherent perspective that allows for more focused deliberation, discussion, and inquiry (Piantanida, Tananis, and Grubs 2004).

Reimagining Genetic Counseling Practice

Reimagining grounded theory from a more interpretive perspective ultimately provided me with an opportunity to empathize with the stories of individuals facing genetic risk in a way that my life as a practitioner in a busy genetic counseling clinic setting failed to do. Looking back, I fear my preoccupation with time constraints led me to focus on the delivery of genetic information, rather than the stories and emotions of my clients. My study allowed me to imagine how at-risk individuals might experience and respond to the offer of genetic testing. As Halpern (2001) notes, "The work fundamental to empathy is imagining how it feels to experience something" (85). She also writes, "The empathizer does not just happen to resonate; she cultivates the capacity for imagining perspectives to which she lacks immediate access" (84–85).

After the completion of my dissertation, Maria Piantanida wisely asked, "Robin, in your dissertation you argue that existential angst is embedded in the stories of participants; what might that mean for genetic counselors?" By asking this question, she helped me recognize the importance of connecting my theoretical portrayal to genetic counseling practice. Although I had discussed the implications of my grounded theory in my dissertation, I had failed to make a compelling connection between the theory and genetic counseling practice. After pondering that question, I met with Maria, who had begun to construct a heuristic to help us probe this connection. After some fine tuning, together along with ideas offered by the study group, we created a heuristic shown in Appendix 2. This heuristic is intended to offer a preliminary conceptualization of genetic counseling practice by outlining four approaches to counseling, each approach stemming from different beliefs about the experience of making genetic-related decisions as well as genetic counseling stances. Not only has this heuristic engendered interesting conversations with my genetic counseling colleagues, but it has also changed my pedagogical endeavors in my work with genetic counseling students. These new insights into genetic counseling practice and education are the ultimate rewards of my dissertation journey.

Appendix 1
Typology of Existential Angst in At-risk Women and Couples Facing Genetic-related Decisions

Containing the Angst. The desire to avoid services such as genetic counseling that have the potential to heighten angst (by reviewing genetic risks, relevant testing options, and psychosocial ramifications of testing, for example).

Evading the Angst. The recognition that a decision about testing needs to be made but allowing time to pass until testing is no longer an option, thus evading the angst generated by being at-risk and facing genetic-related decisions.

Facing the Angst with Faith. The notion that faith in God will provide a protective shield against the risks associated with a woman's age and will ensure a destiny free of unmanageable challenges.

Focusing the Angst. The act of focusing fears on issues unrelated to being at-risk so that the implications of facing genetic risk and the consequences of making genetic-related decisions can be ignored.

Sharing the Angst. The commitment to sharing experiences and making decisions together as a couple to cope jointly with the angst created by being at-risk and facing a decision about prenatal genetic testing.

Submerging the Angst. The perception that prenatal genetic testing offers a sense of control and a way to transcend one's "biological destiny" (Newman 1997), thus allowing the woman or couple to submerge the angst associated with the possibility of receiving an abnormal result. In addition, when a woman believes that the primacy of the pregnancy and prenatal testing experiences belongs to her, she may submerge her partner's angst while she focuses primarily on her own feelings and wishes.

Appendix 2
Toward a Grounded Theory of Professional Practice for Genetic Counselors

The *horizontal axis* depicts two different views of the experience of making decisions related to genetic counseling and testing. The left side of the axis shows a fairly traditional view grounded in a biomedical model that treats the decision as a one-time event with a discrete outcome. The right side of the axis shows the experience as part of an ongoing existential experience fraught with dilemmas and angst.

```
                    Responsiveness to existential angst
                                    ↑
         Question                         Responsive
         Facilitation                     Empathy

                              ┌─────────────┐
                              │  GC's Stance │
                              └─────────────┘
  ←─────────────────────────────┼─────────────────────────────→
  Discrete      The Experience of Making Decisions    Ongoing
  biomedical                                          existential
  decision                                            experience

         Information                      Detached
         Acquisition                      Concern (Halpern 2001)

                                    ↓
                         Information Transmission
```

The *vertical axis* depicts a range of stances genetic counselors might take toward clients. The position at the bottom of the axis casts the counselor as a transmitter of information. The position at the top of the axis emphasizes responsiveness to the existential experience of the clients.

The *cells of the matrix* depict various approaches to counseling and have implications for genetic counseling practice. For example, an approach of responsive empathy would recognize the need for responsiveness to the angst associated with the ongoing existential nature of the experience of making genetic-related decisions.

Notes

1. Genetic counselors are healthcare professionals who work with individuals and families at risk for developing or transmitting genetic conditions.
2. Amniocentesis and chorionic villi sampling are prenatal genetic tests capable of identifying chromosome abnormalities and certain genetic conditions during pregnancy.

References

Annells, M. 1996. Grounded theory method: Philosophical perspectives, paradigm of inquiry, and postmodernism. *Qualitative Health Research* 6, no. 3: 379–93.

Charmaz, K. 1994. The grounded theory method: An explication and interpretation. In Glaser, *More grounded theory*, 95–115.

———. 2000. Grounded theory: Objectivist and constructivist methods. In *Handbook of qualitative research*, 2nd ed., ed. N. K. Denzin and Y. S. Lincoln, 509–35. Thousand Oaks, CA: Sage.

Corbin, J. M. 1998. Alternative interpretations: Valid or not? *Theory & Psychology* 8, no. 1: 121–28.

———. 1999. Data analysis. Pre-conference workshop presented at Advances in Qualitative Methods. Edmonton, Alberta, Canada.

Corbin, J., and A. Strauss. 1990. Grounded theory research: Procedures, canons, and evaluative criteria. *Qualitative Sociology* 13, no. 1: 3–21.

Glaser, B. G. 1978. *Advances in the methodology of grounded theory: Theoretical sensitivity*. Mill Valley, CA: Sociology Press.

———. 1992. *Basics of grounded theory analysis: Emergence vs. forcing*. Mill Valley, CA: Sociology Press.

———. 1994. *More grounded theory methodology: A reader*. Mill Valley, CA: Sociology Press.

———.1998. *Doing grounded theory: Issues and discussions*. Mill Valley, CA: Sociology Press.

Glaser, B. G., and A. L. Strauss. 1967. *The discovery of grounded theory: Strategies for qualitative research*. Hawthorne, NY: Aldine Publishing Company.

Grubs, R. E. 2002. *Living with shadows: Contextualizing the experience of being at-risk and reaching a decision about prenatal genetic testing*. UMI ProQuest Digital Dissertation #AAT 3078844.

Halpern, J. 2001. *From detached concern to empathy: Humanizing medical practice*. New York: Oxford.

Labaree, D. F. 1998. Educational researchers: Living with a lesser form of knowledge. *Educational Researcher* 27, no. 8: 4–12.

Lippman-Hand, A., and F. C. Fraser. 1979. Genetic counseling: The postcounseling period II. Making reproductive choices. *American Journal of Medical Genetics* 4: 73–87.

Miller, S. I., and M. Fredericks. 1999. How does grounded theory explain? *Qualitative Health Research* 9, no. 4: 538–51.

Newman, J. 1997. *Religion and technology: A study in the philosophy of culture.* Westport, CT: Praeger Publishers.

Piantanida, M. E. 1982. *The practice of hospital education: A grounded theory study.* UMI ProQuest Digital Dissertation #AAT 8317299.

Piantanida, M., C. A. Tananis, and R. E. Grubs. 2004. Generating grounded theory of/for educational practice: The journey of three epistemorphs. *International Journal of Qualitative Studies in Education* 17, no. 3: 325–46.

Rennie, D. L. 1998a. Grounded theory methodology: The pressing need for a coherent logic of justification. *Theory & Psychology* 8, no. 1: 101–19.

———. 1998b. Reply to Corbin: From one interpreter to another. *Theory & Psychology* 8, no. 1: 129–35.

Richardson, L. 1990. *Writing strategies: Reaching diverse audiences.* Vol. 21. Newbury Park, CA: Sage.

Smith, J. K., and L. Heshusius. 1986. Closing down the conversation: The end of the quantitative-qualitative debate among educational inquirers. *Educational Researcher* 15, no. 1: 4–12.

Stern, P. N. 1994. Eroding grounded theory. In *Critical issues in qualitative research methods*, ed. J. M. Morse, 212–23. Thousand Oaks, CA: Sage.

Strauss, A. L. 1987. *Qualitative analysis for social scientists.* Melbourne, Australia: Cambridge University Press.

Strauss, A., and J. Corbin. 1990. *Basics of qualitative research: Grounded theory procedures and techniques.* Newbury Park, CA: Sage.

———. 1994. Grounded theory methodology: An overview. In *Handbook of Qualitative Research*, ed. N. K. Denzin and Y. S. Lincoln, 273–85. Thousand Oaks, CA: Sage.

———. 1998. *Basics of qualitative research: Techniques and procedures for developing grounded theory.* 2nd ed. Thousands Oaks, CA: Sage.

Tananis, C. A. 2000. *Discursive evaluation: The journey of an "epistemorph" toward an interpretive practice and inquiry.* UMI ProQuest Digital Dissertation #AAT 9974482.

van Manen, M. 1977. Linking ways of knowing with ways of being practical. *Curriculum Inquiry* 6, no. 3: 205–28.

CHAPTER 7

Embracing a Language of Spiritual Inquiry

Marilyn Llewellyn

Embracing the Study

"Marilyn, when you speak about education, you often draw on the language of democratic schooling rather than from a traditional spiritual language." This observation, offered by my friend Noreen during the course of a dinner conversation about my dissertation, troubled me deeply. We had just been talking about my desire to explore the notion of understanding curriculum as theological text. My interest in this view of curriculum had been piqued when I read Dwayne Huebner's (1995) "Education and Spirituality." Of particular significance to me was Huebner's belief that education should be concerned with and attend to the journey of the self; everything that gets in the way of or limits this journey, he argued, should be rejected. I was intrigued with his critique of how educators describe what is happening in a person's life as "learning theory" or "developmental theory" (Huebner 1995, 18), theoretic constructs that remove the journey of the self from its sacred realm and reduce it to a technical process. These ideas spoke to some of my most meaningful experiences of being with persons in educational settings over the course of more than twenty years. Thus, the accuracy of Noreen's comment about my language stirred something deep and troubling within me.

My reluctance to use what might be characteristically thought of as spiritual language in my conversations is ironic. I am a member of a religious community of women within the structure of the Catholic Church. I struggle to remain connected to an institution that excludes, oppresses and undervalues women as a group. I am suspicious of and often reject a Eurocentric male theology and spirituality with doctrines and ideologies that are deeply embedded with exclusionary language and oppressive practices. I also find the language used by some religious groups, particularly conservative fundamentalists within all faiths, to be very irritating, judgmental and essentialist. Furthermore, there is often a lack of connection between religion and concern for persons in our world who are suffering from social and economic injustices. Consequently, I have resisted using language that resembles this traditionally religious language. At the same time, however, I found it compelling to think about spirituality related to pedagogy. The incongruity of striving to express a spiritual way of being with others in the classroom through a rational technical language opened a dark space within me.

Although darkness can project a sense of danger, within the Hebrew scriptures images of darkness often precede creation. I trust the generative possibilities within darkness, not just theoretically, but with the core of my being. So, I was drawn into the dark space engendered by Noreen's comment. In living with the darkness I found the genesis of my study; in moving through it, I came to imagine a dissertation (Llewellyn 1998) and to envision a method of inquiry, which I named spiritual inquiry that embodies who I am as an educator.

Spiritual inquiry describes both what was under study—my spirituality and pedagogy—as well as the manner in which I engaged in the study. In brief, this method of inquiry entailed my crafting an educational memoir through recollection of a lifetime of kairotic moments. Through contemplation of the memoir, my attention was drawn to compelling issues, anomalies, and important aspects in my life that revealed my spirituality and pedagogy which, in turn, became the focal point of meditative writing. To draw pedagogical implications from the meditations, I entered into a process of exegesis. Although this language may be unfamiliar to many readers, and may seem at odds with the very notion of research, claiming it connected me to traditions of religious and theological inquiry. These traditions, more than scientific ways of knowing, resonated with who I am as a person and my way of being in the world.

I begin by contextualizing my inquiry process with vignettes that exemplify two *kairotic* moments drawn from my memoir. Then I offer a meditative writing on the notion of faith in classroom relationships. Hopefully, this will give a sense of what I came to in my dissertation and create a shared context within which I can elaborate on the concepts introduced above.

Faith in Classroom Relationships–Two Kairotic Moments

My First Parent-Teacher Conference

I walked to school that crisp autumn morning filled with a mixture of excitement, anxiety and fear. It was my first year of teaching, and today was my initiation into parent/teacher conferences. I was certain the parents would make many criticisms of me. As I nervously waited for my first parent to arrive, I thought of how my life had turned out differently than I had expected.

I had switched from an elementary education major and sociology minor during my junior year of college to a history major and secondary education minor. I did my student teaching in the early 1970s in an urban Catholic high school for girls. After my first day of student teaching, the teacher with whom I worked said that she would like me to be responsible for three of her social studies classes; she gave me the textbooks for the freshman and sophomore classes and told me to prepare lessons for the next day. I went home and spent the evening figuring out how I would present the material for these history classes. Following the homeroom period the next morning, I stepped up to the front of the room and began the lesson. After the first 10 minutes, the teacher went out of the room and left me to conduct the class by myself, as she would every day for the entire semester. I struggled to make the material interesting. I tried to create a fun and relaxed atmosphere while retaining some semblance of order and control. I learned so much about teaching during those five months, and I was convinced that I should continue to teach high school students.

But instead of high school, the administration of my congregation had assigned me to teach sixth grade at the urban Catholic elementary school where I now sat waiting for parents to arrive. Sitting there, I remembered how unprepared I had been for elementary teaching—but under the guidance of some excellent teachers in the school, I had come a long way.

When I had prepared my classes in August, I wasn't aware that it was the norm to place students into ability-based reading groups, and so every day we did some activity in language arts that defied the need for any arbitrarily assigned groupings based on skill assessments. We read recipes (and then made fudge), mapped trips across the United States on the floor, played grammar games, wrote creative writing exercises, group poetry, limericks and drama—activities that allowed great diversity in the student groupings.

I had ignored the conventional wisdom "don't smile until Christmas," taking the chance that if I allowed the students to laugh and enjoy themselves, perhaps I would not spend the rest of the year trying to regain control. It was a struggle. I made plenty of mistakes. However, I continually learned from the students, and there was one teacher who helped me a great deal, not only with the content of my classes, but also in the manner of my teaching. She was a wonderful teacher, able to encourage academic excellence while allowing incredible fun. As I remembered how helpful she'd been to me, the first parent, Barry's mother, arrived for our conference.

Barry was an extremely bright and conscientious young boy. As I looked over the folder of his work that I had prepared, I was sure I was not challenging him to his full potential, and I expected to be told so. I took a deep breath, smiled and invited Barry's mother to take a seat across from me.

Her first words to me were, "Thank you." I know the stunned look on my face prompted her to go on. "I'm sure you don't know this," she said, "but during Barry's first five years of school, he complained of a stomachache every morning. He begged to stay home and often cried before leaving the house for school. When I spoke with his teachers about it, they had no answers.

"Then this year," she continued, "for the first time since Barry started school, all of that stopped. He got up in the morning and felt fine. He was happy and anxious to get to school. When I asked him why he'd changed, Barry said that school was fun now. He said that you were nice and that you don't yell. You joke and laugh in class, and he's not afraid to make a mistake. Barry said he's not afraid of school anymore."

As I drifted off to sleep later that night, I thought about how powerful the words of Barry's mother were. "Barry said that he is no longer afraid in school."

Nicki and the Principal's Office

Nicki sat down on the brown vinyl chair in the principal's outer office, and I sat beside her. The principal came out of her main office when she learned we were waiting to see her and pulled up a chair across from us.

"I brought Nicki down here to see you," I said, "because everything I've tried doesn't seem to be helping and, frankly, I don't know what else to do. I'm particularly concerned because Nicki is not doing her work; she is often tardy, and she is very disruptive during class. I've tried a number of things to help her, but nothing seems to work. I'm hoping you can give us some suggestions."

Before I could continue—about how I thought Nicki and I needed some assistance in communicating clearly, even though Nicki seemed to be trying—the principal interrupted me with a long list of unacceptable behaviors she wanted Nicki to change "or else." Her list included things Nicki had done from years past as well as a list of complaints from other teachers. In the background, the steam radiator hissed as the principal rattled off Nicki's vices, her voice louder and louder. Meanwhile, Nicki's head dropped lower and lower. I couldn't listen anymore. What had I done? At the first pause, I quickly stood up.

"Come on, Nicki, or we'll miss English class," I said, gently touching her on the shoulder.

Nicki and I walked silently down the school hall toward the classroom. Just before we reached the classroom door, I turned to her and said, "I'm sorry; I never meant for that to happen."

I was never quite sure what Nicki's nod back to me meant. I do know that I promised myself that I would never do that again. I would figure out other ways to handle difficulties with a student on my own, without asking someone else to take care of conflicts for me. It was an important lesson for my first year of teaching—one that both haunted and helped me in the years that would follow.

Meditative Writing on the Notion of Faith

When I look back at these two experiences, complicated feelings and self-images invite me to examine how differently I responded to Barry and Nicki and how I might better understand the teacher/student relationship. For Barry, I had created a space in the classroom where he felt safe and affirmed through interacting in very real and human ways. Because Nicki had low grades, broke rules, and wasn't doing her work, I justified taking her to the principal on the premise of helping her academically. When I realized that I had placed Nicki in a situation where her already minimal self-worth was exposed to further diminishment, I was forced to probe the merit of my action and vowed I would never knowingly do that to a student again. My different ways of interacting with Barry and Nicki represented a choice I would have to make about what kind of learner/teacher relationship I valued. I could not give credence to both paradigms as I came to see them as more and more incompatible. The first paradigm the learner/teacher relationship as grounded in faith, while the other is rooted in an ideology of achievement (Macdonald 1995).

Faith, although often associated with religion, can also be viewed in a much wider sense as the core of connection in human relationships. Etymologically, faith can be traced to the Greek word *pistij*, the Latin *fides* and later, the Middle English *feith*. According to the *Oxford English Dictionary* (Simpson & Weiner 1989), the principle senses of faith are a trust and belief in someone or something. Additionally, faith yields confidence and engagement. Faith, as the core of connection in human relationships, involves acts of trust that risk placing my belief in someone or something beyond myself. Faith yields the belief that something is possible beyond what I can know, prove or even describe both within myself and in another. Infinite possibilities come to light in placing my life in relationship to another in faith, yet there is also a great deal of fragility that is present within this exchange because faith is intricately linked to human freedom.

The human dimensions of faith as linked to human freedom have been given some of its clearest expression within the discourses of liberation theology. In response to the question, "What is faith?" comes the perception from one black liberation theologian that "it is a contextual faith which comes out of the commitment to the struggle" and "is born in the womb of the struggle itself" (Goba 1990, 22). For Goba, faith is "deprivatized . . . communal . . . calls for resistance in any situation of oppression and dehumanization . . . and the central axis which shapes and directs every aspect of life (1990, 23–25)." In this sense, faith is not an individual act of assent to a body of hidden truths, but rather faith is coming to see what was previously unseen about the reality of our shared lives.

In a similar way, learners and teachers express a relationship based on faith not through articulation of formal doctrines, but rather through openness to contextual, experiential meaning and trust in ordinary, day-to-day exchanges. When relationships between teachers and learners—and learners and learners—are rooted in faith, being and learning together becomes less about individual achievement and more about the communal shaping and sharing of knowledge that benefits everyone. Relationships rooted in faith call us to support those among us who suffer most from forms of oppression—such as can be found in tracking and grading—and to resist the dehumanizing effects of schooling manifested in textbook-driven curriculum, high-stakes testing, rigid control and strict codes of discipline.

Educational relationships rooted in faith defy being expressed in the technical language of behavioral objectives and student measurement. Teaching and learning relationships rooted in faith are very different than those based on the ideology of achievement. Macdonald (1995) describes the ideology of achievement in the following manner:

> It is the rhetoric of behaviorism, scientism, and psychologism. People are "learners," who have to be "motivated" and "measured," and who possess certain "traits," "capacities," and "needs" which we "diagnose." Goals are talked about in "behavioral" terms. This rhetoric has the effect of lifting the burden of our moral responsibility to children (and other people). It creates a mystique about schooling into which one must be initiated through a teacher education program and the rite of certification, and it creates a jargon which obscures our fundamental moral concern.
>
> Thus, it becomes easy to keep our focus upon the achievement of learning goals and to forget the fundamental goal of freeing persons for self-responsible and self-directed fulfillment of their own emerging potential. It is easy to talk about norms, percentiles, concepts, skills, methods, and so forth; and it is equally as easy to forget about the person involved. (52)

A relationship based on faith invites us to risk seeing the other person in fresh and new ways, to believe that the possibility for growth is always present in the other person and within oneself. Relationships grounded in faith actuate a human response to students and peers within the school setting.

Revisiting the Language of Spiritual Inquiry

Spiritual Memoir and Kairos

As I reflected on a lifetime of being in classrooms as a child, a teacher, a principal, a number of incidents like those with Barry and Nicki began to surface from memory. Initially I referred to these as "defining moments." As I struggled with why I needed to tell them, how I would tell them, and what they represented, I began to craft vignettes. As the vignettes accumulated, I came to see them as portrayals of *kairos*.

I chose to use *kairos*, the biblical notion of time, as a way to portray and contemplate life events that have shaped my spirituality and my pedagogy because *kairos* is an expression of time as a period or periods of significance: a fulfilled moment or event(s) that make a difference in one's life. *Kairos* is time expressed as decisive time, the fullness of time, or the coming into being of a new state. This differs from *chronos* or chronological time, which is seen as sequential and unbroken. Laurel Richardson (1995) refers to Husserl in expressing an understanding of time in this manner: "Unlike the clock and calendars that measure out life in moments, days and years, people do not experience time as a succession of instants or a linear linking of points in space but as extended awareness of the past and the future within the present" (208). I used the concept of *kairos* as an organizing principle to reconstruct the life events that form the "extended awareness of the past and the future within the present," events that led to my new ways of being. *Kairos* allowed me to express these life events as emergent and interrelated rather than individual and fixed.

I came to see something that I wanted to study related to my pedagogy. I approached this challenge by constructing a "spiritual memoir" as the textual representation of my curriculum praxis. As a way to reveal the *kairos*, I recollected significant events in my life. A variety of sources—persons, places, events, letters, journals and other artifacts—provided the landscape of my life. But without reflective distillation of these collective memories and artifacts, they remained simply an undifferentiated record of raw life experiences. Accordingly, I selected some life events and chose to craft them as a series of vignettes that I constructed as memoir, thus making an external (albeit partial) text of my life.

William Zinsser (1995), in his book *Inventing the Truth: The Art and Craft of Memoir*, distinguishes autobiography from memoir by describing memoir as "some portion of a life" (11). He goes on to to explain,

> Unlike autobiography, which moves in a dutiful line from birth to fame, omitting nothing, memoir assumes the life and ignores most of it. A memoir writer takes us back to a moment in his or her life that was unusually vivid, such as childhood, or that was framed by war or travel or some other exceptional event. By narrowing the lens, the writer achieves a focus that's not possible in autobiography. Memoir is a window into a life. (Zinsser 1995, 11)

My memoir was intended to create a window into my pedagogical life. I don't claim the memoir as "true" in the sense that I am able to verify all aspects of it as factual; the events all occurred, but I have no written record of most of them. The memoir represents what Madeline Grumet (1988) terms fidelity. That is, I constructed it as my honest version of these life events recollected from memory.

My inquiry process began with engaged contemplation, followed by meditative writing, and concluding with exegesis of the text I had written.

Engaged Contemplation

Engaged contemplation was a way for me to enter deeply into the life events to reveal the *kairos* and discern what emerged for further study. It required that I enter into the stories using my imagination, thoughts and feelings. "Contemplation" derives from the Latin *templum*, translated as "time"; it is a diminutive of *tempus* and primarily used to express a separation, partition, or segment of time. In Greek, the closest approximation is *theoria*, meaning "to intently look at something for a purpose." For the Romans, *templum* designated the spatial; it was an actual space sectioned off for the augurs to read signs and omens gleaned from looking at the viscera of birds. But while the temple was originally an actual place where sacred persons came to portend, predict, and give witness to divine promises, "contemplation" came to mean not a physical place but the act of beholding, gazing or looking attentively at the insides (the metaphorical viscera) of something or someone (Downey 1993, 210). One central dimension of contemplation is awareness. It was within this contemplative space of deep awareness that I experienced a unitive encounter in which there was an interrelatedness of mind, body, and spirit.

Contemplation was a way for me to hear, see, taste, smell, and touch embodied themes in order to distill the significant issues and anomalies from life events that revealed my spirituality and pedagogy. These issues and anomalies then became the focus of the meditative writings. The stillness and solitude before dawn invited contemplation. Rising in the morning, it was often difficult to resist immediately turning on my computer to produce something tangible and concrete; within this process of spiritual inquiry, though, I found it imperative to move at a more contemplative pace. Here in this cosmic space of darkness, the space between claiming what was from what was not, I waited for the concealed aspects of the text to be revealed. When I tried to rush the process, I felt blocked and empty.

I found no single or prescriptive way to enter into the contemplations, but usually I began with a ritual to help me enter into bodily calm and inner stillness. I asked for the gift of openness in order to receive what might be revealed. Sometimes I would just sit quietly or listen to music and allow the rhythmic sounds to flow into my body. At other times, I needed physical movement to enter fully into a contemplative space of stillness and openness.

When it felt appropriate, I would then choose some aspect of my memoir and through imagination and the use of my senses, become actively engaged in it. I allowed the text to speak to me in ways that invited me to "re-vision" in Adrienne Rich's (1979) sense of "looking back, of seeing with fresh eyes, of entering an old text from a new critical direction" (35) and of letting the mystery continually unfold. After spending time in contemplation, I would then write in a journal some of the thoughts, images and ideas that were revealed. The entire process required my openness to the notion that revelation occurs in multiple, mysterious and natural ways. Consistent time spent in periods of contemplation proved to be vital and were a source of profound grace for me.

Meditative Writing

My intent in using memoir as the text for contemplation was to reveal what of my spirituality and pedagogy was embedded in it. This process required that I spend periods of time immersed in the texture of the memoir in an actively engaged and sustained manner. Entering into the contemplations led to a deeper awareness and enabled me to see my memoir in new ways. The wonder, questions, revelations, and insights that emerged from the contemplations shaped the meditative writings. The contemplations flowed into the meditations, and within this cyclic hermeneutic process of contemplation and the crafting of the meditative writings, I grappled with and elaborated upon some of the pedagogical and spiritual issues embedded in my memoir. Conversations with other people as well as engagement with the scholarly literature, particularly in the curriculum field, were also part of the ongoing interpretive process. The meditations portrayed the themes and meanings that were revealed through engaging in contemplation. I entitled my resulting meditative writings as follows: 1) Fractures, Awakenings, Bitter Wisdom and Conversion; 2) Faith–Belief in Unseen Reality; 3) Beyond Caring to Compassion; 4) Revelation–Curriculum in Process; 5) The Divine Wisdom of Lived Experience; and 6) Sacred Space.

Exegesis

In remaining faithful to a language that best expressed the spiritual inquiry, I chose exegesis to explicate the text and portray the essential lessons of spirituality as pedagogy. Richard Palmer (1969) traces the use of the word "hermeneutics" to mean "the principles of biblical interpretation" (34), thereby offering some insight into exegesis:

> The distinction between actual commentary (exegesis) and the rules, methods, or theory governing it (hermeneutics) dates from this earliest usage [1654] and remains basic to the definition of hermeneutics both in theology and, when the definition is later broadened, in reference to nonbiblical literature.
>
> When the usage of the word is broadened in English to refer to nonbiblical texts, it is notable that the texts are obscure, so as to require special methods to extract a hidden meaning. . . . In English usage, then, the word may refer to nonbiblical interpretation, but in these cases the text is generally obscure or symbolic, requiring a special type of interpretation to get at its hidden meaning. The more general definition in English has remained that of the theory of scriptural exegesis.
>
> While the term "hermeneutics" itself dates only from the seventeenth century, the operations of textual exegesis and theories of interpretation—religious, literary, legal—date back to antiquity. Thus, once the word is accepted as designating theory of exegesis, the field it covers is generally extended (retroactively, one might say) in biblical exegesis back to Old Testament times, when there were canons for properly interpreting the Torah. (34–35)

Exegesis provided a way for me to engage in a critical interpretation of a text, to uncover the ideas that were embedded and represented in it and to evaluate the possible contribution of those ideas to the field of curriculum studies. The texts included my memoir, the meditative writings, ideas generated in dialogic relationships and the scholarly literature that informed my study. Through exegesis of a text, I was able to plumb the complexities of the various events, accounts, situations, relationships, difficulties and ideas.

My study began with a troubling question, one that required self-inquiry. Through exegesis I came to a clearer understanding of the ways that my spirituality shaped my pedagogy. I engaged in genuine questioning which invited me into a more authentic way of seeing myself as a teacher and opportunities for new ways of being. The stories of Barry and Nicki exemplify aspects of the process. Ultimately I was shaped by the story I wrote. Graced with a renewed desire, I made a commitment to live and teach more authentically.

Embracing a Spiritual Language

The spiritual offers a language, a way of knowing and a way of being to draw on in imagining schools as places where education is for life and for the enhancement of one's life journey. Within the realm of the spiritual there is vital language, mythic language, a way of knowing that is useful to draw on in education that helps to express a way of being in the world and to shape the transformative possibilities in being and learning together. It is language that can transcend the often-articulated narrow and utilitarian goal of schooling as connected to preparing young persons for the workforce. Exploring the language of the spiritual and its usefulness in education is an invitation to "re-vision," in order to articulate an educational language in which to express one's being. Garman (1994) states, "We are being challenged to pay attention to how language influences the thought and conduct of those we work with, and more important, what our language tells us about our own dispositions and motives"(1). We have a great deal to gain by drawing on the spiritual and envisioning schools as places where education is seen as a journey into a deeper and fuller life.

New metaphors are needed to help shape an understanding of schools as places where growing as a human being is of the utmost value and teaching is a human encounter rooted in relationships marked by faith, trust, care and love. Spirituality as pedagogy is not a technique for becoming a good teacher. Spirituality as pedagogy is the embodiment of the act of teaching as inseparable from one's very being.

References

Downey, M., ed. 1993. *The new dictionary of Catholic spirituality*. Collegeville, MN: Liturgical Press.

Garman, N. 1994. Beyond the reflective practitioner and toward discursive practice. *Teaching and Teachers' Work* 2, no. 4: 1–7.

Goba, B. 1990. What is faith? A black South African perspective. In *Lift every voice: Constructing Christian theologies from the underside*, ed. S. Brooks Thistlethwaithe and M. Potter Engel, 21–30. New York: Harper and Row.

Grumet, M. R. 1988. *Bitter milk: Women and teaching*. Amherst: University of Massachusetts Press.

Huebner, D. 1995. Education and spirituality. *Journal of Curriculum Theorizing* 11, no. 2: 13–34.

Llewellyn, M. J. 1998. *Bringing forth a world: Spirituality as pedagogy*. UMI ProQuest Digital Dissertation #AAT9825673.

Macdonald, J. B. 1995. A vision of a humane school. In *Theory as a prayerful act: The collected essays of James B. Macdonald*, Vol. 2, ed. B. J. Macdonald, 49–67. New York: Peter Lang.

Palmer, R. E. 1969. *Hermeneutics: Interpretation theory in Schleiermacher, Dilthey, Heidegger, and Gadamer*. Evanston, IL: Northwestern University Press.

Rich, A. 1979. When we dead awaken: Writing as re-vision. In *On lies, secrets, and silence: Selected prose 1966–1978*, ed. A. Rich, 33–49. New York: W. W. Norton & Company.

Richardson, L. 1995. Narrative and sociology. In *Representation in ethnography*, ed. J. Van Maanen, 198–221. Thousand Oaks, CA: Sage.

Simpson, J. A., and E. S. C. Weiner, eds. 1989. *Oxford English dictionary*. 2nd ed. Oxford: Clarendon Press.

Zinsser, W. 1995. Introduction. In *Inventing the truth: The art and craft of memoir*, 2nd ed., ed. W. Zinsser, 1–20. New York: Houghton Mifflin.

PART 3

Claiming a Way of Being in Practice through Inquiry

CHAPTER 8

Coming to Know through the Text of Talk: From Interviews to Inner Views Storied to Interpretation

Kathleen M. Ceroni

Opening

By 2005 ten years had passed since I wrote my dissertation, an interpretative study of a lead teacher reform initiative that was playing itself out in some Pennsylvania school districts during the late 1980s and early 1990s. The national political context spawning this specific state initiative was thick with the rhetoric of teacher empowerment, reflecting policymakers' reconceptualized belief that top-down reform management strategies failed because they didn't include the voices of teachers. I was seduced by this rhetoric; it tugged at my own embedded need to believe in the possibilities it promised. So powerful was its hold that I crafted my dissertation to explore the initiative, to talk with teachers who had firsthand experience with it, and to uncover the root of my desire to believe in educational reform despite its history littered with failures. The culmination of that study was my dissertation, *Promises Made, Promises Broken: A Literary Criticism of the Pennsylvania Lead Teacher Experience* (Ceroni 1995).

Since completing my study, I have struggled to understand how writing it changed me. Denzin (1995) tells us, "The qualitative research text is a distinct form of cultural representation, a genre in its own right. The educational researcher creates, through his or her textual work, concrete experiences that embody cultural meanings and cultural understandings that operate in the 'real' world. These texts carry news from one world to another" (8). Writing in this genre of qualitative research, I engaged in an act that was recursive, multilayered, and meaning-making. As the text evolved, I wove and rewove pieces in startling ways, making discoveries about myself and the reform under study. I had to be attentive to the nuances of the process and willing to follow the twists and turns it took. I had to relinquish control to a certain extent, giving myself over to where the writing was taking me, trusting Dillard's (1989) assertion that the writing "digs its own path" (3). The meanings I made in creating the text were powerfully significant for me, and when finished, I was satisfied I had conveyed what the writing had revealed to me at the time. Now, I am aware that the meanings I constructed were partial, contextual, and historically situated and as such, open for reinterpretation, for yet to be made discoveries.

Acting on this insight, I author this chapter, seeking to surface meanings that were previously veiled from me and to discover and name those junctures where the knowledge of my evolving researcher-self and teacher-self were hidden from me.

The Faculty Room and the Floating Text of Talk

To begin I must travel back to the fall of 1973 when I started teaching, long before I ever imagined I would write a dissertation. Like most beginning teachers, I entered my profession carrying constructed images of what a teacher was, images based on the teachers who had taught me. But once I became a teacher myself, I was afforded a dramatically different view—the view of an insider. Behind the closed doors of the faculty room where teachers gathered to talk about themselves and their work, I felt the earliest tugs of a professional dissonance that grew over the years leading up to my doctoral work.

In the private domain of the faculty room, I listened as teachers shared instructional strategies, inventive approaches to content, and anecdotes recounting successful encounters with students. But over time, the floating talk of the faculty room more often reflected a pervasive sense of teachers' discontent about their lives as teachers and their lack of agency. Their professional discontent fractured my schoolgirl image of what it means to be a teacher. But being one of them, I became conflicted by both the need to accept their professional self-portraits and the need to reject them to match my own. My struggle became an effort to bring the two into closer alignment.

Fragments of faculty conversations about recurring, particularly troubling topics would linger with me for months. As I replayed conversations in my head, I could hear the voices of my colleagues and my own in concert with them. When this mental chatter became unmanageable, I began to record it periodically in a journal. Though the entries were sketchy, they reflected my effort to capture the floating text of talk and thus contain it for examination. This text of talk—in both written and unwritten forms—led me to assume a reflective posture. As a participant in those conversations, I began to examine myself as a practitioner, critiquing not only what I contributed to the conversations but also the ways in which I framed my contributions. I began to "see" how I was constructing myself in practice in relation to others like myself. Gradually, as I became more attentive to what I said and how I said it, I also developed an increased sensitivity to the nuances of my colleagues' speech, interpreting unspoken meanings embedded in their text of talk.

My heightened awareness of the roots of my discontent created an ancillary empathic awareness of theirs; I wanted to portray the dilemmas we were experiencing in our professional lives. During this time, I was a doctoral student at the University of Pittsburgh. There I became caught up in the discourse of teacher empowerment, which further fueled my desire to believe that positive changes in the professional landscape of teaching were imminent. But fragments of faculty room conversations replaying in my mind tempered my optimism.

With a degree of a caution, then, I set about studying the Pennsylvania Lead Teacher Initiative and teachers' experiences with it. Since the proclaimed purpose of the initiative was to empower teachers to exert more agency in their professional lives (Pennsylvania Department of Education 1990), portraying and interpreting the stories of the teachers involved with it shaped the intent of my dissertation. Examining this particular reform strand also provided a potential means for me to come to terms with the contradictory images of teachers' lives I had internalized and to possibly find a release from my underlying professional discontent. I hoped to open the door to the faculty room door, inviting outsiders in to experience the text of talk that had so powerfully affected me.

The Interviews and the Captured Text of Talk

Many of the decisions I made in the early stages of my research were guided by intuition. I knew I wanted my interviews to replicate the give and take of talk, but to do that, I had to come to terms with how I perceived myself in the researcher role. I wanted to establish a connection with my participants by being one of them, one who had chosen to take on the researcher role as well. Given this, my decision to reject an objective, detached interviewer stance in favor of active participation in the interviews fit my purpose as well as my worldview, which is rooted in an idealist-oriented epistemology. In this epistemology, according to Graft (1979),

> Our view of the world and our knowledge of it are inevitably based on our interests, values, dispositions, and so on. Because idealism says that reality is to one degree or another mind dependent, we cannot "get outside ourselves" and conduct investigations divorced from our own particular world. Investigating the social and historical world is a process that is socially and historically bounded; that is, our values and interests will shape how we study and discuss reality. (10)

Following the line of thinking that had been guiding me, I knew that the traditional question/answer interview format would not suit my needs. Instead, I designed an open-ended approach and began each interview by asking my participants simply to share a story of their experiences with the lead teacher initiative. I listened to each story and responded by offering insights, asking questions, making comments, and sharing pieces of related stories. As my voice mingled with the voices of my participants, each of us had opportunities to construct and reconstruct meaning in a dialogical interplay, serving to equalize power relations inherent in the interview process and create a conversation not unlike what Tripp (1983) calls "a protracted intimate affair" (34).

My identification with my participants was further reinforced by the fact that all of them were women. Accordingly, I drew on what was then a relatively new approach to the study of language—the relationship between language and gender. Studies focused on women talking with women suggested that women participate more actively, informally, and collaboratively than men talking with men, mutually sharing feelings and personal knowledge while respecting one another's conversational space (Thorne, Kramarae, and Henley 1983; Fishman 1983). These traits aptly describe all my interview conversations, each of which lasted two or more hours.

I conducted all seven interviews by phone, recording them with the interviewees' permission. Not being part of their specific school environment or privy to the personal and political ethos of their particular school privileged me to a certain extent. I was someone interested in their stories because of our shared teacher status, but also someone who could not potentially betray their confidence. As a researcher with the privacy protection sanctioned by my university's human subjects' agreement, I tried to provide a safe outlet for teachers to speak of things they may have otherwise chosen not to disclose.

Even though I trusted the choices I was making during this phase of my research, there were times throughout the months I was conducting the interviews when I was plagued by doubts about the potential usefulness of the data I was collecting. Taking the risks I took, however, was necessary for me in order to own my study. In the intervening years since I wrote my dissertation, I have discovered that trends in interviewing have shifted, that "interviewers are increasingly seen as active participants in interactions with respondents, and interviews are seen as negotiated accomplishments of both interviewers and respondents that are shaped by the contexts and situations in which they take place" (Fontana and Frey 2003, 91).

With the aid of a device that attached to the phone receiver and connected into the tape recorder, I was free to engage in the interview conversations unencumbered. And when the process was complete, I had before me a stack of audio tapes containing the detailed, specific terrain of the interview conversations as they had naturally occurred. Transcribing them was the next methodological step, a step I perceived would be tedious and time-consuming. I shared my concerns with members of my dissertation study group. One colleague suggested I hire a transcriptionist; another suggested I use a computer program. As a beginning researcher, I was unaware that these options even existed, yet once they were pointed out, I immediately rejected them, intuiting my need to stay closely connected with my data. Trusting this insight, I made the decision to transcribe the tapes myself.

Still, I approached the task with a functionalist attitude, incorrectly assuming what Silverman (2003) cautions against: "that the preparation of transcripts is simply a technical detail prior to the main business of analysis" (356). What I discovered, instead, was that my efforts to capture the taped text of talk in written form were not only pleasurable but also powerfully significant in terms of conceptualizing the subject under study and myself in relation to it. I also became aware of the methodological implications of what I now see as the transcription *process* rather than the transcription *step*.

Transcribing the taped interviews by hand, playing and replaying them as I captured them in written text, I re-experienced each conversation, focusing more consciously on the texture of talk: pace and volume, cadence and rhythm, pauses, intonations, and inflections. This ear for texture expanded my understanding of how we were using language to shape meaning in our conversations. Though I was unaware at the time of the actual dissertation writing, the transcribing process enabled me to construct a kind of auditory mirror; as I heard my participants' voices, they appeared in sharper focus, and I appeared in sharper focus in relation to them and to myself.

In this respect, the process highlights Bakhtin's contention that there is no such thing as a "general language," a language that is spoken by a general voice divorced from a specific saying charged with particular overtones. Language, "when it *means*, is somebody talking to somebody else, even when that someone else is one's own inner addressee" (Holquist 1981, xxi). Working against the conventional interview protocol, I wrote myself into each interview, becoming a persona in them. By capturing those conversations in writing through the transcription process, I created both auditory and visual texts. I now understand that in them was lodged, in embryonic form, the ontological stutterings of my coming to know.

The Inner Views Storied and the Narrative Text of Talk

Up to this point on my dissertation journey, the dissonance fueling my study was both born out of and healed by the text of talk. But at this juncture, with the writing of the interview transcriptions completed, I did not understand fully the paradoxical nature of this tacit knowing. As a consequence, I spent months unsuccessfully trying to find meaning *in* the data rather than to construct meaning *from* it. Residual functionalist tugs were pulling at me again, causing me to exert my energies trying to report my data rather than portray it. Fortunately, my chair, Dr. Noreen Garman, came to my aid, offering sage advice to trust myself and rely on my experience as an English teacher and my scholarship in literary theory and criticism to find my way. "Write about what you know," she advised. Her encouragement, coupled with my now more conscious need to continually re-establish a trust in my intuitive and interpretive sensibilities, prompted me to turn to the discourse on narrative as a method of inquiry to study educational experiences. Connelly and Clandinin's (1990) views—that "education is the construction and reconstruction of personal and social stories" and that "humans are storytelling organisms who, individually and socially, lead storied lives" (2)—inspired me to imagine my interviews as narratives.

I became excited by the prospect of finding a way to transform the simple stories of my interview encounters into stories with plot, theme, characters, and mood. I wanted my stories to capture the intimacy of the conversations I had with my participants, who "walk in my shoes," who have an experiential authority I trust, and who speak a language I know and use. I wanted my stories to convey my understanding of my participants' words, their intonations, pauses, breaks, and the self-critical, apologetic stance they—and I—often assumed when speaking. I wanted *my* stories to convey my empathic understanding of *their* stories. But how to proceed remained a mystery for a long time until one day, in conversation with a colleague, I used the phrase "inner views" for the first time. At that moment, in hearing myself speak out loud, the concept for the "inner views storied" came into language.

Though I found no exemplar in the literature for the stories I set out to write, I found grounding to experiment with a new form of representation in the works of Spanos (1987), who encourages the use of forms that disrupt received forms and undermine "an objective, disinterested stance" (271). After writing the first story, a pattern emerged: each story would be constructed around a core theme I interpreted as the participant's dominant response to her experience with the lead teacher initiative. Each title would frame the story and include a pseudonym for the participant followed by a descriptor of the story's theme. This descriptor would also serve to develop each character in a consistent and believable manner. Through this process I created the stories of "Grace—The Dutiful Lead Teacher," "Sarah—The Disillusioned Former Lead Teacher," "Mary Jane—The Outspoken Lead Teacher Trainer," "Debbie—The Cynical Non-Lead Teacher," "Ann—The Detached Non-Lead Teacher," "Maggie—The Acquiescent Lead Teacher," and "Sue and Kate—The Hopeful Lead Teachers."

Each story begins with an exposition that includes the grade and subject(s) the participant teaches, some general traits about the size and locale of her district, and some carefully selected interview excerpts describing her as she describes herself in the actual interview. Next, I weave in my assessment of the interview's conversational terrain, its energy and pace, inserting it early in the story to provide the reader with a sense of context for interpretation. From this point, the narrative action begins to rise as I carefully weave in selected threads of conversation to scaffold the story line and embed the theme. The auditory imprints from repeated playings of the interview tapes serve me well at this point as I work to establish mood by capturing the textuality of blended voices, arranged to convey the struggle to discover understandings through the narrative text of talk. I sequence the seven inner views storied that comprise chapter 4 of my dissertation to create a transtextual aesthetic tension. Taken as a whole, the stories portray a range of responses to a reform initiative that failed to fulfill the promise of empowerment its rhetoric espoused.

As I was writing my literary portrayals, I was struck by the realization that I could not portray anything literally or completely, that stories are selective, and that I had to decide content and structure by attending to what mattered, to what fit my purpose, and that these decisions would be based on my own "inner views." Even though I was a participant in the inner views storied and even though I understood that the stories were filtered through me as author, it did not occur to me then that "in empathy we discover and construct our own version of the life narrative of another self and reconstruct our own" (Barone and Blumenfeld-Jones 1998, 142). When one of my dissertation committee members pointed out at my defense that the stories I had written were really "my story," I was shocked and then bewildered when my other committee members agreed. Even in that moment, I still believed I was telling my participants' stories through myself. It was not until long after my defense that I came to understand that I was telling my story through them.

Retrospectively, I realize that my "inner views" of my own professional dissonance surfaced in the writing of the inner views storied and that the characteristics I set out to portray in my participants' experiences are the very characteristics I exposed for examination in myself. In each of their stories and across all of them, I am illuminated. As Richardson (2003) says, "Writing is a process of discovery." She continues, "The researcher's self-knowledge and knowledge of the topic develop through experimentation with point of view, tone, texture, sequencing, metaphor, and so on. . . . The deepened understanding of the Self deepens the text" (521). Following the path that writing unfolded, I positioned myself to come to know through the narrative text of talk.

Interpretation and the Hermeneutic Text of Talk

By creating the inner views storied, I fixed the narrative and in so doing made it an object for interpretation and reinterpretation. Taken individually and collectively, my inner views storied represented an act of discourse signifying primary meanings that are easily accessible given their explicit, denotative, semantic qualities, as well as secondary meanings that are more latent given their implicit, connotative, affective qualities (Foulkes 1975). This dualism created fertile ground for me to employ literary and educational criticism to examine surface and embedded meaning. From the broad range of literature I reviewed in the early stages of my work, the writings of the critical theorists had the most profound effect on my thinking. These scholars, skeptical of reform rhetoric proclaiming teacher empowerment and professionalism, advocate a view that such rhetoric often masks policymakers' agendas to disempower teachers and promote deprofessionalization. The fact that a significantly higher number of teachers involved with the Pennsylvania Lead Teacher Initiative were female (Piscolish 1993) further reinforced my decision to employ a critical theory lens to interpret the inner views storied. Many scholars in the field associate proletarianization with teaching because it is predominately and has been historically, a feminine pursuit (Apple 1985; Ginsburg 1987; Ozga 1988; Zeichner 1991). Thus, though making no claims to be schooled in feminist literary criticism, I presented my interpretations from a feminine perspective.

Confident in my ability to construct meaning through the interpretive process in the hermeneutic tradition that values the primary role of language in human understanding, I crafted my interpretations. I began with an introduction describing my perception of the conversational ethos of the story and frontloading the themes I had selected to tease out for critique. With the conceptual frame for analysis in place, I composed the body of the text by taking apart the theme-related language each teacher used to describe her experience with the initiative. I excavated contradictions around issues of power, resistance, domination, collegial relationships, and role identity buried in the stories.

Assuming the stance of literary critic allowed me to step outside of the stories, to view them with an aesthetic detachment. From this position, I became aware of the role I played in each story, which led me to close each interpretation with a section titled, "The Role of the Researcher in the Story." This move, which occurred quite naturally as an integral phase of the interpretive act, represented a turning point for me, a conceptual leap of great import achieved through all of the writing that had brought me to this place. An exemplar of the researcher's role taken from "Maggie's Story—The Acquiescent Lead Teacher" follows:

> I am disturbed throughout Maggie's story, frustrated and angered by her response to the experiences she describes. Appalled by her acceptance of the injustices she and her colleagues endure, I plead with her to help me understand why she continues to pursue leadership activities. The struggle to understand Maggie's behavior parallels my own struggle to come to terms with my own attitude of persisting in spite of overwhelming odds. Maggie's story helps me to see how domination plays itself out in the professional lives of teachers and how females, especially, are more prone to permit such domination and even participate in it. But in the story, I am as ignorant as she of the forces working on us. But I am adamant in my desire to continue to give voice to my outrage. I feel compelled, driven, to speak loudly about the injustices, about the ways in which teacher commitment is eroded and dedication is destroyed through schemes designed to make teachers believe that they have control over their professional lives. What angers me, no what frightens me, is that Maggie may not even feel the outrage. Is it because she refuses to allow herself to "see" what is happening, or is it because she does not want to "see" what is happening because to "know" or admit to "knowing" would then require taking action? Does she "know" and not speak, or does she "not know" and is therefore unable to speak? In the story I want Maggie to feel the outrage because I came to discover that to admit to the subjective response is the first step in being able to begin the process of critical reflection that is necessary for transformation. In this respect, the effect of Maggie's story on me is cathartic.

In this section and others like it, I brought to light issues of power and powerlessness, agency and helplessness, trust and despair that had been building in me over the course of my professional career.

The development of a personal identity, a set of curricular beliefs, and a stance occurs, according to Barone and Blumenfeld-Jones (1998), "within a *hermeneutical* process; self-understanding comes about through acts of interpretation. *What* is interpreted are the phenomena that, in the course of our daily lives, we *experience*" (138, emphasis is original). The issues I began to explore in "The Role of the Researcher in the Story" segments were less about the lead teacher initiative than about all the negativity, mistrust, and frustration I had been assimilating from faculty room conversations, interactions with the "powers that be," and my own way of being in the world. In them, I am grappling with my own reaction to authority and my own sense of professional integrity, autonomy, power, and agency.

By engaging in the hermeneutic text of talk, I unmasked myself and came to an understanding not only of how the dominant ideology functions to oppress my class and gender, but also of how I had acted in complicity with the very forces I had been struggling to combat. "Self-reflexivity," as Richardson (2003) points out, "brings to consciousness some of the complex political/ideological agendas hidden in our writing" (520). For me, this coming to consciousness was painful and the wisdom, bitter.

Closing

A journey takes us to places unknown, making us vulnerable, open to new understandings and self-revelations. Writing my dissertation was such a journey for me. The bitter wisdom I came to understand was that the political, cultural, and institutional context of schools does not seem to support teacher efficacy. And in the absence of a nurturing context, teachers may willingly or unwillingly assume attitudes, behaviors, and ways of being in the world that can potentially hinder the development of ontological awareness. These ways of being can become the norm and consequently are seldom held up to scrutiny. But their negative effects can and often do seep out into the world of the classroom, the world of the school, and the world of the teacher.

Constructing this version of reality—of "the way things are for me"—and framing my understanding of it as bitter wisdom has been helpful and to a certain degree, comforting. But in revisiting the dissertation to author this chapter and in mining my concept of how I come to know through the text of talk, I now have an understanding of why I resisted owning the inner views storied as *my* story for so long. My inability to claim them was directly proportional to my inability to let go of my underlying construction of the way things "ought to be." Thus, my notion of bitter wisdom was rooted in resignation and bound to a grief I was acknowledging but not fully accepting. Now, I am ready to accept the self who emerged through the conversations I had with my participants and see myself *in* my professional context in a revised, less conflicted way.

Arriving at this place, I have chosen to let go of and move away from the residual anger that attends to "the way things are for me." In this space, I am better able to draw on the power within me, the power I've possessed all along to make choices that support and nurture me. Accepting this responsibility is tantamount to accepting the view that no external educational reform initiative can empower me, for the empowerment I seek can come only from within. *This* coming to know is liberating and the wisdom, sweet.

References

Apple, M. W. 1985. Teaching and "women's work": A comparative historical ideological analysis. *Teachers College Record* 86, no. 3: 455–73.

Barone, T. E., and D. S. Blumenfeld-Jones. 1998. Curriculum platforms and moral stories. In *Curriculum problems, politics, and possibilities*, ed. L. E. Beyer and M. W. Apple, 137–55. Albany: State University of New York Press.

Ceroni, K. M. 1995. *Promises made, promises broken: A literary criticism of the Pennsylvania lead teacher experience*. UMI Pro Quest Digital Dissertations #AAT9529124.

Connelly, M. G., and J. D. Clandinin. 1990. Stories of experience and narrative inquiry. *Educational Researcher* 19, no. 5 (June/July): 2–14.

Denzin, N. K. 1995. The experiential text and the limits of visual understanding. *Educational Theory* 45, no. 1 (Winter): 7–18.

Denzin, N. K., and Y. S. Lincoln, eds. *Collecting and interpreting qualitative materials*. Thousand Oaks, CA: Sage.

Dillard, A. 1989. *The writing life*. New York: Harper Collins.

Fishman, P. M. 1983. Interaction: The work women do. In *Language, gender, and society*, ed. B. Thorne, C. Kramarae, and N. Henley, 89–101. Rowley, MA: Newbury House.

Fontana, A., and J. H. Frey. 2003. The interview: From structured questions to negotiated text. In Denzin and Lincoln, *Collecting*, 61–106.

Foulkes, A. P. 1975. *The search for meaning*. Berne, Switzerland: Herbert Lang & Co. Ltd.

Ginsburg, M. B. 1987. Teacher education and class and gender relations: A critical analysis of historical studies in teacher education. *Educational Foundations* 1, no. 2: 4–36.

Graff, G. 1979. *Literature against itself*. Chicago: University of Chicago Press.

Holquist, M. 1981. Introduction to *The dialogic imagination*, M. M. Bakhtin, ed. M. Holquist and trans. C. Emerson and M. Holquist, xv–xxxiv. Austin, TX: University of Austin Press.

Ozga, J. 1988. Teaching, professionalism and work. Introduction to *Schoolwork approaches to the labour process of teaching*, ed. J. Ozga, ix–xv. Milton Keynes and Philadelphia: Open University Press.

Pennsylvania Department of Education. 1990 (March). *Lead teachers and lead teacher training centers concept paper*. Harrisburg, PA: Author.

Piscolish, M. A. 1993. *The Pennsylvania lead teacher program 1992–93 evaluation report*. October. Harrisburg, PA: Pennsylvania Department of Education.

Richardson, L. 2003. Writing: A method of inquiry. In Denzin and Lincoln, *Collecting*, 499–541.

Silverman, D. 2003. Analyzing talk and text. In Denzin and Lincoln, *Collecting*, 340–62.

Spanos, W. 1987. *Repetitions: The postmodern occasion in literature and culture*. Baton Rouge: Louisiana State University Press.

Thorne, B., C. Kramarae, and N. Henley. 1983. Language and society: Opening a second decade of research. In *Language, gender, and society*, ed. B. Thorne, C. Kramarae, and N. Henley, 7–24. Rowley, MA: Newbury House.

Tripp, D. H. 1983. Co-authorship and negotiation: The interview as an act of creation. *Interchange* 14, no. 3: 32–44.

Zeichner, K. M. 1991. Contradictions and tensions in the professionalization of teaching and the democratization of school. *Teachers College Record* 92, no. 3: 363–79.

CHAPTER 9

Imagining Reflective Artmaking: Claiming Self as Artist-Teacher-Researcher

Wendy M. Milne

This chapter represents a "portrait" of my concept of "reflective artmaking" in relation to educational research. The portrait comprises both the sketch in Figure 1 and the words I use to explicate the meanings of its images.

I invite readers to view Figure 1 much as you would a portrait hanging in an art gallery. Spend a bit of time considering the images. How do they speak to you? What do you make of them? What thoughts do they call forth?

Figure 1. Self-portrait as reflective artist-teacher-researcher

As the artist of "Self-Portrait as Reflective Artist-Teacher-Researcher," I hope the piece has piqued the reader's curiosity. I recognize, though, that the reader may be a bit perplexed, for the symbolic meanings of the images are highly personal. Therefore, in this chapter, I take the stance of an artist-teacher-researcher who has been invited to speak at a viewing of her own work. As we pause before this particular piece, I call attention to the various images within the composition and explain the ideas I am aiming to express through the sketch. However, because the act of offering an interpretation of my own artwork may be seen as problematic, I first address the role of interpretation in relation to arts-based educational research. Also, as is often the case in creating a piece of art, the piece on display in this chapter has gone through much revision. Although space limitations prevent my including precursors to the composition in Figure 1, I share some of the process that led to its final form as a way of illustrating my way of reflective artmaking.

The Role of Interpretation

Art educator and author Terry Barrett (2000) states that providing an interpretation of art aids in "enlarging a person's understanding of the artwork, the world, as we know it, and ourselves" (8). Piantanida, McMahon and Garman (2003a/b) also remind us that one of the goals of arts-based educational research is to contribute to the educational discourses. Doing so may entail providing a verbal explanation that communicates meanings found through artmaking processes as well as meanings found in the symbolic images of the artwork itself. I chose to use both words and visuals in my dissertation (Milne 2000) because I wished to speak to art education communities. Furthermore, I took on several different roles in my dissertation: artist, museum curator and museum docent. To critique my own visual/verbal portraits, words were necessary. Parsons (1992) states that words are not necessary when thinking in art but, when viewing an abstract art object "we need to talk about artworks as well as look at them . . . we need to connect them with aspects of both the art world and the world in general" (82). He continues,

> On the interpretive view, then, language becomes an essential part of the cognition in the art. If an object is unclear, we try to express our sense of it in words. In practice, this means we must try to say it as well as see it. More accurately, since only part of the sense will be more clear in the interpretation than in the object itself, and

vice versa, we must be able to discuss what is hard to see and to see what is hard to say. And then the two kinds of thinking—that is thinking in two different media—will be interactive and combine to form one understanding. We clarify in words relations of the object so we can see those relations in the object. It follows that the words are not just a crutch. They are as important as the looking. Not more important but equally so, because both the talking and the looking are constitutive of the artwork, of the qualities it has and the meanings it carries. If we stayed with thinking in one medium, interpretation would be impossible and the object would remain obscure. (Parsons 1992, 82)

We must be careful with Parson's quote that "two kinds of thinking will combine to form one understanding" because some might argue that forming *one* understanding goes against what artists and interpretive researchers often strive for—that is, for each reader/viewer to come to his/her own interpretation. Some might feel that when an artist offers an interpretation of his or her work, readers may see that as the "right" or "only" interpretation and will be reluctant to form their own interpretations. This risks shutting down the conversation about the artwork and the ideas it represents. Barrett (2000) reminds us, however, that "artworks attract multiple interpretations and it is not the goal of the interpretation to arrive at a single, grand, unified, composite interpretation" (6). I believe, as do Piantanida, McMahon and Garman (2003a/b) that in an arts-based educational inquiry, the art does not stand on its own.

In my arts-based dissertation and in this chapter I choose to include my artwork first so that the viewer might pause to consider his or her own interpretations of the work. Therefore, the interpretation I offer in the following sections of this chapter as an arts-based educational researcher does not stand as the correct and sole version, but as another informed opinion readers may integrate into their initial interpretation. I invite the viewer/reader into dialogue with me. With this in mind, I now offer a brief explanation of the process that led to the creation of Figure 1.

Creating "Self-Portrait as Artist-Teacher-Researcher"

Sitting on the floor, I silently placed my pencil to the white page of my sketchbook. Thoughts were swirling about who I had become since I concluded my doctoral work in 2000. I lightly sketched my features in the center of the page, for this drawing process was going to help me reflect on my growth from a child artist into a teacher and later, arts-based educational researcher.

As I started to sketch my initial ideas, I drew a figure in the center and then, in the background, transposed texts directly from my dissertation to merge both the visual and verbal. In my dissertation and afterwards, while speaking at conferences, I stressed the importance of the researcher's obligation to communicate her processes, products and insights to a variety of audiences, who may or may not be versed in "reading" visual art. The text-filled background of my initial sketch represented this belief that interpretation is necessary when creating an educational inquiry. I decided that the sketch was completed in this form and set it to the side for a time when I could examine the ideas more carefully.

My sketch remained with the figure and text until months later when I attempted to critique it. It was not until that moment that I sensed that something did not "feel right" about it. I wondered, "Was I only trying to explore the importance of interpretation through words and visuals?" Reading over my notes I saw that I had scrawled "teacher," "imagination," "power," "artmaker," "researcher." This wasn't solely about interpretation; it was about me—artist, teacher, researcher—reflective artmaker. I had been given (as well as gave myself) the authority to imagine a dissertation that fit my ontological orientation. The image sitting before me did not represent what I was striving for.

Although the sketch I had created did not wholly depict what I wanted it to, parts of it did. I decided to create a second version by retaining the central image of me holding a framed picture and eliminating the words in the background. By removing the background text I created a large open space in which to include my teacher-self. I collaged two actual student portraits drawn by second-graders into the space. This altered sketch helped me reflect upon how I come to know my pedagogy.

As Pat McMahon eloquently describes in chapter 13, time does not unfold in her narrative research in a linear, chronological sense. Likewise, my final sketch represents various times throughout my life. In Figure 1, I am represented at once as the child-artist, the tentative novice researcher, the teacher, the student and the adult artist.

Interpreting "Self-Portrait as Artist-Teacher-Researcher"
Images of Self as Artist

I call the reader's attention to the center of Figure 1, where I've depicted images of myself as an adult and child. The adult image holds a smaller black-and-white copy of a self-portrait I made in second grade. While gluing this childhood drawing into my lightly sketched hands, I recalled my elementary art teacher coming to the room once a week to teach the class various art techniques and to introduce us to exciting new media that our classroom teacher never let us use. Although I do not recall the art teacher's name, I remembered the day we drew our self-portraits. The art teacher taught us the techniques to draw a face in proportion and then allowed us to draw ourselves with any supply we wished. I preferred the pressed crayons, because we had used them a few times before this lesson, and I was confident in my ability to create a masterpiece with them. I drew myself with my hair in ponytails and wearing a favorite new yellow striped dress that I had worn on a family trip. Prior to this drawing experience, I recall, I drew everyday at home, my favorite gifts being new art supplies. I rendered my world in these drawings—my parents, my home, my yard, my friends, my pets—all were scrutinized through my child-artist eyes.

I was an artist until second grade. In future grades, the art teacher taught us techniques, rather than letting us explore our world through art. My art teachers developed the artistic problem we were to solve and the media we were to use. I was no longer able to decide for myself what I wanted to draw with or what the subject matter should be. Years later, despite being an art education major, I continued to be told what to create throughout college. I began to forget what it was like to find my own artistic problems because everyone else was creating an artistic problem for me to solve.

The next time I was challenged to be an artist, I was sitting in a graduate research class. As I fumbled to explain a possible dissertation topic, Maria, the instructor, asked why I didn't simply draw what I was thinking. Although I was enrolled in an art education program, I rarely made art for my courses. Research papers were regularly required, so I was quite surprised at my professor's suggestion. I pulled out my old sketchbook the next day and sat for several hours trying to decide what to draw. I was excited about the opportunity to create again but could not decide what to draw. Maria had only told me to draw; she hadn't said what to draw or what to use. Along with the excitement of returning to my sketchbook, I felt fear and confusion:

"How could I possibly draw something for a doctoral course?" "What should I draw?" In the end, I timidly sketched my thoughts on being the lone art teacher in an elementary setting.

In that moment, Maria had given me the opportunity to claim myself as artist once again. In eight years of teaching art to students, I had rarely drawn or painted as an artist. In her powerful question—"Why don't you just draw what you think?"—Maria gave me authority to become the artist I had been so many years earlier. I immediately embraced this notion of making art and searched for others who had created art as a form of inquiry, leading me to the newly emerging field of arts-based educational inquiry research.

I noted that art education discourses supported the notion of creating art (Anderson 1997; Ball 1990; Bayles and Orland 1993; Bolanos 1986; Feldman 1993; Kellman 1999; Szekely 1978; Thompson 1986; Wix 1998). Art teacher and researcher Thompson (1986) urges art teachers to create art because she believes that in creating art we "link ourselves to our students in ways that mere knowledge of theories of creativity cannot produce" (47) and that "producing art can lead to improved teaching skills, personal renewal, and a better understanding of the creative process, including its struggles, obstacles and rewards" (48).

The center of the sketch shows me as the adult artist holding my child-artist self-portrait as a reminder to myself of who I had been and who I have been reclaiming both during and after my dissertation inquiry. The dissertation process allowed me to return to the ways that I come to know best—through artmaking. Like other artists, I began to make art to come to a deeper understanding about myself that I might not otherwise have been able to discover. Indeed, Ellen Winner (1982) states that artists frequently say they create not only as a way to express themselves, but also as a way to "discover, to understand, and to know" (34). Furthermore, Reid (1980) suggests that it is indeed possible to make meaning of ideas through artmaking:

> In the making or composition of any art the meaning comes into being, is created, or if you like is gradually discovered, in the process of working in a medium. . . . But in the process of making, or struggling to make, out of these preliminary on-goings there emerges, in the process of working with and forming the material, a new thing, the artistic meaning. (6)

As I worked and reworked my sketch, I used the black marker and pencil to search for ways to share how my artistic process, which I named reflective artmaking, helped me to come to know myself as an artist, teacher and researcher.

Images of Self as Artist-Teacher

I now direct the reader's attention to the large faces and overlapping hands peering out of the background. These portraits were created by two of my second-grade students. After I realized that my sketch was not solely about the necessity of interpretation, I focused on my overlapping roles of artist and teacher. While the images included in the sketch may have multiple interpretations, these particular faces are symbolic of my role as an elementary visual art teacher—a role upon which I closely reflected during my inquiry process by immersing myself in select educational discourses.

I noted these discourses promoted reflecting on one's own practice (Brubacher, Case and Reagan 1994; Dewey 1933/34; Henry 1999; Livingston 1999; Onslow and Gadanidis 1997; Posner 1993; Schon 1987; Thunder-McGuire 1995; Tremmel 1993). Purposeful reflection allows teachers to observe themselves and their pedagogical practices in order to determine if changes are necessary. Reflection, some may argue, is commonly associated with linguistic symbols (Stout 1993; Yinger and Clark 1981) rather than visual images. Houston and Clift (1990) however, contend that "language can either facilitate or limit our ability to reflect" (209), suggesting that some may benefit by reflecting in ways other than verbal. Based on these assumptions, I decided to wed the processes of artmaking and reflection as a way to draw upon my natural inclination for artmaking as a form of reflection about my pedagogy.

While reworking my sketch, I reflected on my role of an artist-teacher by reviewing past sketches in my sketchbook as well as the drawings in my students' portfolios. I kept returning to the self-portraits my second graders had drawn, thinking how the ways in which I taught my students to draw were similar to those of my own elementary art teacher. Of the many student self-portraits from which I had to choose, I selected a drawing by a young girl who seemed to enjoy art class very much. I knew from her mother that she drew all the time at home and often in her homeroom. When I saw that she, too, had drawn herself with long curls pulled up on the sides of her head, I knew that this portrait would reflect how I strive to create a classroom where the children can be real artists who find and solve their own problems.

As Maria Piantanida did for me, I now try to do for my students; to give them the authority to remain artists.

The second image I selected was from a shy new student who had not, I was told, been academically successful in his previous school. Sometimes students who are not academically inclined are excellent artists. I glued his image into the background to represent my belief that all students can find a place to fit in school.

Finally, I drew numerous overlapping hands behind my own hand, all raised, as if asking questions. My hand merges with theirs as a symbol of our desire to know and learn together. I also added the words "art" and "teacher" into the sketch to show that neither role takes precedence over the other. I am both the artist and teacher.

Images of Self as Artist-Teacher-Researcher

While the roles of artist and teacher were balanced and equal, the role of researcher did not come easily at first. Look closely at the remaining images of the arms emerging from my central image and the upturned face in the lower left corner. These wing-like arms are not meant to evoke angels, but rather flying and the freedom to fly—the freedom to imagine and create. At the same moment of this freedom, however, there is hesitation, questioning, a hand pulling the arm down: Can I, a neophyte researcher, engage in a non-traditional form of research? Am I strong enough to break these boundaries, to imagine something different? The hesitation was strong. Perhaps the hand pulling down the arm is protecting me from the possibility of failure and the fear of the unknown associated with an arts-based educational dissertation. I added the upturned face as a way to show my surprise that, despite my fear, I made the decision to engage in an arts-based educational inquiry.

Entering into an arts-based dissertation was intimidating because not many researchers at the time had incorporated visual art. Therefore, I could not rely on other examples. I knew as I set forth on my dissertation journey that I could have chosen an easier route, one that may have helped me earn my degree more quickly or one that may have been less challenging. In the past I would have chosen that simpler path. Indeed, my time as a public school student was spent determining what it was the teacher wanted and how much I would have to do to get an A. This way of proceeding through school remained with me even while I was a practicing teacher enrolled in graduate courses. Somewhere along the journey, though, I realized that my role was no longer to figure out what the teacher wanted, because I had become the teacher.

Merging my roles of artist and researcher with that of teacher occurred as I crafted an arts-based educational inquiry. The inquiry enabled me to return to art in a meaningful way while still devoting my energy and curiosity to teaching.

Reflecting Theory in Practice

After examining the idea of using reflective artmaking to study my practice, I had to decide how I would incorporate it into my roles of full-time and cooperating teacher. To juggle these demanding responsibilities, I decided to combine them. I asked my student teacher, Heide, to engage in reflective artmaking with me for the seven weeks we would be working together. Daily we created drawings about our teaching experiences in a sketchbook and wrote journal-like entries to accompany our art. We also engaged in weekly videotaped conferences to discuss the works in the sketchbook and created a sketchbook log to document the procedures of our reflective artmaking. During one of our weekly meetings, I noted that Heide did not sign her sketches. She responded by saying that she did not consider these finished artworks worthy of a signature. I, on the other hand, had been signing all of my sketches. I felt that each sketch represented deeper understandings about my practice that I had not previously known and therefore deserved a signature. Likewise, the last images represented in "Self-Portrait as an Artist-Teacher-Researcher" are my signature in the lower right hand corner and my fingerprints creating a border. These are symbolic of my individuality. Signing my name helped me claim the authority to imagine myself as a reflective artmaker. Reflective artmaking brought an aesthetic order (Eisner 1985; Cohen and Gainer 1971) to the pedagogical event(s) I was examining, thus allowing me to communicate with myself and to others the thoughts, insights and perspectives surrounding my teaching in my dissertation, which I titled "Reflective Artmaking: Implications for Art Education (Milne 2000).

References

Anderson, R. 1997. A case study of the artist as teacher through the video work of Martha Davis. *Studies in Art Education* 39, no. 1: 37–56.

Ball, L. 1990. What role: Artist or teacher? *Art Education* 43, no 1: 54–59.

Barrett, T. 2000. Studies invited lecture: About art interpretation for art education. *Studies in Art Education* 42, no. 1: 5–19.

Bayles, D. and T. Orland. 1993. *Art and fear: Observation on the perils (and rewards) of artmaking.* Santa Barbara, CA: Capra Press.

Bolanos, P. 1986. Agents of change: Artists and teachers. *Art Education* 39, no. 6: 49–52.

Brubacher, J., C. Case, and T. Reagan. 1994. *Becoming a reflective educator: How to build a culture of inquiry in the schools.* Thousand Oaks, CA: Corwin Press, Inc.

Bruner, J. 1996. *The culture of education.* Cambridge, MA: Harvard University Press.

Cohen, E. and R. Gainer. 1971. *Art, another language for learning.* New York: Schocken Books.

Dewey, J. 1933. *How we think: A restatement of the relation of reflective thinking to the educative process.* Boston: D.C. Heath.

Dewey, J. 1934. *Art as experience.* New York: First Peligree Printing.

Diamond, C., T. Patrick and C. A. Mullen, eds. 1999. *The postmodern educator: Arts-based inquiries and teacher development.* New York: Peter Lang.

Eisner, E. 1985. Aesthetic modes of knowing. In *Learning and teaching the ways of knowing: Eighty-fourth yearbook of the national society for the study of education,* ed. E. Eisner, 23–36. Chicago: University of Chicago Press.

Feldman, E. 1993. Best advice and counsel to art teachers. *Art Education* 46, no. 5:58–59.

Henry, C. 1999. The role of reflection in the student teachers' perceptions of their professional development. *Art Education* 52, no. 2: 14–20.

Houston, W. and R. Clift. 1990. The potential for research contributions to reflective practice. In *Encouraging reflective practice in education,* eds. R. Clift, W. Houston, M. Pugach, 208–224. New York: Teachers College Press.

Kellman, J. 1999. The voice of an elder: Jo Leeds, artist teacher, a personal perspective on teaching and learning. *Art Education* 52, no. 2: 41–46.

Livingston, D. 1999, Fall. Highly accomplished teachers. *NAEA Advisory.*

McVikar, P. 1972. *Imagination: Key to human potential.* Washington, DC: National Association for the Education of Young Children.

Milne, W. M. 2000. Reflective artmaking: Implications for art education. UMI ProQuest Digital Dissertation AAT 9974457.

Onslow, B. and G. Gadanidis. 1997. Mirroring practice: Reflections of a teacher educator. *Education Canada* 37, no. 1: 24–51.

Palmer, P. J. 1998. *The courage to teach: Exploring the inner landscape of a teacher's life.* San Francisco: Jossey-Bass.

Perry, L. 1984. The arts judgment and language. *Journal of Aesthetic Education* 18, no. 1: 21–32.

Piantanida, M., P. McMahon, and N. Garman. 2003a. Sculpting the contours of arts-based educational research within a discourse community. *Qualitative Inquiry* 9, no. 2: 182–91.

———. 2003b. On the value of "leaky boundaries": A response to Patrick Slattery. *Qualitative Inquiry* 9, no. 2: 198–201.

Reid, L. A. 1980. Meaning in the arts. In *The arts and personal growth*, ed. M. Ross, 1–15. New York: Pergamon Press.

———. 1983. Aesthetic knowledge in the arts. In *The arts and personal growth*, ed. M. Ross, 19–41. New York: Pergamon Press.

Schon, D. 1987. *Educating the reflective practitioner*. San Francisco: Jossey-Bass.

Stout, C. 1993. The dialogue journal: A forum for critical consideration. *Studies in Art Education* 35, no. 1: 34–44.

———. 2000. In the spirit of art criticism: Readings and writings of women artists. *Studies in Art Education* 41, no. 4: 346–60.

Szekely, G. 1987. Uniting the roles of artist and teacher. *Art Education* 31, no. 1: 17–10.

Thompson, K. 1986. Teachers as artists. *Art Education* 39, no. 6: 47–48.

Thunder-McGuire, S. 1995. *Art teaching, dialogue, and reflection: Constructing meaning through narratives of experience*. Doctoral dissertation, The University of Iowa.

Tremmel, R. 1993. Zen and the art of reflective practice in teacher education. *Harvard Educational Review* 63, no. 4: 434–59.

Winner, E. 1982. *Invented worlds: The psychology of the arts*. Cambridge, MA: Harvard University Press.

Wix, L. 1998. Book Review, *Studies in Art Education* 39, no. 3: 281–84.

Yinger, R. and C. Clark. 1981. *Reflective journal writing: Theory and practice*. East Lansing: Institute for Research on Training, College of Education, Michigan State University.

CHAPTER 10

Imagining in the Forest Dark: The Journey of an Epistemorph in the Land of Ologies

Cynthia A. Tananis

Several years ago, I found myself speaking to a group of doctoral students gathered for a class on qualitative research, and in a somewhat surreal moment of post dissertation clarity, I heard myself saying that as I came to *author* my dissertation by journeying toward an interpretive logic of justification for grounded theory, I was in turn *re-authoring* my own practice of educational evaluation.

My dissertation, "Discursive Evaluation: The journey of an 'Epistemorph' toward an Interpretive Practice and Inquiry," traced my journey from an educational program evaluator steeped in the science-based traditional approaches of the field toward a more discursive practice grounded in interpretive worldviews (Tananis 2000). The grounded theory study offered a heuristic for my own journey in exploring what I call the "ologies" (ontology, epistemology and axiology).[1] In it I struggled with the embedded and core issues of the relationship of "self" (as an evaluator) and "other" (my clients and the programs I evaluate) in practice, as well as with the sources, interpretations and values of knowledge in a field that is designed to illuminate processes and outcomes, if not judge and validate them.

The relatively short history of the field (educational evaluation didn't really emerge as a field until the 1960s) was built on the postpositivist empirical research tradition of random-assignment experimental studies. Over time, the discourses of the field evidenced a great deal of exploration beyond this more limited frame to include a variety of quantitative and qualitative methods and approaches. More currently, scholars in the field have turned attention to issues of ontological stance, as evidenced by the volume of literature focused on issues of ontology and epistemology in relation to evaluator stance and role and the design and conduct of the evaluation (Abma 2002; J. C. Greene 2000, 2001; King and Stevahn 2002; Mertens 1999, 2002; Schwandt 2002).

The Quest—To Tackle the "Troubles"

My dissertation inquiry was closely linked to my evaluation practice and became a study of the shifts in my perspective and worldview that I had long been experiencing in my practice. I had yet to codify and give meaning to those issues through scholarship even though they had become palpable and recurring "troubles" in practice.

I had been socialized as an evaluator within the strong empirical and functionalist traditions of educational assessment and evaluation. Early in my practice, and even into my early doctoral study, I had not given much thought to alternative ways of framing either my practice or research. I refined my practice by learning new methods and mastering new tools and skills. I was well schooled in a number of data-gathering and analysis techniques, both qualitative and quantitative. I had exhausted the limits of my methodological expertise but still found myself unable to resolve nagging issues such as how to deal with the complexities of involving stakeholders more fully and how to link evaluative inquiry with other inherent processes of an organization.

While these issues were addressed in the literature in terms of practical suggestions, the "answers" did not adequately address the complexity I was experiencing in my practice across various educational organizations. Rather than primarily technical issues, these concerns involved every aspect of evaluation practice—how I viewed my role as an evaluator in relationship to others, how others expressed their values and concerns with the evaluation, and how evaluation findings might be used and misused, for example. Schwandt (1996) makes the case that the paradigmatic "fuss" may be wrongly focused on "method and procedures" when it is in fact "arguing about different ways of knowing and being" and the "moral and cognitive commitments" that are inherent with these choices (81).

I spent a good deal of time focusing on technique and method in my practice, framing challenges in my practice as problems to be solved through increased knowledge and refinement of models or tools. I refer to this initial stance as the "insulated expert," in which as an evaluator, I attempted to remain distanced from the "objective" reality and those close to it as a way to control and account for bias (Tananis 2000).[2] My insulation wore thin, however, as I bumped up against unsolvable problems and persistent concerns. My functionalist worldview no longer provided adequate answers. Rather than continuing a search for more and better-refined tools to *do* evaluation differently, I began a deeper inquiry to *think* about evaluation differently and felt a call to explore potentially more useful responses through immersion in more expansive discourses. Entering those discourses clarified—and further confused, for a time—issues related to my practice and doctoral inquiry.

The intersection of my practice and inquiry—so much reflecting what seemed a growing mismatch in technique and approach—drew my dissertation further along a journey into the realm of epistemology, tugging me further to the connected roots of ontology and axiology. I experienced an equal set of troubles with the dissertation study and writing. Unlike colleagues who seemed, on the surface, to relish the very act of writing the dissertation and even more the processes of research within it, I felt that I had become the poster child for the reluctant, the ambivalent and the uncomfortable. Without my colleagues and advisors, I most certainly would have abandoned the struggle. It was wrenching at a core level.[3] Perhaps because the origin of the issues (the "ologies") was the birthing ground for difficulty in both my practice and my dissertation, I found little comfort from the dilemmas of my practice in my research and little comfort from the dilemmas of my research in my practice. It was not the research itself; I can easily lose myself in the complexities and elegant subtleties of "data" even as a functionalist researcher/evaluator. It was not the expectation of rigor and worthiness; I had long lived and worked in a world of grant-funded initiatives and deadlines, a world in which most of my work had very high-stakes consequences attached. It was not the inquiry; if anything, I suffer from too much curiosity coupled with an intellectual restlessness, qualities that often lead to and sustain inquiry. No, it was not the process of the research or dissertation that left me so miserable (although, with no other known target for my angst, it became the focus both for me and those around me during that time anyway). It was, in fact, the deep discomfort that is part of metamorphosis—in my case, what I came to call my journey as an "epistemorph" (Tananis 2000).

Wandering in the Land of Ologies

My troubles with the ologies surfaced when I tried to move forward with the study. I found myself often paralyzed, not able to rely anymore on comfortable habits of third-person scientific narrative nor yet able to embody and bring language to the foreign currency of the interpretive stance. This paralysis was further deepened by my resolute search for "the" strategy that would work—the one that I was sure existed, though it continued to elude me. I was still driven by framing worldview as a discrete, if not dichotomous, choice, rather than a process, perhaps even a journey, that would evolve over time with its own nuances. More simply, I had abandoned my own metaphor—I had eschewed the inherent meaning of "journey."

This was especially apparent as I struggled with how to best approach my data. Interpretivists often find useful the distinction between "data" and "text." For the interpretivist, the essence of a phenomenon is revealed in the created and evolving "text"—the dialogic interplay between the phenomenon and the researcher, often situated in discourse with others. The difference between "data" and "text," for me, lies less in where they originate than in how they are used. From a functionalist perspective, researchers use data as raw material and *reduce* the information to more meaningful constructs through any number of data-analysis techniques. Contrarily, the interpretivist seeks to *extend* and expand text through interpretation, to draw from it conceptual meaning.

When I first approached my rather large data sets (lines upon lines of email correspondence), my first inclination was to apply grounded theory coding techniques to *reduce* the complexity of the data. I viewed my data as lines or "chunks" of information that through reduction could yield meaning, rather than looking at the whole of a conversation represented by the lines of E-mail, from which I might generate an interpretive text. I spent a great deal of time coding data,[4] but in the end, I generated the concepts of the theory only after I began to write—and *later* code—interpretive vignettes. Interpretive inquiry, and its reliance on the evolving interpretation of texts, requires extensive writing as a way of coming to know and make meaning of experience. By placing too much emphasis on coding—and only talking about what I was sensing with the "data"—I kept myself from a fuller immersion in the interpretive writing process.[5]

My discomfort with technique and my sense of disconnect from what had been familiar were compounded by my suspicion that I was somehow defective for not enjoying—and at times, not even understanding—my own dissertation. While I joked and smiled at comments by others, for example, members of my study group who sometimes saw more relevance and meaning in my dissertation than I did, my perceptions only fed the growing suspicion that I was incompetent to continue, let alone succeed. A vicious cycle began. Having moved from the safe ground of science and postpositivist "certainty" that had provided me with predictability and direction for many years of practice and learning, I not only fumbled about as a neophyte with little skill in this new landscape of qualitative study, but I did so in what felt like a horribly public, high-risk undertaking: the dissertation.

I chose to engage in an inquiry process that I needed to learn *how* to do *as* I was doing it—to engage in an emerging process that I trusted could simultaneously reflect and change my practice in meaningful ways. This choice was not made in a cavalier manner—in fact, much of my coursework leading up to and even including preliminary dissertation documents reflected my desire to find what I considered to be a well-defined and manageable topic and inquiry method. The road I took to a more interpretive study of my own practice was particularly challenging. On any given day throughout this process, both my practice and the inquiry were open to near-constant revision as a dynamic interrelated process that defied prediction and the type of a priori planning that previously marked my academic and professional career. Rather than representing learned expertise, the dissertation process came to represent my engagement in a learning process—learning about practice and about inquiry—and what I bring to both as a scholar-practitioner.

With the best functionalist reasoning I could muster, during most of the dissertation process, I believed that I needed to eradicate all vestiges of my positivist roots before I could embrace a more interpretivist worldview, let alone complete an interpretive inquiry. After a long and frustrating battle with myself, I finally turned to the more interpretivist call within me and abandoned my "all or nothing" framing to come to accept myself as what I now claim as a result of this inquiry: an epistemorph. I can no more shrug off all of what it means to have positivist roots than I could will myself a new eye color. Once I surrendered that battle, I found that far from needing to claim epistemological purity, I needed to embrace my diverse perspective as an epistemorph as that which sets my signature to both my practice and my scholarship.

A notable characteristic of that signature includes what I have described as "functionalist" and "interpretivist drift." I don't claim a stable and secure footing as an interpretivist; it is quite clear that my functionalist roots influence how I view and structure my work and inquiry. As I frame a task or issue, I may inadvertently "drift" to a more functionalist approach—at times I catch myself—and pull back to regroup. At other times, I may not even realize how much I have drifted until I move further along the path to arrive at a different frame of reference. In large part my journey as an epistemorph has been about learning to recognize my own drifting and then navigating the terrain more consciously. One of the most tangible artifacts of my "functionalist drift" is what Miller, Nelson, and Moore (1998) refer to as "conflicted research voices," in which speech and writing reflect a duality of functionalist and interpretivist language (400). Bakhtin (1981) refers to this as a "hybrid construction" of voice in which a single speaker represents two voices that include two social languages or worldviews simultaneously (304–5).

I do not mean to suggest that one can or should attempt to blend or mix epistemological and ontological perspectives—in fact, I agree with Lincoln's (1991) assertion that the two worldviews of positivism/functionalism and interpretivism are quite irreconcilable. One cannot simultaneously hold perspectives of a single objective truth and of multiple socially constructed truths. Had it been possible to mix perspectives, I would have resolved the issues at the core of both my practice and dissertation long ago. In fact, as a more naïve explorer, I attempted to straddle the two, only to find it both unproductive and dysfunctional. I am proposing, however, that while my functionalist colleagues recognize my perspective as far different from theirs, my interpretivist colleagues would also take issue if I were to claim myself as an interpretivist. I am what I have claimed here: an epistemorph.

The "Forest Dark"—Claiming Myself as an Epistemorph

My original discomfort was a product of the lack of familiarity and the sense of fear as I entered a journey into the "forest dark." One of my colleagues early in the dissertation process offered Dante's *Inferno* as an apt metaphor for my journey:

> Midway in our life's journey, I went astray
> > from the straight road and woke to find myself
> > in a dark wood. How shall I say
>
> what wood that was! I never saw so drear,
> > so rank, so arduous a wilderness!
> > Its very memory gives a shape to fear.
>
> Death could scarce be more bitter than that place!
> > But since it came to good, I will recount
> > all that I found revealed there . . .
> > > (Dante, *The Divine Comedy, Inferno*, Canto I)

I rejected the metaphor on several occasions; I was uncomfortable with the images it conjured, perhaps even more so because all I could feel around me was the pressing darkness of uncertainty. For most of my inquiry and dissertation writing, I felt unsure, a woman without an inquiry "home," someone lost, perhaps tricked by shadows, wandering until she came to find she had only circled back to where she began. I struggled to maintain direction and progress, to hear the calls from colleagues, who seemed so much clearer about my inquiry while I was feeling utterly lost in murkiness. The *Inferno* metaphor never really left completely, sticking uncomfortably in the recesses of my mind only to be prodded loose too many times at my colleague's insistence that the metaphor was apt for the journey.[6]

This is not to say that there were no illuminated and even illuminating turns in my trail. There were. But they did not appear as bright beacons to lead me through the "forest dark"—no, they were often small flickers in the soft waters flowing through the wood, glimmers that a weary traveler could easily miss. But glimmers they were, nonetheless, and they often led me, if I was willing and able to follow, to areas of rest and comfort, shade and coolness.

In my evaluation practice, I was comforted by alternatives to an experimental or otherwise purely quantitative design. Certainly, compelling accounts of case studies and anecdotal portrayals have the ability to bring the reader closer to the lived experience of those involved in educational programs and projects, and many evaluators have had exemplary success in using them (Stake 1995). During the 1999 national conference, the American Evaluation Association offered a well-attended session exploring the use of narrative in evaluation, and prior to the conference, the first professional development seminar to fully "book" was a day-long session focused on narrative evaluation. At more recent conferences, the quantity and quality of interpretive sessions continue to increase. While these sessions indicate a growing interpretive discourse community among evaluators, the mainstream of my evaluation colleagues are still to be found attending sessions firmly planted in the postpositivist paradigm. To choose to frame my practice more interpretively carries with it the embedded choice to step further away from some colleagues and toward others. So, too, while I have had the pleasure of long-standing evaluative relationships with a number of clients and stakeholders who value discursive deliberation as the lifeblood of evaluative inquiry, I have also been turned down in response to proposals that required an a priori design and instrumentation to qualify as an evaluation contractor. Identifying and resonating with a worldview involves trade-offs.

As of mid-2005, there has been a renewed focus on framing educational evaluation and research from a postpositivist perspective. Projects receiving federal funds (from the Department of Education and National Science Foundation, for example) are being *required* to show "rigorous evidence" of impact documented via "randomized controlled trials" as the "gold standard" of research (U.S. Department of Education 2003). This unfortunate trend may well marginalize not only a variety of forms of evidence that are not quantitative, but also practitioners in education and evaluation who seek to document experience more richly and fully through interpretive studies.

My journey as an epistemorph included a fundamental shift in my view of the "nature, limits and certainty of knowledge" (Kitchener 1983) as I moved from a functionalist stance as an "insulated expert" to a more interpretive stance of "discursive deliberator" (Tananis 2000). In doing so, I came to envision knowledge as more tentative, as a construction of evolving dialogue. Similar to the transformative processes of other colleagues in evaluation as well as in other fields (Heshusius and Ballard 1996), my journey represented new "agreements about what counts as real and how we allow each other to claim knowledge" (2). My educational experiences (Kitchener and King 1981) and challenges in practice (Baxter Magolda 1994) encouraged me to question my epistemic and ontologic assumptions and to allow myself the freedom to be both more vulnerable in my interactions with colleagues and less "certain" in my own expertise. My particular journey included a somewhat protracted period of dissonance as I struggled to reframe "problems" from my practice as "dilemmas" that invited me to think differently about the nature of evaluation and my role as an evaluator—to question my assumptions. Living in and working through dissonance may offer the promise of excitement and vitality in the "aha" moments of breakthrough, but it is also particularly uncomfortable, unsettling, and tiring. Reconstructing one's view of the world is neither easy nor for the weak of heart.

It is important to note, however, that as I moved through the discomfort, I was able to embrace re-imagining and authoring both my dissertation and practice. As I came to claim my own journey, messy and uncertain as it seemed, I began to "move beyond to what is not yet, to what might be; . . . to break *through* boundaries" (M. Greene 1990, 149, italics added).

In the imagining, I began to "awaken, to disclose the ordinary unseen, unheard, and unexpected" (M. Greene 2001, 28) that had been all around me but ignored in the "forest dark." In the imagining, I had to let go of the notions I had continued to carry with me from the safety of prior certainty—to allow the experience to *be* my teacher, to raise the experience and present to an interpretive prominence rather than relegating it to the insignificant or trivial.

Looking Back—Seeing More than the Dark

I wish I had been able to come to some of these more comforting thoughts while in the *midst* of the dissertation. I suspect that my colleagues, advisors and I would all have been happier folks. But I have come to see that the process of imagining—of authoring—does not, for me, begin and end with the written document. It is a much more extended process of coming to know than I can capture in the writing. The real authoring, the real imagining, for me, has been in coming to claim myself most authentically—as an epistemorph rather than as someone simply passing through the "forest dark" on her way to some form of enlightenment as an ontological purist. My assumption through most of the dissertation was that I had to indeed *become* an interpretivist to lay claim for my practice and research outside of the more traditional postpositivist realm. Many of my struggles were bound to that assumption—that I needed to *get through* the forest—and stake a claim on the other side of the wood in a place I seemed unable to reach. In trying to hurry to the other side, I was ill prepared to claim myself emerged from the forest as an "interpretivist." Equally as important, I feared the shade of the forest as an enemy instead of seeing it only as another version of illumination. Today, I am content to explore the forest more fully, to examine valleys and summits I at first was unable to see. I have discovered a complex world revealed in the shade, one that provides a more comfortable home for both my practice and my study.

I don't offer my journey as either universal or unique. Many of my evaluation colleagues never find a need to reframe their practice; they seem able to find their "answers" within the more prevalent functionalist traditions of the field. Without some perhaps latent interpretive proclivities, I too, may have been content to continue refining my practice as a "master craftsperson" (Tananis 2000). However, my journey is not unlike the process of transformation described by Schwandt and Guba,[7] among others in a group of essays presented by Heshusius and Ballard (1996) that explore transitions from postpositivism. Regardless, it is a journey I had to take—one that I was drawn to, first in my practice, and later, in my inquiry. I was pushed forward by my need to better understand the unresolved troubles in my practice. In that sense, while my journey is not unique, it is particularly personal.

Lessons of the Forest Dark—Revealed in the Shadows

Again, I offer my journey more to generate possibilities and invite imagining, not as a map or prescribed direction. While I am still actively engaged in authoring my practice and related research, I do think I have traveled relatively far along the path. From this vantage point, I offer some thoughts that may serve others. Perhaps first and most important is my sense that the journey itself, regardless of its destination, is well worth the effort and struggle.

I have not only learned about myself as a practitioner-scholar, but also have come to a deeper appreciation for the diversity of perspectives that frame our worlds—and how important one's worldview is in both what we deem worthy of our attention and how we frame those issues once we turn toward them (Pallas 2001). I have also found discourse communities that welcome my voice, both in practice and in scholarship, even within a field richly steeped in rational-scientific tradition and history. As I have "morphed," I have come to a deeper appreciation for other voices, both in evaluation and inquiry. Early in my career and graduate study, I was somewhat reluctant to invite different voices into my worlds of practice and scholarship, not out of contempt or criticism, but out of an attempt to "manage" the cacophony of voices. So I shut myself into a world I originally dichotomized as the "real world" versus the world of the academy. I realize now that I cut myself off from an array of resources and opportunities that today serve as the fountainhead of my day-to-day practice. I am enriched because of the diversity of voices available through the discourses of the field and beyond, but until I could envision myself as a potential scholar, those opportunities seemed earmarked for others, not for me.

I have come to know that "morphing" defies neat, linear, well-packaged and controlled change—it is truly a conversion of "turnings" rather than sudden transformation. I often joked with my study group colleagues that I simply did not understand why, if one could conceive and give birth to a fully functional human in such a relatively short time, one could not also complete a dissertation in nine months. I have no doubt that many a dissertation has been and can be completed in nine months, but my dissertation took much longer to conceptualize, experience and write. With each turn in my morphing came repercussions in my practice and inquiry that required extended time to assimilate and resolve. Part of that messiness involved coming to own a worldview that matched my own proclivities rather than accepting some "inherited notion of authority" (Logsdon 2000) or some dysfunctional notion of "mixed" epistemologies/ontologies.

Allowing me the freedom to explore the twists and turns of my journey was at times at odds with trying to complete a dissertation within a planned and finite period. Finding a more interpretive voice—speaking more directly from my lived experience in first person, portraying my journey without the insulation of a more objective, distanced and less impassioned stance—originally felt foreign and cumbersome. While that stance is now more practiced, it remains somewhat uncomfortable. I still struggle with finding a consistent voice. To move toward a more interpretive voice, I have to first set aside my more practiced, functionalist comfort with the third-person narrative of science. Equally daunting is the challenge of moving from a stance of anticipated certainty to one of engaged tentativeness. It is difficult to let loose of the perceived comfort of certainty, even more so when that choice often represents a break with traditions, discourses and colleagues once valued.

All of these choices represent risk and struggle, yet they hold promise to allow me a more genuine engagement in practice and inquiry. Regardless of the potential, all of these issues are charged with various emotions and required trade-offs. It is important for me to think through each of the options as I recognize them and to understand what they represent, both in my practice and inquiry.

Many of the nuances of my journey came into relief only once I had moved further along the trail and could retrospectively reflect on the critical junctures and highlights. I had not anticipated or planned it and often had a sense that I was not able to consciously control it. It was—and remains, as I continue to morph—truly a lived experience. In retrospective writing about a process such as this, I run the risk that my portrayal, presented in a more linear and compact narrative, belies the rather messy and ambiguous "lived" nature of the experience itself.

I still struggle at times to find a more serene rapprochement. I still contend with my multiplicity as an epistemorph, with my functionalist roots and my interpretivist reach. Rather than reaching a finished state, my transformation continues as an extended series of fractures in practice and inquiry that drive me to turn away from one set of epistemic and ontologic assumptions and simultaneously turn toward another. While I seem better able to navigate the shaded paths of the forest, the rough spots on the trails still exist, and I can find myself lost or delayed. As I have from the beginning, I learn more as I continue on the journey. I have come to recognize that thinking I can either control every aspect of the journey or fully prepare myself by anticipating every twist and turn is not only a frustrating remnant of my functionalist thinking, but also an impossibility to enact.

One might be tempted to ask, "Why don't you simply leave the forest?" I have been tempted at times, but then I remind myself I didn't enter cavalierly. I needed to resolve nagging troubles in my practice—and the resources I needed just happened to be *in* the forest. Earlier in my journey, I didn't even look towards the wood—perhaps, didn't even realize more than a few trees existed. When I did turn toward it, I wandered in only slightly, testing my footing carefully as I slowly nudged forward wary of what seemed a threatening darkness. Eventually, to reach for the potential resources I sought, I needed to leave behind the brightness and certainty of the terrain around me, to move further into the depths of the forest and learn to know the forest *as* I experienced it. The resources I have found in its shaded recesses not only address the troubles that urged me to enter in the first place, but also give me a renewed sense of energy, focus and engagement in both my practice and inquiry.

Notes

1. The study is not a philosophical rendering of ontology, axiology and epistemology; rather, it offers an exploration of the assumptions that underpin the grounding of practice (in this case, evaluation practice) in one's worldview as a scholar and practitioner.
2. My use of the "insulated expert" persona of evaluation practice is drawn from a fuller heuristic of evaluation practice developed in the study. The heuristic explores various personae (earnest technician, procedural specialist and master craftsperson) as *insulated experts* as opposed to the personae (naïve explorer, ambivalent convert and inquiring practitioner) of *discursive deliberators*. See Tananis 2000 for more.
3. As other chapters of this book reveal, each dissertation journey holds its own challenges. While it *seemed* to me that the dissertation represented an intellectual respite from practice for some of my colleagues, the lens of my own discomfort may well have distorted my perception, leading to a minimized view of their discomfort and a conversely expanded view of my own.
4. For a fuller discussion of grounded theory coding techniques and an interpretive framing of grounded theory, see Grubs' chapter in this book as well as Grubs 2004.
5. For a fuller review of issues related to the dissertation, see Tananis 2000.
6. Interestingly, the colleague who first suggested the use of Dante's *Inferno*, offered this comment on reviewing a draft of this chapter: "This strikes me as a somewhat functionalist use of the quote. I had always imagined it to be an interpretive heuristic that would give readers the beginning gestalt of what the journey felt like to you. It seems to me it loses power when used in this way." Of course, she is correct! Again, my inability to embrace her interpretive image was yet another manifestation of my struggle of turning *from* a more functionalist worldview *toward* a more interpretive one. Clearly, her suggestion, while appropriate, was lost in my internal struggle, though resurrected here as I embrace the metaphor of the "forest dark" in this chapter.

References

Abma, T. A. 2002. Hidden images of self. In Ryan and Schwandt, *Exploring*, 119–38.

Bakhtin, M. M. 1981. Discourse in the novel. In *The dialogic imagination: Four essays by M. M. Bakhtin*, ed. and trans. M. Holquist, 259–422. Austin: University of Texas Press.

Baxter Magolda, M. B. 1994. Post-college experiences and epistemology. *Review of Higher Education* 18, no. 1: 25–44.

Dante. *The Divine Comedy—Inferno.* Canto I. Translated by J. Ciardi, 28–33. New York: The New American Library.

Greene, J. C. 2000. Reconsidering roles. Paper presented at the Annual Meeting of the American Evaluation Association, Honolulu, Hawaii.

———. 2001. *The Relational and Dialogic Dimensions of Program Quality*. In Visions of Quality: How Evaluators Define, Understand, and Represent Program Quality. Edited by A.P. Benson, M. Hinn, and C. Lloyd. Oxford: Elsevier Science Ltd.

Greene, M. 1990. *Arts education in the humanities: Toward a breaking of the boundaries*. In W.J. Moody (Ed.) Artistic intelligences: Implications for education. New York: Teachers College Press, Columbia University. pp. 147–58.

———. 2001. *Variations on a blue guitar: The Lincoln Center Institute lectures on aesthetic education.* New York: Teachers College Press, Columbia University.

Grubs, R. E. 2004. *Living in shadows: Contextualizing the experience of being at-risk and reaching a decision about prenatal genetic testing.* UMI ProQuest Digital Dissertation #ATT 3078844.

Heshusius, L., and K. Ballard, eds. 1996. *From positivism to interpretivism and beyond: Tales of transformation in educational and social research. The mind-body connection.* New York: Teachers College Press.

King, J. A. and L. Stevahn. 2002. Three fameworks for considering evaluator role. In Ryan and Schwandt, *Exploring,* 1–16.

Kitchener, K. S. 1983. Cognition, metacognition, and epistemic cognition. *Human Development* 26: 222–32.

Kitchener, K. S., and P. M. King. 1981. Reflective judgment: Concepts of justification and their relationship to age and education. *Journal of Applied Development Psychology* 2: 89–116.

Lincoln, Y. S. 1991. The art and science of program evaluation. *Evaluation Practice* 12, no. 1: 1–7.

Logsdon, M. J. 2000. *A pedagogy of authority: Speculative essays by an English teacher.* UMI ProQuest Digital Dissertation #AAT 9998630.

Mertens, D. M. 1999. Inclusive evaluation: Implications of transformative theory for evaluation. *American Journal of Evaluation* 20, no. 1: 1–14.

———. 2002. The evaluator's role in the transformative context. In Ryan and Schwandt, *Exploring,* 103–18.

Miller, S. M., M. W. Nelson, and M. T. Moore. 1998. Caught in the paradigm gap: Qualitative researchers' lived experience and the politics of epistemology. *American Educational Research Journal* 35, no. 3: 377–416.

Pallas, A.M. June/July 2001. Preparing education doctoral students for epistemological diversity. *Educational Researcher* 30, no. 5: 6–11.

Ryan, K.E., and T.A. Schwandt, eds. *Exploring evaluator role and identity.* Greenwich, CT: Information Age Publishing.

Schwandt, T. A. 1996. Notes on being an interpretivist. In Heshusius and Ballard, *From positivism to interpretivism,* 77–84.

———. 2002. Traversing the terrain of role, identify, and self. In Ryan and Schwandt, *Exploring,* 193–207.

Stake, R. E. 1995. *The art of case study research.* Thousand Oaks, CA: Sage.

Tananis, C. A. 2000. *Discursive evaluation: The journey of an "epistemorph" toward an interpretive practice and inquiry.* UMI ProQuest Digital Dissertation #AAT 9974482.

U.S. Department of Education. 2003. *Identifying and implementing educational practices supported by rigorous evidence: A user-friendly guide.* Washington, DC: Institute of Education Sciences.

PART 4

Claiming Self as Writer

CHAPTER 11

Writing Essays: Minding the Personal and Theoretic

Marjorie Barrett Logsdon

Perhaps all relationships—including our relationship with writing or our relationship with a dissertation—form, re-form, and are nurtured or atrophy through a process of letting go and accepting. I know the process of writing my dissertation was this way for me. From comprehensive exams to nine dissertation titles, from journals, narratives, and essays to the crash of my computer "one dark and stormy night," from the question, "What makes a collection of essays a dissertation?" posed at my defense, to now, I've come to understand something about letting go and accepting.

I realize that may sound simplistic, and although I'm somewhat uncomfortable not pinning my experience to profound theory in these opening remarks, still there is method as well as theory waiting in the wings. I can admit now that it took years letting go of "wrongheaded" notions about writing and thinking (Berthoff 1981) for my inquiry to thrive. Decades ago, Berthoff told us that since interpretations aren't amenable to proof or demonstration, our task is to be as authentic as possible in making our best case. She said it well: "If we aren't gods who have perfect knowledge, we are nonetheless powerful creatures who can describe and define, argue and tell stories, encouraging, persuading, entertaining: rhetoric is what we have instead of omniscience" (Berthoff 1981, 43).

So what follows is rhetorical, descriptive, personal, and authentic; it is also an essay. It tells a story about writing as practical and theoretical process (Richardson 1997). It locates memory as the wellspring of my thinking about teaching and authority. It describes what I now find *meaning-full* in writing essays for an inquiry stated in the ninth and final title, A Pedagogy of Authority: Speculative Essays by an English Teacher (Logsdon 2000).

Writing: Preconceptions and Misconceptions

> It's easy, after all, not to be a writer. Most people aren't writers, and very little harm comes to them. (Barnes 1985, 121)

First, I want to dispel an idea that may be forming in the reader about English teachers. We are not all born writers, nor do we all fill summer months composing novels or essays—at least not the English teachers I've taught with in schools. It is probably fair to say we are lovers of language and literature. It may also be fair to say we are often affectionate critics of writing. Too, in terms of academic preparation, colleges and universities require those of us aiming for the classroom to write academic papers about theory and critical or reflective papers about practice. Beyond this, my experience tells me teaching in high school does more to prepare English teachers to critique essays than to write them.

Second, my defensiveness about being an English teacher suggests weightier matters. While I was writing, some colleagues dismissed my struggles, assuming they were fabricated, exaggerated, or symptomatic of an English teacher's desire for perfection. Not so. Writing for me was hard, even if fulfilling. Professional authors say this all the time. Dillard (1989) talks about the terror of beginning, of the blank page "which you cover woodenly" (58). Emig (1983) says: "Nowhere are there hints about preverbal anguishing and the hell of getting underway; of the compulsions and fetishes governing the placement of the first word or phrase on the page— the 'getting black on white' of de Maupassant" (48). Of Montale it was said: "For him all writing was like opening an artery and bleeding out words drop by drop" (Mewshaw 1999, 29).

Yet acknowledging writing is hard is not enough. Some preconceptions about writing confound the thinking process, divert attention from what really matters, from the inquiry at hand. Colleagues who suggested English teachers are "writerly" troubled me because I internalized judgment. Worrying how my writing and thinking might be judged—which focused energy on self instead of the inquiry—not only sapped energy but derailed generative thinking. In other words, my worry closed conceptual possibilities still in draft. In learning to accept my struggle, worry moved offstage, thus allowing the inquiry to take stage center. In attending to the inquiry, I discovered ways to tend to ideas, little realizing that each step prepared the ground from which the figure of a writer emerged.

Attending to the inquiry meant being prepared for ideas, especially those that arrive unannounced. Like melodies, memories, and grief, ideas may arrive in the imagination lacking apparent association. They often defy order. Of course, we may later impose an order on them through reason and interpretation, but initially, we should simply welcome ideas as presents from the unconscious, regardless of where and when they are given. Since they materialized in their own time, I learned to be ready for them. Readiness meant stowing little two-by-three–inch notebooks in my car and next to my bed; access and transportability were key. I liked the small size because no jotting was dwarfed by white space when I later read a phrase or word or even an author's name; no idea was unworthy or insignificant or too small to record. Nor did the process of writing a dissertation seem so overwhelming when ideas could be stored in such diminutive places. Readiness meant *write it*; write it down now—consider, deepen, or discard later.

But I need to offer a caveat here. If it sounds as if I contend that all ideas spring mystically like Athena from the head of Zeus, I do know otherwise. Ideas most often keep company with hard intellectual work, coming with and through much reading and deliberation, rising to coherence through sustained writing. I recall taking lengthy notes, writing abstracts, and storing keywords and themes in an endnote library. Each writing created another reading, each quote shaped a distinctive voice, each source offered me a place to nod agreement, make asides, or begin forming concepts. Keeping company with authors began a conversation, kept thoughts and ideas percolating. Repose and relaxation offer fertile ground for insights to surface, but the intellect needs to be kept vital by continually engaging with all kinds of texts.

The funny thing is that at the time I didn't call what I was doing writing. And even though I believed writing is thinking, and repeated this mantra-like to my students, *I hadn't lived it*. What Berthoff (1981) says was true for me: "It is far easier, I think, to teach those who have had no training in writing than it is to unteach the anticomposing that so many have learned" (3). For her, anticomposing is "outlining as a first step; not writing at all 'until you know what you want to say,' avoiding generalizations, always *making it vivid;* casting so-called thesis statements in the form of simple assertions" (Berthoff 1981, 3, italics in original). Of course, I realized at the time that two decades worth of writing scholars largely agreed with Berthoff and theorized writing as thinking, as process instead of product (Elbow 1998, Perl 1994). And some social scientists, Richardson (2003) very prominent among them, argue for writing as method. But I had to unteach myself to experience writing as a dialectical process (Berthoff 1981).

In naming my actions taking "notes" or "jotting down" ideas, I misapprehended how thoughts and abstractions evolve. While I didn't consider the notes or jottings mechanical tasks, neither did I consider myself forming concepts. Retrospect now shows me that I had wrongly *performed* writing as the result of thinking. I had wrongly *produced* writing as whole, complete, and finished, rather than organic and unfolding. Past experience with writing never demanded that I compose differently. But as Berthoff (1981) explains, "Composing is forming: it is a continuum; it goes on all the time. Composing is what the mind does by nature; composing is the function of the active mind. Composing is the way we make sense of the world; it's our way of learning" (36).

In these ways, my personal education on writing continued, as did learning what to accept and let go. Yet my writing was soon to make a pivotal turn, although not before I became mindful of my past, gathering through memory and dream those experiences that composed my teaching life.

Memory Writing

> There may be no more pressing intellectual need in our culture than for people to become sophisticated about the function of memory. (Hampl 1986, 36)

The turn came after filling notebooks, writing teaching journals, and composing two narratives. Suddenly and surprisingly, after I released two narratives into writing, memory let go of others. The once-stored images rushed into consciousness, and I felt alert, excited, and energized. Everything happened after that: I conceptualized the entire dissertation. I sketched out themes—inherited authority, expert authority, textual authority. I titled the as-yet unwritten memories "cluster stories," locating each one, about thirty in all, within themes. I titled chapters. All of this in a few hours on a Saturday morning in the fall. I'll never forget it.

Some unwritten memories came as voices from the past, like my mother's, "Marjorie, do you have to yell?" Other lines, like this from a student—"I don't know what to use to *prove* my third thesis point"—

expressed an epistemological authority I no longer accepted unproblematically. "Back behind the Podium," a narrative, signaled my discomfort with sharing authority in a discussion circle and my retreat to safer ground. "Nice combination of 'sneak attacks' and calling on volunteers," a principal wrote after observing my class, a militaristic metaphor unsettling at the time, more chilling in retrospect.

Each memory pressed upon me a need to figure out its meaning, and each memory invited review of experience. How could I understand ways I enacted teacher authority unless I sought authority figures from years past whose performance of authority shaped, rewarded, or punished me? How could I understand why authority images proved so intractable in my life unless memory took me to the very formation of those ideas? How could I uncover inherited notions that constructed a pedagogy of authority without memory travel? Memory itself taught me to listen, to recall images, to draw from imagination the times, plot lines, characters, and conflicts that comprise narrative. As Hampl (1986) says, I discovered the "authority of memory" (36), and I began to validate my teaching life.

And I learned something else, this lesson coming from the unconscious: other unwritten texts besides memory may have meaning as well. I turned to dreams. Over the years, disturbing and recurring teaching dreams had stuck with me. I wrote them—past dreams from memory, recent dreams the morning after they arrived. In drawing these texts into the open, I became emboldened. I discovered that my colleagues had teacher dreams also but learned that teaching dreams are so similar in nature that they are often discounted (Tompkins 1996). Dreams of students refusing to be quiet, dreams of not being heard or obeyed, dreams of "students leaving the classroom when we face the board," of "pontificating in nasal tones about subjects [we] know nothing about" (Tompkins 1996, 42). Dreams of the failure of authority.

I believed that something lay behind my dreams. Doll (1995) remarks that she spent half her life interested in dreams. She believes, "These nightly dramas, often of an absurdist nature, will reveal to you the side of yourself you need to visit, your shadow side, which, once revealed, can spiral you into more knowing awareness of and sensitivity towards your experiences, both inner and outer" (Doll 1995, 95). We are wiser than we know, she claims; "or rather, what we know with our conscious minds is only part of our wisdom" (Doll 1995, 96).

Looking back, I realize how writing made permeable the boundaries between the conscious and unconscious. Memory opened "commerce with the unconscious self" (Emig 1983, 48), took me to dreams and the unfinished business on authority they represented. Through the unconscious and its "unmeant knowledge" (Felman 1982, 28), I glimpsed a lifetime of scripts, now pushing forward with urgency.

I see now I was writing my way toward understanding what it means to claim writing as method, but it took living the experience rather than merely theorizing it. I had to live it to really understand what Berthoff (1981) meant when she described composing as forming. I had to perform writing as thinking. What does it mean to author an interpretive dissertation? I know now it first means letting go of the wrongheaded notions. It also means accepting that "Writing is not just a mopping up activity at the end of research" (Richardson 2003, 499). The learning *is* in the doing. Sontag (2001) offers other significant thoughts:

> Writing is finally a series of permissions you give yourself to be expressive in certain ways. To invent. To leap. To fly. To fall. To find your own characteristic way of narrating and insisting; that is, to find your own inner freedom. To be strict without being too self-excoriating. Not stopping too often to reread. Allowing yourself, when you dare to think it's going well (or not too badly), simply to keep rowing along. No waiting for inspiration's shove. (225)

A series of permissions you give yourself. Overworked as the idea of permission has become, it still rings true. I like her emphasis on "series," too, because it seems that the struggle to author is a struggle always unfinished. And we *do* need to just keep rowing along. I continually reminded myself about permission. And I continually reminded myself to trust my experience, right up to my defense. The dream and memory texts, the jottings and journals—each unstaged writing performance carried my personal authority forward into the staged performance of writing essays.

Writerly and Readerly Considerations

> And I shall ask as well . . . what sort of feeling and imagining is called into being by the shape of the text as it addresses the imagined reader, what sort of readerly activity is built into the form. (Nussbaum 1995, 4)

After Maria (see Piantanida this text) suggested I read Schubert's (1991) article on the speculative essay, I reconceptualized the inquiry, moving from narrative to writing essays as method. In changing genre, writerly and readerly considerations also shifted, posing new questions. Who is it who writes?

How is an author situated in or absented from a text? How might a writer's position vis-à-vis the text effect a reader?

Other writerly questions surfaced when I altered the inquiry. What stance does the author of memory texts take to compose and portray the teacher of her past? Her present stance? Or a more speculative stance? I recalled some authority tropes I had enacted as a teacher. "No late papers accepted," I'd say to students. "Think about this metaphor: *dead*line." Portraying the person who made this pronouncement, conveying tone and nuance, working to achieve integrity in the telling and understanding through the speculations—these were writerly and readerly considerations that I faced in new ways when essay supplanted narrative.

In the narratives already written, I tended to plotlines and details, but an essayist, like a memoirist, needs to tell her "mind," not just her story (Hampl 1999, 18). The sensibility that awakened in me after writing memory texts fueled my need to see how ripples of past experience touched my teaching present. I like the way Welty (1984) puts it:

> Experiences too indefinite of outline in themselves to be recognized for themselves connect and are identified as a larger share. And suddenly, a light is thrown back, as when your train makes a curve, showing there has been a mountain of meaning rising behind you on the way you've come, is rising there still, proven now in retrospect. (90)

Memory texts gave me that hindsight, yet I needed more. I needed to follow the pathway of writing and thinking; I needed to theorize and make meaning. Writing speculative essays, "a form of philosophical inquiry put into writing" (Schubert 1991, 66), offered a method to throw a light back on my experience.

On method, Berthoff (1981) is again instructive. She says that method can be simply a procedure or a sequence of activities that may apply to almost anything, from dieting to climbing Mt. Everest. But method in philosophy is a way of "bringing together what we think we are doing and how we are doing it: *meta + hodos* = about the way; the way about the way" (Berthoff 1981, 4); when teachers consider language and thought, theory and practice, when they think about thinking, they are doing what philosophers do. Through all of the writing I had done, especially the memory texts, I was learning to accept that writing doesn't precede thinking, it *is* thinking, thinking in process. As Shaw and Borges both said, we don't work from ideas, we work toward them. Writing speculative essays, characterized as a personal writing *on* a subject, seemed well-suited to my inquiry. The deadlines, the dreams, the taken-for-granted ways I enacted authority—stories about each of these became a means to excavate the assumptions, beliefs, and practices that composed my pedagogy. It was *mind* I was after.

Let me add here that I was mindful of my pedagogy before this. In fact, I thought about it a great deal. But in the past I didn't use writing to make thinking visible. I didn't use writing as mode of inquiry. I had diagnosed my pedagogy on what did or did not "work" with students, what texts they liked or didn't like, how this or that discussion succeeded or failed. Too frequently these reflections were interior monologues, often dramatic in nature but not illuminated by other perspectives. Up until this time, I hadn't taken a long view of my pedagogy, spanning incidents down through the years, seeking patterns through retrospect. Now my questioning intensified and deepened, pointed itself toward making the personal theoretic and public.

The public nature of writing essays turned my inward gaze outward toward others, and I brought other voices into the text besides my own. I became eclectic. I gave myself one of those permissions Sontag (2001) mentioned and moved freely from one discourse to another, borrowing a strand of theory here, a spool there. Sometimes I found that the feminist work that I read for comprehensives served well, especially for the essay on expert authority. But for other essays, I read broadly, in search of new discourses and theory to aid my interpretations. This is how I discovered Doll (1995) and her interest in dreams. Gestalt theory and its use for teacher practice also informed my thinking (Korthagen and Kessels 1999), as did literary theory on myth.

Remembered lines from literature took on new uses when I considered them as foils for my thinking about pedagogy. Sometimes they gave me parallel texts to think through, as when Hamlet says he could be bound in a nutshell and count himself king of infinite space but for bad dreams. Other lines seemed to float in and out of my life, uncannily repeated by one person or another. It wasn't until I taught *King Lear* a decade later that I realized the source of a line often quoted at school by Sister Maria Magdalene, my principal, and at home by my mother: "Her voice was ever soft,/ Gentle, and low, an excellent thing in woman" (Lear, 5.3. 275–76). As a teacher of literature, images, characters, and lines were vital to my teaching and always hovered close to recall. Good (1988) argues that these kinds of citations are not so much sought for authoritative support as they are a way to bring old friends into a conversation (1), and I know these fictional friends settled me into my text with the comfort of the familiar.

Because I was so accustomed to lacing my writing with literary citations, I took the same approach with scholarly references. I did not dedicate a separate essay to a literature review. In keeping a convention of the essay, each voice joined the essay's conversation, complicating and deepening my own, moving what might have remained interior into the open air of discourse, making what might have seemed simple, complex. Too, my habit of taking many pages of notes kept ideas and sometimes lines from scholars near the surface.

I experimented with voice in another way, using the second person pronoun "you" for an essay called "Musings on the Study." I offer some of that writing here for flavor and explanation:

> Then you realize, even as you claim writing as method of inquiry and the "speculative essay" (Schubert, 1991) as the genre for the study, that you still hold on to ideas about writing that you learned in the [60s]. But you school yourself and keep trying to move forward, to write with a "sense of trust" that makes discovery possible (Stafford, 1994). Even today you begin (again) to trust. You dream that you are reading a dissertation by a Study Group member who used second person in a chapter. Why not try this, you think in the dream. Then you awaken and know that she did not use second person in her dissertation. You remember Cate, your student, who wrote using "you" throughout a personal writing. Something caught hold. Why not consider second person, try on different voices, theorize from another vantage point? You had found something lacking in the narratives you had already written. Perhaps in a paradoxical way, avoiding the first person allows you to "open" the text of the dissertation and will also open another layer of meaning, somehow bring you closer to understanding what you need to express. (Logsdon 2000, 5)

Here, entering a text from another direction opened possibilities. In letting go of first person and trying on second, I felt oddly free to challenge convention, to create a new authorial stance and presence. Displacing "I" altered my perspective, gave me another view of "self" and in its mode of direct address, drew a circle taking the reader in. (Remember learning first person as "speaker," second person as "spoken to," third person as "spoken about"?) Writing in another voice added textuality and stretched me as a writer. It gave me another way to "mind" the text of my thinking.

I realize now that I wrote a great deal, experimenting more than I ever intended or imagined. Some of the writings, like the second-person piece, made it into the dissertation. Others only found their way to files called

"Extra Text." Through writing and experimenting, through reading and revision, I was thinking my way through the text of my teaching. Each re-reading and rewriting distilled, clarified, and heightened my belief in the interpretability of experience, teaching me what it means to write and think discursively with self, the texts I authored, and the texts of others.

Through writing essays, I followed the conventions of the genre to think out loud, addressing an imagined reader whom I asked to follow the "undulating trek of [my] thought and feeling" (Schubert 1991, 65). In tracing the pathway of my thinking, I sought the "why," not the "how," behind my teaching: the tyranny and authority of texts; the uses and abuses of time; the influence of inherited knowledge. With each writing, I hoped to pull the reader into my thoughts and into my confidence. The apparent immediacy of composing in this manner asks a reader to enter an "as if" (Nussbaum 1995) world: think along with me, think on this experience, this explanation, this idea.

In an "as if" world, the literary imagination quickens. Like other types of writing that are lifebound, an essayist writes with the hope a reader will question, How is this familiar or strange, like or unlike me? In this way, the literary experience of reading an essay is not unlike the experience of reading a novel. I like what Nussbaum (1995) has to say about this: "The experience of reading a novel implicitly involves reflection about what human activities are the most important, and how political action of various sorts does or does not support those activities. This means that the novel invites us to reflect critically" (44). Nussbaum (1995) lays out an argument claiming that storytelling and the literary imagination are not opposed to rational argument and may in fact provide essential ingredients (xiii). Her claim, that a novel "does not purchase its attention to social content and to individual variety at the price of jettisoning moral or political theory," might also be made for writing essays for educational research (Nussbaum 1995, 45). I want to quote her at length because what she says is important to my thinking about the essay:

> It [the novel] forges a complex relationship with its reader in which, on the one hand, the reader is asked to care about specific features of circumstance and history and to see these as relevant for social choice, but on the other, is reminded always to recognize that human beings in different spheres do have common passions, hopes, fears—the need to confront death, the desire for learning the deep bonds of family. To see this is to engage in theoretical reflection. (Nussbaum 1995, 45)

It seems to me that an essay, engendered in narrative impulse and mindful speculation, has potential to call forth this type of response from a reader. In writing essays that laid out both story and thinking, I extended an implicit invitation to read both with and against the grain of my thinking (Bartholomae and Petrosky 1999). I asked my reader to "read generously," to work with ideas, to enter an "as if" world. In adding multiple voices, both scholarly and literary, I encouraged a reader to go "against the grain," read critically, provide alternative readings, look for limits in my vision (Bartholomae and Petrosky 1999, 11).

Reading a speculative essay, then, invites a reader not only to observe a mind at work in the act of speculating, but also to engage in acts of imagination and speculation as the text unfolds. This type of reading (and composing) is an act of forming or act of imagination that Berthoff (1981) says is a name for the active mind (28). For her, the imagination needs to be reclaimed and "rescued from the creativity corner and returned to the center of all that we do" (Berthoff 1981, 28). Reclaiming the imagination is necessary because "the positivists have consigned it to something they called the 'affective domain' in contradistinction to 'the cognitive domain'"; this false philosophy cannot account for imagination as a way of knowing, Berthoff argues, or as a means of making meaning, because it understands imagination as ancillary or subordinate, not as fundamental and primordial (1981, 28).

In light of these understandings then, I believe that reading a speculative essay that is generated in memory and attentive to theorizing has the potential to draw a reader into a speculative realm, a space where multiple ways of reading are required. If Postman (1996) is correct in saying that scientists "tend to be more conscious of the abstracting process" as they shape inquiries (182), then essays that mine and mind the personal and theoretic may offer possibilities for social researchers to allow readers to witness abstractions as they form. Thus, readerly activity *is* built into the form and that activity is variegated.

References

Barnes, J. 1985. *Flaubert's Parrot.* New York: Alfred A. Knopf.
Bartholomae, D., and A. Petrosky. 1999. *Ways of reading: An anthology for writers.* New York: Bedford/St. Martin's.
Berthoff, A. E. 1981. *The making of meaning: Metaphors, models, and maxims for writing teachers.* Upper Montclair, NJ: Boynton/Cook Publishers, Inc.
Dillard, A. 1989. *The writing life.* New York: Harper & Row.

Doll, M. A. 1995. Dancing the circle: Cambridge School of Weston Graduation Address (1991). In *To the lighthouse and back: Writings on teaching and living*, M.A. Doll, 92–97. New York: Peter Lang.

Elbow, P. 1998. *Writing without teachers*, 2nd ed. New York: Oxford University Press.

Emig, J. 1983. The uses of the unconscious in composing. In *The web of meaning: Essays on writing, teaching, learning and thinking*, ed. D. Goswami and M. Butler, 46–53. Upper Montclair, NJ: Boynton/Cook Publishers, Inc.

Felman, S. 1982. Psychoanalysis and education: Teaching the terminable and interminable. *Yale French Studies* no. 63: 21–44.

Good, G. 1988. *The observing self: Rediscovering the essay*. New York: Routledge.

Hampl, P. 1986. Memory and imagination. In *The Dolphin Reader*, ed. D. Hunt, 695–706. Boston: Houghton, Mifflin Company.

Korthagen, F. A., and J. Kessels. 1999. Linking theory and practice: Changing the pedagogy of teacher education. *Educational Researcher* 28, no. 4: 4–17.

Logsdon, M. 2000. *A pedagogy of authority: Speculative essays by an English teacher*. UMI ProQuest Digital Dissertation # AAT 99–98630.

Mewshaw, M. 1999. Montale as couplet. *The Nation* (March 29) : 29–30.

Nussbaum, M. 1995. *Poetic justice: The literary imagination and public life*. Boston: Beacon Press.

Perl, S. 1994. Understanding composing. In *Landmark essays on writing process.* ed. S. Perl, 99–106. Davis, CA: Hermagoras.

Postman, N. 1996. *The end of education: Redefining the value of school*. New York: Vintage House.

Richardson, L. 1997. Skirting a pleated text: Feminist post-structuralist theory and praxis. Paper presented at the American Educational Research Association, Chicago.

———. 2003. Writing: A method of inquiry. In *Collecting and interpreting qualitative materials*, ed. N. K. Denzin and Y. S. Lincoln, 499–541. Thousand Oaks, CA: Sage.

Schubert, W. 1991. Philosophical inquiry: The speculative essay. In *Forms of curriculum inquiry*, ed. E. C. Short, 61–76. New York: State University of New York Press.

Sontag, S. 2001. Directions: Write, read, rewrite. Repeat steps 2 and 3 as needed. In *Writers [on writing]: Collected essays from the* New York Times. Introduction by John Darnton. 223–29. New York: Henry Holt and Company.

Stafford, W. 1994. A way of writing. In *Landmark essays on writing process. ed* S.Perl, 231–33. Davis, CA: Hermagoras Press.

Tompkins, J. 1996. Look back in anger. *Teacher Magazine* (October): 42–45.

Welty, E. 1984. *One writer's beginnings*. Cambridge, MA: Harvard University Press.

CHAPTER 12

Speculations on the Personal Essay as a Mode of Curriculum Inquiry

Maria Piantanida

> *Speculation.* The mental view of anything in its various aspects and relations; contemplation; intellectual examination.
>
> *Speculate.* To meditate; to contemplate; to consider a subject by turning it in the mind and viewing it in its different aspects and relations . . . to think about or theorize on any subject . . . to reason from assumed premises . . . to conjecture . . . to consider earnestly or with considerable attention.

The speculations in this chapter arise from the interplay between my own foray into essay writing as a mode of inquiry and ideas put forward by noted curriculum scholar William H. Schubert (1991) in his piece "Philosophical Inquiry: The Speculative Essay." To initiate my speculations, I highlight two of Schubert's arguments. In the first, he makes a persuasive case for the philosophical or speculative essay as a mode of inquiry with a long-standing tradition in the field of curriculum. In the second, he suggests that discourses of curriculum might be enriched by studying not only the essays of curriculum scholars, but also the "unwritten essays" embedded in the lived experience of teachers, curriculum leaders, and students.

As an educational practitioner (a teacher and curriculum consultant), I am deeply grateful for Schubert's assertion that knowledge generated through unwritten personal reflection on practical experience might merit serious attention. Yet since completing my dissertation (Piantanida 1982), I have believed passionately that the stances of practitioner and scholar need not be dichotomous. Transforming unwritten reflections into personal essays has become, for me, a process through which I strive to embody and enact an integrated stance of scholarly practitioner. This way of being-in-the-world gives rise to the central speculation of this chapter: that the writing of personal essays might serve as a useful mode of inquiry for other educators inclined toward engagement in scholarly practice. This core conjectural speculation leads me to a second, more meditative speculation: What might help novice researchers ease into the writing of personal essays as a mode of inquiry?

Schubert contends that " . . . there could not and should not be a how-to manual of instruction on constructing curricular essays" (1991, 68). Nevertheless, while avoiding prescriptive instructions, Schubert does recommend five phases of preparation for aspiring curricular essayists. In brief, these phases are:

> (1) to write from experience for which one is a connoisseur; (2) to write from commitment to ideas to which one is deeply committed; (3) to immerse oneself in the general masters of the essay form; (4) to immerse oneself in the abundance of essays on curriculum; and (5) to write a great deal. (Schubert 1991, 71)

In the remainder of this chapter, I speculate upon Schubert's advice in light of my own efforts at essay writing and at introducing doctoral students to qualitative research.

Imagining Myself as Essayist

As I speculate on Schubert's five phases, it seems to me that there is a preceding phase—the decision to try one's hand at essay writing. This may seem too obvious to warrant mention. Yet the very act of imagining myself as an essayist made possible a way of scholarly writing that I had not previously considered.

The idea of naming myself an essayist came to me on April 10, 1996. I can pinpoint this date because I was sitting in a hot, over crowded room at the annual meeting of the American Educational Research Association (AERA). As I listened half-heartedly to a highly rational technical presentation on professions education,[12] my mind began to wander, and I felt again the constriction of writing to satisfy others rather than myself. Having grown increasingly weary of the demand for functionalist writing—in which parsimony is valued over nuance, brevity over substance, answers over questions, certitude over inquiry—I longed for a mode of writing that would allow me to muse about the complexities of teaching and learning and to portray in a more personal way the lessons learned from my work in curriculum making. Suddenly the idea of becoming an essayist popped into my mind. Instinctively and immediately, it felt right.

It wasn't until some time after I embraced the notion of essay writing that I serendipitously encountered Schubert's argument for the philosophical/speculative essay as a form of curriculum inquiry. From the moment I happened across his piece, however, my intuitive decision to adopt the stance of essayist took on a heightened meaning for me. As Schubert explains:

> For the essayist, writing is a special way of thinking. It is a method of inquiry, one that allows the reader to follow along the often convoluted journey that leads to greater illumination. Perhaps traveling such a journey allows the reader to embark on his or her own byways and even pursue other journeys at the same time. In a sense, then, the essay is a process of inquiry that transcends the problem of reducing human experience to an objectified commodity, a snare of all formal systems of inquiry. The essay, a fluid and less formal form, retains the vitality of lived experience by creating method of inquiry within its presentation. Perhaps, too, it is not mere coincidence that both the essay, as a form of inquiry, and curriculum are often described by journey metaphors. (Schubert 1991, 69–70)

This perspective of the essay is both daunting and affirming. It is daunting in the expectation that I should lay bare not only what I think, but also the processes through which I think. It is affirming in the sense that my way of thinking about my curriculum praxis might count as legitimate inquiry.

When I say "my way of thinking," I am alluding to two facets of my proclivity for meaning-making. First, my way of thinking is to ruminate on (some might say, obsess over) personal and professional experience. I am endlessly fascinated by the complexities and challenges of enacting discursive curricula. Typically, my ruminations center around my failed attempts at such curriculum-making endeavors. Second, my way of thinking entails writing, for it is through writing that I move from rumination (and often recrimination) to reflection and understanding. This compulsion to write my way toward understanding brings me to my next point of speculation.

A Compulsion to Write

As I reflect on nearly forty years of writing experience, it strikes me that Schubert's advice to "write a great deal" is deceptively mild. From the moment I entered college in 1964 to the present, I have written a great deal:

academic papers, administrative briefings, grant proposals, program descriptions, curriculum plans, policy and procedure manuals, publishable articles, informational pamphlets, newsletters, minutes of meetings, memoranda, on and on. I can imagine others with similar experience saying to themselves, "I've had to write a lot as a professional, so I'm prepared to use the personal essay as my research method." Should any reader be harboring such thoughts, I cannot say firmly enough, "Proceed with caution!"

Required writing imposed by teachers (e.g., term papers) and employers (e.g., reports) bears little resemblance to essay writing as a mode of inquiry. While I realize that a doctoral dissertation can be seen as a required writing project, such a view hardly provides sustaining energy for a scholarly inquiry. What sustains me is the compulsion to understand myself and my experiences through the process of writing.

It is this compulsion that makes me, not just willing, but eager, to sit alone at my computer day after day. It is this compulsion that engenders a guilty sense of nonproductivity when life's obligations impose a writing hiatus. It is this compulsion that draws me back to my workstation even after hours of staring fruitlessly at a blank monitor screen, even when a day's worth of typing yields a meager paragraph or two—even when I know that this meager output will be discarded when I again put finger to keyboard.

Knowing what I want to say and conveying that clearly in writing are challenging enough. Even more challenging is first *discovering* what I want to say through writing. For me, the admonition to "write a great deal" has little to do with voluminous production and everything to do with devoting a great deal of time to sitting with myself, my ideas, and my computer.

"But," I can hear my good friend and colleague Noreen saying, "don't you also have to spend time with literature that can inform your thinking? If you write only about yourself and what you already know, don't you run the risk of solipsism or naïveté?" This admonition brings me to the next three speculations.

Hearing Myself Think

Schubert's advice to read the great essayists and to immerse oneself in curriculum essays evokes in me a disquieting flow of emotions—resistance, tension, studied ambivalence. The wellspring of these emotions is fed by subterranean streams of my psyche—a need to please authority figures (especially those whom I respect); a need to appear reasonable, intelligent, learned; a need to be authentic; a need to be heard, acknowledged, affirmed. The older I get, the more these needs conflict.

In my younger years, I sought acknowledgment and affirmation by conforming to the expectations of authority figures. If they said I should write in a certain way, I practiced that form of writing until I won their approval. If they said my ideas had no merit until I read what others had written, I put aside my thoughts and attended to the thoughts of others. If my efforts fell short of the mark, if I didn't receive the approval I craved, I went into intellectual hiding, watching chameleon-like to discern what expectations I had yet to meet.

Perhaps the onset of middle age has engendered my resistance to this authority-pleasing way of being. Yet, the vestiges linger. So I adopt a stance of studied ambivalence, acknowledging the reasonableness—even necessity—of immersing myself in literature, while tentatively suggesting that may not be the only way to enter into essay writing as a mode of inquiry.

Let me elaborate a bit on why I resist reading the great essayists. As an undergraduate and graduate student, I majored in English literature. During the semester I studied *Beowulf*, I composed a quasi-epic poem in honor of my brother-in-law's graduation from medical school. During the semester I studied Spencer's *Faire Queene*, I composed an abbreviated epithalamion to commemorate my sister's wedding. This tendency to mimic the style of whatever literary genre I'm currently reading persists even today. Not long ago, I read Brenda Ueland's inspiring book, *If You Want to Write: A Book about Art, Independence and Spirit*. Several hours into my next writing session, I suddenly realized the cadence of my writing had subtly shifted to resonate with Ueland's. Given this penchant for mimicry, I fear reading the master essayists, for their voices might ring so loudly in my ears that I would be unable to hear my own voice or find my own style as an essayist. Losing myself in the thinking and style of others is problematic, if as Harris and others suggest, "authorial presence" is a central characteristic of the personal essay. As Harris (1996) puts it,

> The immediate effect of the successful personal essay is simply the consciousness of participating in an individual way of looking at things, of savoring the striking or pungent phrasing that gives force to the author's individual point of view, or of pursuing fresh thoughts of one's own for which the unique mental organization of the author has somehow been a catalyst. (936)

To appear reasonable I must acknowledge that Schubert's advice to read the masters points to an important issue: if one claims to be writing or inquiring within a particular genre, one should know something of its traditions and conventions. At the same time, however, it is crucial to cultivate the inner sensibilities that ultimately manifest as "authorial presence." Perhaps, then, a different avenue of preparation for essay writing might be helpful. Consider Ueland's advice to the aspiring writer:

> There is much, much in all of us, but we do not know it. No one ever calls it out of us, unless we are lucky enough to know very intelligent, imaginative, sympathetic people who love us and have the magnanimity to encourage us, to believe in us, by listening, by praise, by appreciation, by laughing. . . .
>
> If you are going to write you must become aware of this richness in you and come to believe in it and know it is there so that you can write opulently and with self-trust. If you once become aware of it, have faith in it, you will be all right. But it is like this: if you have a million dollars in the bank and don't know it, it doesn't do you any good. (Ueland 1938, 148)

When I immerse myself in the writing of great essayists and noted curriculum theorists, I lose this sense of inner richness. Any incipient feelings of self-trust are swept away in waves of self-doubt. Who am I to think I can write like these giants? What can I possibly add to the curriculum conversations that hasn't already been said with greater scholarship and elegance? Who would want to read my humble musings? What value does my experience with curriculum have in comparison with those who work at the national and international level? When I contemplate the writings of noted curriculum theorists, I despair of ever having anything important to say about curriculum. Again, Ueland expresses the feeling quite eloquently:

> It is because of the critics, the doubters (in the outer world and within ourselves) that we have such hesitancy when we write. And I know the hesitancy just mars it. And it does not make it better at all.
>
> As I write this I many times have had the chilling feeling come around my heart because of the thought: "What if it may not be true? People will say I am crazy. Where is my logic? I haven't a Ph.D. in philosophy or psychology." (Ueland 1938, 174)

Well, I do have a Ph.D., and I still fall prey to such debilitating doubts, doubts that are exacerbated by the haunting refrain "don't run the risk of naïveté." More energizing is the stance advocated by Ueland:

> I believe now in speaking from myself, as I want you to do when you write. Don't keep marshaling thoughts like: "I must prove it."
>
> You don't have to prove it by citing scientific examples, by comparing and all. Say it. If it is true to you, it is true. Another truth may take its place later. What comes truly from me is true, whether anybody believes it or not. It is my truth.
>
> Therefore, when you write, speak with complete self-trust and do not timidly qualify and feel the ice of well authenticated literary usage and critical soundness—so afraid when you have finished writing that they will riddle you full of holes.
>
> Let them. Later if you find what you wrote isn't true, accept the new truth. Consistency is the horror of the world. (Ueland 1938, 174–75)

"That's all well and good," my friend Noreen would counter. "However, good scholarly writing does entail warranting one's ideas as well as placing one's thinking within a tradition of discourse. It is not enough to state uninformed opinions." This concern brings me back to the other point of speculation I mentioned above—having something to say.

Having Something to Say

Schubert advises would-be essayists to have something important to say about curriculum matters. The cautions against naïveté and solipsism evoke within me the question, "Is what I have to say important?" This question, however, is premature, for it leapfrogs over a more fundamental question: "What do I want to say?" Ueland's encouragement to write authentically and with self-trust frees me to risk putting my thoughts on paper. Fear of my own banality can suspend me in a state of perpetual preparation, for there will always be more to read, more to study, more to learn. Neutralizing the paralysis associated with prejudging everything and anything I might have to say depends upon several critical sensibilities.

First, I must accept that writing and thinking are recursive and reciprocal processes. Each draft allows me to see new possibilities; each essay opens onto more pathways beckoning for exploration. "Completed" essays are only resting points in an ongoing inquiry. I take as givens that new truths will continue to emerge for me and that the search for these new truths will entail iterative cycles of writing.

Second, I am propelled toward unrecognized truths through processes of discursive deliberation. I belong to two writing groups where I can receive supportive, yet critical, responses—not to my writing, but to my thinking.

Through these deliberative exchanges, I confront the limitations of my current understandings and am drawn to new ways of seeing and thinking.

Third, I must be vigilant against making claims that overreach the experiential context and the genre within which I write. Sometimes the experiential context might consist solely of reflections on personal life events, as, for example, in an essay called "Lessons from Art Class" in which I portray my anxiety about learning to draw. In this essay, the "experiential context" is broader, including personal efforts at writing, literature on the essay as a genre, and over twenty-five years of conversation with Noreen about curriculum. Still, in framing this as a personal essay, I make no claims to broadly generalizable knowledge or truth, as I shall discuss later. But first, I want to touch on the last sensibility which focuses on the issue of audience. Determining the importance of one's ideas cannot be accomplished in a vacuum. Nor can the determination of naiveté. Consideration of audience interconnects my compulsion to write, hearing myself think, and having something to say.

Considering My Audience

I suggested above that asking, "Is what I have to say important?" leapfrogs over the more fundamental question of "What do I want to say?" Now I would like to suggest that that question is also incomplete, for it begs the question, "Important to whom?" Perhaps it is solipsistic, but first and foremost what I write must be important to me; if I don't care about the ideas, why would I expect anyone else to?

Claiming the stance of personal essayist symbolized a declaration of independence from the utilitarian writing I had done for most of my professional life. I could no longer accept the illusion that writing functionalist memos, accountability-oriented administrative reports, and rational-technical curriculum plans was meaningful or fulfilling. The personal essay as a genre grants me license to explore myself in relation to life experiences, including my connections and disconnections with others.

Often, my sense of disconnection from those with whom I work as teacher or curriculum consultant activates my need to write. This need points to another audience to whom I write. In *The Tact of Teaching*, van Manen (1991) calls attention to the "pedagogical moment," to situations that are "pedagogically charged because something is expected of the adult" (40). I envy those who always seem ready and able to respond in the pedagogical moment. Too often, I find myself at a loss for words, my thoughts an incoherent jumble. Even if I manage a response on the spur of the moment, I'm likely to feel it was incomplete or slightly off the mark. So I replay the conversations, trying to figure out what I could have said or should have said; trying to figure out how to bridge the gulf between my way of thinking about curriculum and the thinking of others; trying to figure out how to mend the breaches in relationships that come from misspoken ideas and misunderstandings. My imagined co-conversationalists in these exchanges that have gone awry serve as my audience. I often write with a particular person in mind, striving to express in my essay what I failed to communicate during a real-time exchange. Thus, the act of essay writing externalizes the conversations that play endlessly in my mind. This, too, is characteristic of the personal essay as a genre, for as Lopate (1994) observes, "Personal essayists converse with the reader because they are already having dialogues and disputes with themselves (xxiv).

Lopate also suggests, "The conversational dynamic—the desire for contact—is ingrained in the form and serves to establish a quick emotional intimacy with the audience" (1994, xxv). Regardless of whether my readers experience this sense of intimacy, I do, and I find it cathartic. Schubert, in building the case for the essay as a form of curriculum inquiry, reflects on the centrality of public space to curriculum concerns. He speculates:

> A public space essentially refers to a community of growth through liberating dialogue and open communication. If the essay is a form of writing that relates to the public space, and if curriculum . . . represents a striving to build a public space, then it would seem that there exists a compatibility of substantive concern and form of expression in the joining of curriculum and essay. (Schubert 1991, 68)

Much of my consulting on curriculum is with higher education faculty in schools of the health professions (e.g., pharmacy) whose teaching is grounded in the natural and biomedical sciences, who have minimal interest and little time for extended deliberations about processes of teaching and learning. Despite repeated calls for educational reform in health professions education, curriculum still tends to be equated with the organization of disciplinary subject matter into lecture notes or handouts. Despite my longing for liberating dialogue and open communication about curriculum matters (e.g., what is worth teaching; how is authentic learning engendered and supported within licensure-driven curricula), I frequently feel marginalized and silenced. The writing of personal essays has become a way for me to create a public space in which to share my thinking. For although I often write with a particular person in mind, by sharing my essays, I make an effort to reach out to broader audiences. This leads to several speculations on the nature of knowledge embodied in personal essays.

On the Nature and Value of Knowledge in the Personal Essay

My point of departure for thinking about the personal essay lies within the opening sentence of Schubert's essay: "To claim that the philosophical essay can be a form of curriculum inquiry requires the characterization of the essay as a form of rhetoric embodying speculative or personal knowledge" (1991, 61). Schubert's wedding of personal knowledge with the literary genre of essay evoked a sense of excitement and possibility within me. Almost instantaneously and unconsciously, I reframed Schubert's genre of *philosophical essay* into *personal essay*. On one hand, this might be seen as a cavalier misreading of Schubert's text. I prefer, however, to see it as a manifestation of Schubert's notion that the reader of essays is not only invited to share the journey of the essayist but to "pursue other journeys at the same time" (Schubert 1991, 70). Still, it is worth considering the nature and value of knowledge put forward in a personal (as compared to philosophical) essay.

Schwab (1969), in a now-classic essay on the need for the practical in curriculum inquiry, asserts that "curriculum is brought to bear not on ideal or abstract representations but on the real thing, on the concrete case in all its completeness and with all its differences from all other concrete cases on which the theoretic abstraction is silent" (108). The genre of the *philosophical* essay pushes my writing away from the concrete toward more abstract, formal, and propositional knowledge: lived experience, having provided the springboard for inquiry, recedes to the background. By contrast, the personal essay maintains a focus on the specifics of experience which, as Schwab suggests, lies at the heart of curriculum. Good (1988), in tracing the historical development of the essay as a genre, contends, "Empirical science aims to be cumulative and progressive, though in a critical and selective way, preserving and building only on proven observations and laws. The essay does not aim at system at all; its empirical data are used in a much more limited way" (3). Good goes on to draw rather sharp distinctions between the personal essay and discipline-based inquiry and writing, including the thesis and the scientific article. In claiming the personal essay as a mode of curriculum inquiry, I am not sure that the distinctions are as clear and fixed as Good suggests. I do, however, resonate with his observation that the "truth of the essay is a limited truth, limited by the concrete experience, itself limited, which gave rise to it. The essay is a provisional reflection of an ephemeral experience of an event or object" (Good 1988, 7).

Harris (1996) and Lopate (1994) also stress the provisional, tentative, and reflective qualities of thinking and writing characteristic of the personal essay. As a genre of writing and inquiry, then, the personal essay suits my desire to express and explore the uncertainties of curriculum work. The aim of these explorations is not to arrive at universal abstractions about what content should be taught, how it should be taught, or how curriculum should be developed. Rather, my aim is for deeper understanding of who I am and what I am able to bring to the pedagogical moments in which I strive to enact curriculum in concert with others. This centers my curriculum inquiries on what I don't know. As Lopate notes:

> Personal essayists are adept at interrogating their ignorance. Just as often as they tell us what they know, they ask at the beginning of an exploration of a problem what it is they don't know—and why. They follow the clue of their ignorance through the maze. Intrigued with their limitations, both physical and mental, they are attracted to cul-de-sac: what one doesn't understand, or can't do, is as good a place as any to start investigating the borders of the self. (1994, xxvii)

This quest for personal understanding may seem of little value to those who long for a science of curriculum. I am reminded of colleagues who also work in schools of health professions and whose research strives to demonstrate conclusively that some curriculum innovation will result in more effective learning outcomes for students. This rational technical ontology of curriculum practice values, in turn, a scientific epistemology.

I cannot claim the understandings I gain through the writing of personal essays as scientific knowledge, for they are not reliable, valid, or generalizable within the conventions of scientific research. The inquiry itself is not replicable, nor does it rely on strict adherence to specific procedures for the collection and analysis of data to warrant its truth claims. Rather, as Lopate (1994) suggests, "At the core of the personal essay is the supposition that there is a certain unity to human experience" (xxiii). This unity affords the possibility of shared knowing, not through verifiable generalizations of science, but through universal chords of aesthetic expression.

A well-conceived, well-crafted personal essay creates possibilities for experiential connections between author and reader. A sense of connection may be established as an essayist's experience evokes memories of a similar experience in a reader. Or a connection may be vicarious, grounded in a reader's empathetic response to an author's experience. In either case, *personal experience*, not scientific evidence or philosophical argument, sets the stage for understanding.

Schwandt (1999) draws from the work of Gadamer (1989) and Kerdeman (1998) to argue for the relational and existential nature of understanding, an understanding that

> requires an openness to experience, a willingness to engage in a dialogue with that which challenges our self-understanding. To be in a dialogue requires that we listen to the Other and simultaneously risk confusion and uncertainty both about ourselves and about the other person we seek to understand. (Schwandt 1999, 459)

Within this notion of relational understanding lies the possibility of transformation as I gain new insights into myself and new perspectives about those with whom I strive to enact curriculum. Transformative possibilities arise for readers who resonate with the ways in which I portray and probe my personal experiences with curriculum. It should be noted that transformations need not lie in a reader's agreement with understandings I derive from my inquiries; indeed, their transformations may occur as they depart from my own avenues of thinking. In any event, the knowledge that accrues through the personal essay as a mode of curriculum inquiry is not the grand stuff of hard science.

As I was working on this essay, I had an opportunity to hear an internationally renowned biochemist talk about cutting-edge research on methods for the early detection of cancer. The challenge in this form of research, he explained, is like finding a needle in a haystack. To be successful a diagnostic test must be reliable in two ways. First, it must indicate that cancer is lurking somewhere in the body; second, it must differentiate as precisely as possible the type and location of the cancer. Without this level of precision and reliability, the economic, clinical, and emotional costs of searching through the haystack are too great.

As I listened to this researcher, I marveled at the creativity of his thinking. Already he had evidence suggesting that a drop of blood might be sufficient for clinical diagnosis of cancer. Using his knowledge of biochemistry, he is designing laboratory experiments to zero in on minute protein patterns that correspond to various forms of cancer. His quest is a quest of "hard science": a quest for certainty.

I think it is safe to say that those of us who are haunted by the specter of cancer wish this scientist and his team of investigators speedy success. Indeed, his passionate belief in the promise of this research caused one member of the audience to murmur, "It makes me want to be a scientist." I identify with this wishful longing—to be on a quest of heroic proportions—to aid in the eradication of cancer, if not in our lifetime, in our children's. This is heady, seductive inquiry. Working as I do in the world of health professions education, I feel its siren call. But the truth is, I am not a scientist and to pretend otherwise is to be inauthentic. This issue of authenticity brings me to a final speculation—the "fit" between my way-of-being in practice and my way-of-being in inquiry.

Ontological Fit between Practice and Inquiry

Labaree (1998), in a thoughtful analysis of traditional hierarchies of knowledge within the academy, contrasts the hard knowledge of scientific research with the "lesser form of knowledge" generated through educational research. In an interesting conceptual turn, Labaree then points out the "softness" of all forms of knowledge:

> In the past decade or two, there has been a strong and highly effective series of attacks on positivism and on the validity of quantitative research. This process has been played out in a wide range of fields, beginning with the philosophy of science and moving eventually into education. . . . [T]he consensus has shifted toward a position that asserts the essential softness of hard knowledge and the essential uncertainty at the core of the validity claims made by the hard sciences. (1998, 11)

Labaree's comments on the privileging of hard science remind me of my attempts to demonstrate the scientific rigor of my grounded theory dissertation (Piantanida 1982). At the time, I drew upon the work of Guba and Lincoln (1981) to construct what Smith and Heshusius (1986) describe as a "logic of justification" for my research procedures. I was pretty pleased with my efforts until a mutual acquaintance arranged for me to have dinner with Egon Guba. In the course of a remarkably awkward evening, Guba made only one comment about my dissertation: "You're more of a positivist than you think," he pronounced. I was too devastated, too embarrassed to ask what he meant. For the first ten years after that meeting, I chafed with re-sentiment over his dismissal of my thinking. In the subsequent decade, I've been grappling with the accuracy of his observation. These more humble and humbling musings have driven home the importance of sorting through the way my mode of inquiry is congruent with my mode of practice. What unites the two is not the use of particular method, but rather the worldview that I embody. As van Manen (1977) suggests, "underlying every orientation is a definite epistemology, axiology and ontology, i.e., a person's orientation is composed of what he believes to be true, to be valuable, and to be real" (21).

I skate on thin conceptual ice if I purport to hold forth philosophically about the notions of ontology, epistemology, and axiology. Instead, I try to be mindful of how I relate to others in my curriculum practice as well as in my inquiries into that practice. The reality of curriculum, I've come to believe, lies within each person. My curriculum plans, no matter how well conceived or executed, are still only that—my imaginings of what might happen during an educational encounter. The reality of what happens lies in the meanings that individuals make of their experience within that encounter. I can neither predict nor control what those meanings will be. I can only hope. Whether these hopes are fulfilled—or even justified—entails careful attention to what learners are willing to reveal about their meaning-making.

The "truth" about these personal meanings is not discerned by treating others as objects, nor by assuming I understand them better than they understand themselves. If I am worthy of learners' trust, they may enter into a discursive relationship with me, and through our discursive exchanges I may be privileged to gain some insight into their truths about the curriculum as they have lived it. These insights hold transformative possibilities for how I think about, plan, and enact curricula in the future.

If, as I believe, the reality (ontology) and truth (epistemology) of curriculum lie within individuals, what is the point of curriculum inquiry? Of what value are personal insights into ephemeral educational encounters? In grappling with these questions, I find Schwandt's (2001) discussion of responsiveness in evaluation practice to be illuminating:

> Responsiveness is also (and perhaps primarily) something like an *epistemic and moral virtue*—a particular kind of human excellence that we strive for in our efforts to understand others and the social world. . . . Responsiveness has an epistemic aspect because it is about "knowing" others; it also has a moral dimension because responsiveness . . . is concerned with "what it is good to be" as a human being. As an epistemic and moral virtue, responsiveness is a distinctive capacity for, or way of, interpretively moving about the world. . . . Responsiveness is a quality or virtue we

strive for in all human endeavors like evaluating, teaching, administering, providing social services, and so on. (74–75, italics in original)

Drawing upon Aristotle's notion of *phronesis*, Schwandt goes on to argue that responsiveness entails a capacity for discernment or wise judgment, which he explains "requires bringing together two sets of considerations simultaneously. . . . On one hand, one *always attends first and foremost to the concrete or situational particulars of the immediate case.* On the other hand, one brings into view principles, goods, criteria, standing commitments, and the like" (2001, 78, italics added).

The cancer researcher, working in his laboratory, has the luxury of framing the situational particulars of immediate cases as "extraneous variables" and then factoring them out of experiments designed to ferret out generalizations applicable to large populations. As a curriculum practitioner, I do not have this luxury, for it would create an ontological rupture between my research and my practice: in my research I would be relating to others as objects whose individuality (and humanity) is stripped away, while in my practice I would be striving for responsiveness to individuals within specific pedagogical moments. The personal essay as a mode of inquiry affords an ontological congruence between practice and inquiry by focusing my attention on situational particulars. By appreciating the particulars, I hope to increase my capacity for discernment and wise judgment. To the extent to which my personal essays evoke a responsive chord in readers, they, too, might gain insights that lead to wiser judgments.

Note

1. For an extensive critique of rational technical approaches to professions education, see Schon 1983 and 1987.

References

Gadamer, H-G. 1989. *Truth and method.* 2nd rev. ed. Trans. J. Weinsheimer and D. G. Marshall. New York: Crossroad.
Good, G. 1988. *The observing self: Rediscovering the essay.* New York: Routledge.
Guba, E. G., and Y. S. Lincoln. *Effective evaluation.* San Francisco: Jossey-Bass.
Harris, W. V. 1996. Reflections on the peculiar status of the personal essay. *College English* 58, no. 8: 934–53.
Kerdeman, D. 1998. Hermeneutics and education: Understanding, control, and agency. *Educational Theory* 48, no. 2: 241–66.

Labaree, D. F. 1998. Educational researchers: Living with a lesser form of knowledge. *Educational Researcher* 27, no. 8: 4–12.

Lopate, P. 1994. *The art of the personal essay: An anthology from the classical era to the present.* New York: Anchor Books.

Piantanida, M. 1982. *The practice of hospital education: A grounded theory study.* UMI ProQuest Digital Dissertation #ATT 8317299.

Schon, D. A. 1983. *The reflective practitioner: How professionals think in action.* New York: Basic Books.

———. 1987. *Educating the reflective practitioner: Toward a new design for teaching and learning in the professions.* San Francisco: Jossey-Bass.

Schubert, W. H. 1991. Philosophical inquiry: The speculative essay. In *Forms of Curriculum Inquiry*, ed. Edmund C. Short, 61–76. Albany: State University of New York Press.

Schwab, J. 1969. The practical: A language for curriculum. In *The curriculum studies reader*, eds. D. J. Flinders and S. J. Thorton, 101–119. New York: Routledge.

Schwandt, T. A. 1999. On understanding understanding. *Qualitative Inquiry* 5, no. 4: 451–64.

———. 2001. Responsiveness and everyday life. In *Responsive Evaluation, New Directions for Evaluation*, eds. J. G. Greene and T. A. Abma. 73–88. San Francisco: Jossey-Bass.

Smith, J. K., and L. Heshusius. 1986. Closing down the conversation: The end of the quantitative-qualitative debate among educational inquirers. *Educational Researcher* 15, no. 1: 4–12.

Ueland, B. 1938. *If you want to write: A book about art, independence and spirit.* Saint Paul, MN: Graywolf Press.

van Manen, M. 1991. *The tact of teaching: The meaning of pedagogical thoughtfulness.* Albany: State University of New York Press.

———. 1997. Linking ways of knowing with ways of being practical. *Curriculum Inquiry* 6, no. 3: 205–28.

CHAPTER 13

Narrative Yearnings: Reflecting in Time through the Art of Fictive Story

Patricia L. McMahon

> The tectonic layers of our lives rest so tightly one on top of the other that we always come up against earlier events in later ones, not as matter that has been fully formed and pushed aside, but absolutely present and alive.
>
> Schlink 1997, 217

When I was in the midst of writing my dissertation (McMahon 1993) over a decade ago, I could not have imagined how my narrative study would come to be the touchstone inquiry upon which I would build an understanding of my past, present, and future life as a teacher. Since that time, I have written to explore my relationship with narrative and have come to a much fuller awareness that narrative is more than a research method by which I pursue specific inquiries to inform my thinking about educative issues. Narrative is also the means by which I articulate my way of being in the classroom and therefore lies at the root of my ontological orientation. I am continuously interpreting and recreating both my pedagogy and myself through narrative. Over the years, I have experimented with my natural tendency to apprehend experience through story by writing fictive representations of what transpires in the classroom. I do not wish to claim these stories as corresponding to some reality; in fact, because I conceive experience as story, I am more comfortable reflecting from my authorial stance, one that enables me to assume an inquiring eye. Such a stance does not bind me to chronological time. I am free to explore the dilemmas, contradictions, and ambiguities that arise in the classroom, and I am compelled to make connections between my research method, my teaching, and my way of being in the world. In one section of this chapter, I include one of my fictive stories about teaching and, embedded in that story, I refer to others I have written. I suppose this chapter in its entirety is a larger representation of my ongoing relationship with narrative, specifically literary narrative (Brodsky 1987). By this I mean my use of fiction as a means of coming to know.

Time, Space and the Need to Story

Philosophers speak of events in our lives as marking the passage of time; I feel this passage through a teacher's sensibilities. Each semester brings new faces, fresh beginnings, revised curricula, and a renewed energy for inquiry and discovery, for embracing pedagogical moments[1] (van Manen 1991). But because I am so aware of time as an unfolding story, a story of the teacher I am and the teacher I wish to become for my students as we interact in the deeply meaningful enterprise of teaching and learning, each new semester is also a reminder of the past and a signpost to the future. The space I occupy in this endeavor is seemingly miniscule when I think about what Ricoeur refers to as "cosmic time—the time of the world that unfolds as a sequence of uniform, qualitatively undifferentiated moments in which all change occurs."[2] I am sure that my need to story events from my teaching life is partly a response to my existential sense of mortality; through literary narrative, I assuage the vast expanse of cosmic time, and "temporality becomes interpretable in human terms. Time is made human; narrative is a condition of temporal experience" (Richardson 1990, 2).

Viewed this way, so much of my perception of time is informed by the space I inhabit within the context of my practice of teaching and researching—my[3] professional knowledge landscape.[4] My desire to story significant episodes from my practice emanates from a wish to discern what underlying meaning resides in the often intricate sequence of events that transpire on any given day. Robinson and Hawpe (1986) explain that "stories are a means for interpreting or reinterpreting events by constructing a causal pattern which integrates that which is known about an event as well as that which is conjectural but relevant to an interpretation" (112).

Inclination and Reflecting on Moments of Learning

My existential angst aside, I am also powerfully motivated to tell stories simply because it is my nature. In this regard I am no different from any other person except perhaps in degree. All human beings are both consumers of stories and storytellers, and so the potential for story is everywhere. In my family, story was a spontaneous means of conveying information and making observations about all facets of life. I grew up listening to the many stories of my parents and grandparents, aunts and uncles, delighting in their ability to dramatically render plot lines not only of momentous occasions but also of the more common incidents from daily life. In the process of telling their stories, these familial storytellers revealed their desire to be understood and to connect with their listeners and their need to work out connections among seemingly discrete incidents that somehow led to a particular conclusion. They were organizing knowledge through the interpretive lens of story. For someone like me, immersed in the fictive lives of an endless stream of characters from novels and short stories, the result was powerful. From a very early age, narrative became my primary means of making sense of the world. I developed a heightened appreciation not only for the power of story to render experience, but also for the potential for drama in everyday life.

All these years later, I feel this sense of drama most profoundly in the classroom when my students and I engage in inquiry in order to make meaning. Each student has his or her unique part to play in the process of discovery. About the "drama of the classroom," Garman (1991) tells us, "Learning happens when the events of the classroom unfold, when participants feel the nuance of conflict and motive, dissonance and emotion, as part of the intellectual process . . . they must feel their own sense of belongingness, their own place in the drama" (280).

It is incumbent upon the teacher to facilitate such dynamic educational encounters. The drama is what transpires in the moment, but that moment has both a history and a legacy that are equally dramatic: a space in the past as I remember what learning has come before in order to build a sense of momentum—and a space in the future as I envision a multiplicity of places we might reach as a result of our work together. So much of a teacher's knowledge is "event structured" (Carter and Doyle 1987, cited in Carter 1993, 7). For me, there is no better way to access the significance of these educative events than through story, which inherently captures the element of time.

Polkinghorne (1997) tells us that "narrative transforms a mere succession of actions and events into a coherent whole in which these happenings gain meaning as contributors to a common purpose" (13). But attaining coherence from the spontaneity of an educational encounter is possible only if the teacher regards those learning moments as the epicenter of her research. "The sense of coherence," Bochner (1997) reminds us, "does not inhere in the events themselves. Coherence is an achievement, not a given" (429). The teacher becomes the conduit for coherency when "the meanings of events flows [sic] from their appearance in the researcher's reflections on them from the perspective of what has happened" (Schon, 1983, cited in Polkinghorne, 1997, 15). My ability to reflect on classroom interaction is crucial, then, to my understanding the significance of what has occurred.

Reflecting on a Method of Inquiry

The interpretive lens through which I view my practice has enabled me to explore my natural tendency to story events from my teaching life. For more than a few years, I have been writing literary narratives, or fictive representations, of what transpires in the classroom. Most of these reflections could best be described as "mildly" fictional, or what Barone (1995) terms "weakly" fictional texts. In other words, these texts are not "created solely out of [my] imagination" (Barone 1995, 175), as are other reflections of mine, texts that I refer to as "wildly" fictive. All of my stories, be they mildly or "wildly" fictive, are borne of difficulty; as Pinar says, "whatever difficulty exists, there is a story behind it, often 'whole, bright, deep with understanding' " (1981, 173–88). I write because I am trying to reach a place of understanding. I am working out a teaching problem that presents itself to me in a way I cannot ignore or define. Something has created a dissonance within me, but I am not sure enough to label what it is exactly, because it seems complicated or because it presents itself to me as uncomplicated. Either way, I do not want to rush to terminology that does not reflect the layers of meaning I suspect lie beneath the interactions of the classroom. I want to write my way into understanding what it is I feel and think about the situation. I write my literary narratives because, in doing so, I come face to face with the nature of my unrest.

Eisner (1985) tells us that "all experience is the product of both the features of the world and the biography of the individual" (25). When I explore the trouble I sometimes collide with in the classroom, I feel that I really am digging in to see myself more clearly as well, and I want to see myself as clearly as possible, because, as Palmer (1998) states, "We teach who we are" (1). If my stories are to be of any worth to me, I must be authentic in both my portrayal of the felt experience and my interpretation of it. I should note here that an integral part of both my mildly and wildly fictive pieces is my interrogation of the fiction for meaning. In other words, as I write my interpretation of a fictive story, it becomes an extension of the story itself, because it is there, in my interpretation of the story, that I have my moments of illumination. My fictional portrayal of events speaks to me, and I am able to see something I previously could not, and in this sense, there really is the feel of a narrative arc for me. I, the teacher narrator, make a discovery. The discovery may be subtle or profound, but writing literary narratives enables me to conceptualize knowledge, knowledge often submerged at the tacit level of understanding, tough to access because it is accompanied by pain or confusion.

I wholeheartedly agree that "researching difficulty through narrative is self-work; the narratives constitute a kind of daily, practical, if lyric, philosophy" (Zwicky cited in Fowler 2003, 165). Gradually, I have become aware that my affinity for writing in storied form as a method of inquiry is directly related to what, I am coming to realize, is the essence of my ontological orientation, an ontological orientation so deeply rooted in narrative that as I explore what confuses or concerns me in my teaching life, I sense "a congruence between the topic and the method of inquiry" itself (Oberg 2003, 126). It seems that my fictive portrayals of difficult teaching and learning moments inevitably lead me to explore concepts of time and space, the very stuff of literary narrative.

Image and Story

Often, my decision to create imaginative renderings of what occurs in the classroom provokes questions about journaling instead. My response must begin with some commentary about the power of image, specifically as it is defined by Fleckenstein (2002):

> An image—regardless of whether it is mental, graphic, or verbal—consists of an array of relationships that marks or punctuates an unknowable reality in a particular way. Counterintuitive though it may seem, neither graphic, mental, nor verbal imagery is a thing; instead, all imagery consists of a pattern of mutually creating folds crafted by a metaphoric logic. (6)

Journaling does not afford me the fluidity of movement I need to be emotionally present in the images attached to my teaching experiences. For that, I must rely on the conventions of fiction as a means of capturing design and pattern in the texture of classroom interactions. I am compelled toward reflection by the sights, thoughts, and sounds of teaching that I absorb and store in my memory. Writing techniques such as plot, conflict, dialogue, and point of view work together to slow down the pace of how I play back classroom scenes in my mind's eye. By making the invisible visible, I notice connections, draw parallels, and reveal nuances, and so the everyday moments of life in the classroom take on a heightened sense of clarity. Journaling tends to keep me to a chronological order; I think about classroom events in a linear way bound by the realities of "school time." This view of time, according to Laidlaw and Sumara (2000), "usually occurs within educational settings, often embodies Cartesian notions and demonstrates the Newtonian clockwork understanding of the universe (or certainly the 'universe' of schooling)" (11). Significantly, this conception of time "influences and determines the ways in which pedagogy is structured, enacted, and experienced" (Laidlaw and Sumara 2000, 11). To this I would add that it may also determine how a teacher *reflects* on what takes place in the classroom.

I first began thinking about this a few years ago in the midst of writing the following mildly fictive story about one of my students. This next section is a story of my interactions with a student teacher. It is important to keep in mind that my insights about our interactions are also part of this story.

Reflecting in Time: 'Storying' as a Mode of Teacher Inquiry

A few years ago, while working with a small group of student teachers on their portfolios, I became aware of something that both surprised and concerned me: I saw no evidence of reflection in the journals they were keeping about their student teaching experience. I first became aware of this during an onsite conference with one of these students. When I asked where her reflective journal was, she pointed to the section in her huge binder I had just reviewed. "You just read it," she said quietly.

"Oh," I said, hoping I had read too quickly, but knowing otherwise. When I looked back at Kim, she looked me straight in the eye and stated,

"I'm not really sure about how to reflect. My methods instructor sometimes talked about it, but I never really understood what she wanted reflection to look like in a journal. I'm not reflecting, am I?" She looked troubled.

Our conversation was the start of a series of group mini-lessons devoted to the subject of reflecting through writing.

The next time I visited Kim, she proudly opened her binder to her journal. "I think you'll see that I am really reflecting now," she announced. While her entries were noticeably longer, they were only slightly more reflective than they were the first time I read them.

"Well," I said, "what you've got here is a pretty lengthy explanation of what occurred during each of your classes, and I notice you also indicate moments in your lessons when you had to revise your original lesson plan, and sometimes you say you were 'surprised' or 'upset' about something. Without a doubt this is a valuable record of the progression of your lessons, but..."

Before I could continue, an exasperated, worried Kim cut in, "But I'm still not reflecting! Darn it! I am never going to understand how to do this!"

I began to fear that *my* concern about her writing had now become hers, and I felt the need to stop what I sensed was an insidious momentum building in her mind, one that might distract her from what she really was doing so well—teaching.

"Listen," I said, "let me ask you something, Kim. Are you getting anything out of your journal? Is it working for you in any way?"[5]

Looking guarded, she replied, "Well, I can't imagine planning my lesson for the next day without doing the kind of writing I'm doing now in this journal. It helps me to get everything down and just honestly write about what I did. Once I write about what happened during the day and see what I did, I'm able to move on to start thinking about the next day."

"Then, for now, that's good enough for me," I said. "Let's take this one step at a time. In time, you may want to revisit some of these entries, maybe at the end of the semester, but for now, because your journal seems to be working for you, keep doing what you feel you need to do."

What I needed to remember in my interactions with Kim is that an individual cannot summon reflection to occur. Kim was doing what novice teachers do. She was stuck in time. Her journal was a "frank transcription of experience" (Ricoeur 1984, 12) in which she adhered to a chronological sequencing of events in order to replay the effectiveness of her lesson planning. As a more seasoned teacher, I have a very different perspective of time; in fact, when I write, perhaps because I story my memories of classroom events, I am aware of time as a "quality." As Lightman (1993) describes it,

> In a world where time is a quality ... events glide through the space of the imagination, materialized by a look, a desire. Likewise, the time between two events is long or short, depending on the background of contrasting events, the intensity of illumination, the degree of light and shadow, the view of the participants. (127)

The idea of time as a quality resonates with me. It becomes a certain ineffable feeling of which I am sometimes aware when I am in the classroom teaching. Time as a quality is an accessory to the act of reflection; it can filter out extraneous occurrence. For some of us, what remains is an invitation to reflect through story.

Fictionalizing events from my professional life allows me to think about those events in a way that would not be possible were I to produce a nonfiction account. In shifting to a form of representation that privileges an aesthetic way of knowing, I am able to inquire into an experience as a result of creating "a structure ... that gives rise to feeling" (Eisner 1985, 27). For me, story provides that structure. This is especially true, I think, when an experience is unsettling or scary, when there is a lingering angst associated with that experience, or when a particular classroom occurrence haunts my thoughts, signifying relevance, demanding me to deconstruct its import. Story, then, is both the result of capturing the emotional texture of my interior landscape and the means by which I make instinct and intuition explicit in order to construe meaning. Much of my need to write literary narratives emanates from my wish to endow a sense of wholeness to the disturbing bits and pieces of emotional residue of memory.

In writing my brief portrayal of Kim's attempts at reflective journaling, I began to understand that my perspective of time as a quality may very well be the reason I find myself writing *mildly* fictive stories about some teaching episodes and *wildly* fictive stories about others. I often wondered how or why I make this decision when attempting to capture the essence of classroom events. What does it mean that some of my stories in no way mirror lived events while others do? If I use Kim as a guide, I can work my way through this question. As a novice teacher, Kim was bound to the chronology of events as they actually occurred because for the first time she was a teacher, knee-deep in the demands of real-time classroom action. She was, more precisely, a student teacher recording her experiences, her version of reflecting, because she was getting ready to plan the next day's lesson. For Kim, time was a very literal translation of reality. She quite literally needed to reflect in time in order to be prepared for the following day. I am beginning to suspect that I write mildly fictionalized stories for much the same reason.

Let me use an example as a means of clarifying my thinking. A number of years ago, I wrote a story entitled "May Have Trouble Seeing" about a student of mine named Margaret. Margaret created a scene in class one day, and I was the target of her emotional outburst. I was so upset and confused about the incident that for days I was unable to think of much else. Her behavior seemed inexplicable. I could not shake the memory of Margaret, who had stopped attending class, from my mind. Soon afterwards, I found myself writing a mildly fictive narrative about the episode and the days leading up to it. I want to stress that, despite my labeling it as mildly fictive, the story I wrote about Margaret completely adheres to what I consider the essential ingredients of all fiction. I conveyed my experience by using language that is, in Richardson's (1994) words, "metaphorical and evocative" (521). In fiction, Richardson suggests, by "using dramatic recall, strong metaphors, images, characters, unusual phrasings, puns, subtexts, and allusions, the writer constructs a sequence of events, a 'plot,' holding back on interpretation, asking the reader to 'relive' the events emotionally with the writer" (1994, 521).

As I interpreted my story about Margaret, I was able to see why this student acted the way she did, and I was also able to understand my own culpability. Ultimately, it was a story of two individuals unable to connect because their assumptions about one another, though perhaps benign, kept them moving on different planes of perception.

In the story, I offer Margaret an invitation to think creatively, which she sees as an opportunity to write a shockingly disturbing essay filled with violent imagery and hatred directed at her family. As a reader, I am mortified by the graphic display of malevolence; as her teacher, I am deeply concerned about her frame of mind. I am also confused, because Margaret's essay seems so far removed from the intent of the actual writing assignment. Not knowing exactly how to respond in writing to her, I choose to be brief and direct. At the bottom of her paper, I simply state, "If it is your intention to pass this class, you will need to do the assignment you were given." I didn't want to write anything else; I wanted to talk with Margaret. I was sure we could have a conversation after class to clear up any misunderstanding.

Despite the strangeness of what she had written, I felt I knew Margaret. She was extreme in her likes and dislikes and in her passion for self-expression. Here was a person, I reminded myself, who had covered her textbook with a photocopied picture of Frida Kahlo's painting "Self-Portrait with a Thorn Necklace and Hummingbird." I thought I understood the dramatic quality of her expression. I did not want to extinguish Margaret's fire; I just wanted her to be more aware of when it was safe to burn.

But my written note to her destroys any chance for communication. Margaret feels as though she's been betrayed by me, that her unique expression of emotion has been rejected by someone she assumed had invited it. I, too, feel betrayed—by the terseness of my own note, which completely eclipses my good intentions and leaves me feeling misinterpreted, and by Margaret's extreme and public reaction to it. By the end of the story, the emotional damage takes its toll; the level of bewilderment and hurt is so deep, there really is no hope for us to see past the wall of misunderstanding we built between us.

"May Have Trouble Seeing" was extremely enlightening to me; it made the invisible web of emotion visible. What might have remained in the realm of intuition surfaced very clearly, in time for me to learn a lesson. I stayed close to the chronology of actual events in this story, because the emotional truth was buried in that time and because I felt a sense of urgency to understand what had happened with Margaret, *in time*, before I inadvertently repeated history.

In this regard, my motivation to write mildly fictive representations is not all that different from my student Kim's need to provide herself with chronological accounts of her teaching. Yes, the writing that we created looks different, but our treatment of time as we reflect on classroom events is similar. Ultimately, Kim was able to see how she could prepare for her next lesson, and I was able to put language to what had previously been an emotional blur so that I did not get stuck in time, recalling unpleasant images from my episodes with Margaret but not understanding their significance. Like Kim, I was able to learn and move on.

Sometimes, however, what happens in the classroom is too unpleasant or too complex to deal with at the time. In these cases, it seems that writing wildly fictive narratives allows me to distance myself and unpack the emotions. Creating stories solely from my imagination gives me this flexibility with time. I am now thinking of a story of mine entitled "Helicopter Man" that was published in the *Journal of Curriculum Theorizing* (McMahon 2000). It bears no resemblance to anything that transpired in the classroom, but it captures the tension existing in the deeper, invisible currents beneath the surface of classroom action. At the heart of this piece are my feelings about one of my students, a man whose behavior both confused and frightened me. Absorbing him into a completely fictional representation of reality, I gained a different view of him because I moved him beyond the classroom space, and in doing so, was able to study him from an unfamiliar perspective. My fictional representation of this student was not tied to the realities of time; he was not bound by any of the familiar trappings of the classroom, nor was he constrained by the explicit and implicit rules governing his behavior. I was able to distill the lessons to be learned by observing his motives in this new setting, from a safe distance. I would not have been afforded this distance had I chosen to write about him in a journal. I felt too threatened by him. Perhaps I did not want to understand him completely when he was still a student sitting in the back of my classroom. But, safe and away from him in my wildly fictionalized setting, I had the freedom to work the image of him any way I chose (McMahon 2000).

I believe that, for me, the potential lesson of a wildly fictive piece of writing is not buried in the actual-time sequence of events. The lesson for me as a teacher lies in the power of my suppressed emotions attached to those events. Emotions do not cooperate with time constraints; they transcend time. Because I do not have to adhere to an actual chronology of experiences when I write wildly fictional narratives, my sense of time filters everything but the intensity of my feelings. What impact, if any, "Helicopter Man" has on a reader should not be measured, therefore, in terms of its capacity to validate actual "real" details about the incidents that took place in the classroom between my student and me, but rather in terms of its potential to convey a verisimilitude about my felt sense of our encounters.

After so many years of teaching and reflecting on my developing pedagogy, my relationship with time is different from what Kim experienced during her student teaching. Kim was building a repertoire of lessons, and she often voiced concern about going "over time" or "falling short on time" in the classroom. Understandably, her writing at this point in her teaching career reflected these matters.

Reflecting in Pedagogical Time: An Authorial Stance

Merleau-Ponty (1962) states that "time is not a real process, not an actual succession that I am content to record. It arises from my relation to things" (412). This conception of time gives me room to reflect on my teaching in a manner more in keeping with who I am and what I believe about the process of learning. Those "arrested moments" (Gallagher 2001, 155) of troubling teaching incidents that I have stored in my mind occasionally bang into other memories—strands of dialogue, visual images, questions, and persons. In confronting the problem a student may represent for me, I instinctively "relinquish linear structure so that . . . experience [can] be examined from many sides, each revealing another response and interpretation" (Grumet 1976, 162). There isn't a sequence or order to my reflection when I am in the midst of a troubling reality, only images that demand my attention. This kind of reflection requires what Anne Michaels refers to as "vertical time." In other words, "each present understanding or experience is embedded within a historical past, and interconnects within a web of memory, within narratives of self. . . . As our interpretations of the world, our interpretations of ourselves, and the interpretations we receive from others shift and evolve, we recreate ourselves" (cited in Laidlaw and Sumara 2000, 20).

In the act of portraying a student such as Margaret, then, I am aware that at the very least I am obliged to interpret my pedagogy, that place where she and I met unsuccessfully. To see Margaret and what she represented and so claim a more conscious understanding of my pedagogy, I turned to my imagination, my use of metaphor, and other conventions of fiction. According to Lepage, "metaphorical telling is like seeing a piece of theatre where there are many levels, where things seem to be connected in a vertical way" (cited in Gallagher 2001, 151). These stagings, according to Gallagher, "[move] up and down rather than across the horizon—[and allow] for . . . contradictions . . . spiritual quests and . . . material realities to co-exist" (2001, 151).

This vertical movement is possible in pedagogical time, which, according to Laidlaw and Sumara (2000), differs from "modernistic understandings of time, experience, and 'self,' where these are viewed as fixed for all intents and purposes, and where the individual is viewed as making a linear progression along a line of development" (19). Fictionalizing events from my life affords me an authorial stance: I am free to sense where the story begins and to make decisions about the sequence of events. I am purposefully crafting the memory of those events in order to locate and explore my inquiry, and in so doing, I gain a clearer perspective of the disturbing experience. I can move freely in pedagogical time.

Story and the Lived Curriculum

I do not know what lessons await me until I begin to write my literary narratives. What I do know is that, for me, only story has the potential to convey the emotional weight of what I experience in my teaching practice. Only story has the capacity to hold the images of my students and me as actors moving together in the unfolding drama of an educational encounter in which there is both the grounding of thoughtful planning and the promise of playful spontaneity. Thinking through story, I thrive on this dynamic of purpose and improvisation; it is central to what I believe about curriculum and teaching, and it is best articulated in the philosophy of *currere*,[6] which "understands that the path of curriculum is 'laid down while walking' and that this path will bend, wind, and turn depending on the particular ways relations among students, texts, teachers, and contexts develop" (Sumara 1996, 175). Literary narrative allows me to express the interplay of intention and improvisation as these various unpredictable relationships evolve in the classroom, because literary narrative acknowledges the current of underlying tensions at work when, individually and collectively, students and teacher endeavor to make meaning.

My proclivity for story also causes me to "experience time, [not] as a succession of instants, a linear linking of points in space, but as an extended awareness of the past and the future within the present" (Husserl cited in Richardson 1990, 22). Again, my vision of curriculum tends to honor this sense of time. When I teach, I am very aware that while my students and I are in the midst of a learning moment, laying down the path while walking, we are "always already at the intersection of remembered, lived, and projected experiences" (Sumara 1996, 233). Conceiving time and experience from the perspective of *currere* affects how I might regard the concept of space as well, for *currere* acknowledges that "there can be no fixed and clearly defined boundary between schooling and other lived experiences; events of schooling become inextricable from the path of life" (Sumara, 1996, 174).

Story and the Practice of Research

As I write this, I realize that I am in the process of unfolding knowledge about my narrative yearnings. Writing my dissertation, a memory that is at once so distant and so immediate, was my first foray into an extended narrative of my teaching practice. Weaving theory and practice, I wrote the story of my students and me in our composition classroom and released my narrative impulse. I was powerfully motivated to portray a different kind of college composition classroom, where students and teacher co-author the learning experience by writing as a means of coming to know. The dissertation experience was an extended invitation for all of us to ride continuous waves of trust and uncertainty as we embarked upon our reflective voyage. I have often said that I enjoyed the process of writing my dissertation, because it was such a dramatic time in my life. It was dramatic in the best way—my students and I felt the tug of two simultaneous states of being: we were emboldened by the freedom to explore our assumptions, beliefs, and hunches, and we were vulnerable as a result of such freedom. We found ourselves in wide open space; there were no givens, few guidelines, no models to appropriate. In these wide open spaces was an incredibly productive tension to mine. I wrote my way into making meaning, guided by the spirit of narrative inquiry. In this way, I became a researcher, a practice that, according to Bourdieu, is "characteristically fluid and indeterminate," a practice that "occurs in space and time, is guided by tacit understanding which is neither wholly conscious nor wholly unconscious, and is purposeful and strategic" (cited in Polkinghorne 1997, 11–12). Throughout my dissertation experience, I felt the same wonderfully productive tension in the classroom that propelled me to write mirrored in my practice of research. I had the sense of myself in the midst of a story, a story I was authoring with any number of ways it could develop. The key for me was to remain focused, in the moment, to think "*with* the story, letting [myself] resonate with the moral dilemmas it . . . posed, understanding its ambiguities, examining its contradictions, feeling its nuances" (Ellis cited in Bochner 1997, 436). I understand what Polkinghorne (1997) means when he says, "Researchers are the protagonists in the drama of their quests for understanding. The drama consists of a sequential composition of decisions, actions, chance occurrences, and interactions with subjects and colleagues. Values, desires, inadequacies, skills, and personal characteristics make their appearance at various points in the researcher's performance" (9).

Over the years, as my storytelling seems to have become more complicated, more layered, so, too, has my understanding of teaching. And, as I have interrogated my stories in an attempt to uncover their significance and learn from them, so, too, have I interrogated my use of fiction itself as a genre that has the capacity to move and inform me. In other words, I find myself inquiring not only about ambiguities and contradictions in my practice of teaching but also about fiction as a viable form of educational inquiry. My relationship with narrative, specifically literary narrative, is strong indeed; it is both the method of inquiry and the subject of my research. It is inextricably linked to my way of being in the world, as a teacher and as a researcher. In this sense, there really are no boundaries between my practice of teaching and my practice of researching. There is no time or space that clearly designates one mode of being or the other; both perspectives exist at once and find form through my literary narratives, and they are sustained by the stories of my life.

Often, it seems I find myself in that space where images from my past and present fold into and inform one another, silently undulating and propelling me to a future. The literary narratives I write about my practice allow me to hold on to meaningful moments, and they become part of the narrative of who I am and who I wish to become—the teacher, the researcher, the writer.

Notes

1. The active encounter in any situation when "[pedagogically right] action is required even if that action may be non-action" (van Manen 1991, 40).
2. Dauenhauer, B. "Paul Ricoeur." *Stanford encyclopedia of philosophy*. 2002. Ed. E. N. Zalta. http://plato.stanford.edu/entries/ricoeur.
3. Polkinghorne contends that "researchers are practitioners; that is, they engage in a human activity carried out over time in order to accomplish a purpose" (1997, 3).
4. Clandinin and Connelly argue for "understanding the context for teacher knowledge in terms of individual teacher knowledge [and] the working landscape"; such knowledge is positioned at "the interface of theory and practice in teachers' lives" (1996, 24).
5. Based on the research of my dissertation, reflective writing looks very different from one student to the next. Students use individual strategies to write their way into meaning.
6. From Pinar and Grumet's book *Toward a Poor Curriculum* (1976), in which the concept of *currere* is presented as a method of inquiry for studying the curriculum experience.

References

Barone, T. 1995. The purposes of arts-based educational research. *International Journal of Educational Research* 23, no. 2: 169–80.

Bochner, A. P. 1997. It's about time: Narrative and the divided self. *Qualitative Inquiry* 3, no. 4: 418–38.

Brodsky, C. 1987. *The imposition of form: Studies in narrative representation and knowledge*. Princeton, NJ: Princeton University Press.

Carter, K. 1993. The place of story in the study of teaching and teacher education. *Educational Researcher* 22, no. 1: 5–12.

Clandinin, D. J., and F. M. Connelly. 1996. Teachers' professional knowledge landscapes: Teacher stories—stories of teachers—school stories—stories of schools. *Educational Researcher* 25, no. 3: 24–30.

Eisner, E. 1985. Aesthetic modes of learning. In *Learning and teaching the ways of knowing: Eighty-fourth yearbook of the National Society for the Study of Education*, Part II, ed. E. W. Eisner, 23–36. Chicago: University of Chicago Press.

Ellis, C. 1995. *Final negotiations: A story of love, loss, and chronic illness.* Philadelphia: Temple University Press.

Fleckenstein, K. 2002. Inviting imagery into our classrooms. In *Language and image in the reading-writing classroom: Teaching vision*, ed. K. S. Fleckenstein, L. T. Calendrillo and D. A. Worley, 1–26. Mahwah, NJ: Lawrence Erlbaum Associates.

Fowler, L. 2003. Narrative plains of pedagogy: A curriculum of difficulty. In *Curriculum intertext*, ed. E. Hasebe-Ludt and W. Hurren, 159–72. New York: Peter Lang.

Gallagher, K. 2001. The staging of qualitative research: Authorship, ownership, and artistic expression in social science inquiry. *Journal of Curriculum Theorizing*, 17, no. 3: 145–56.

Garman, N. 1991. The drama of the classroom: Dramaturgy as curriculum inquiry. In *Reflections from the heart of educational inquiry*, ed. G. Willis and W. Schubert, 277–83. Albany: State University of New York Press.

Grumet, M. R. (1976). Toward a poor curriculum. In W. F. Pinar & M. R. Grumet, *Toward a poor curriculum,* 162. Dubuque, IA: Kendall/Hunt.

Laidlaw, L. and D. Sumara. 2000. Transforming pedagogical time. *Journal of Curriculum Theorizing*, 16, no. 1: 9–22.

Lightman, A. 1993. *Einstein's dreams.* New York: Warner Books.

McMahon, P. L. 1993. *A narrative study of three levels of reflection in a college composition class: Teacher journal, Student portfolios, teacher-student discourse.* UMI ProQuest Digital Dissertation # ATT 9329582.

———. 1998. May have trouble seeing. Paper presented at the American Educational Research Association Annual Meeting. San Diego, CA.

———. 2000. From angst to story to research text: The role of arts-based educational research in teacher inquiry. *Journal of Curriculum Theorizing* 16, no. 1: 125–45.

———. 2001. Reflecting in time: "Storying" as a mode of teacher inquiry. Paper presented at the American Educational Research Association Annual Meeting. Seattle, WA.

Merleau-Ponty, M. 1962. *Phenomenology and perception.* London: Routledge.

Michaels, A. 1996. *Fugitive pieces.* Toronto: McLelland & Stewart.

Oberg, A. 2003. Paying attention and not knowing. In *Curriculum Intertext*, ed. E. Hasebe-Ludt and W. Hurren, 123–29. New York: Peter Lang.

Palmer, P. J. 1998. *The courage to teach: Exploring the inner landscape of a teacher's life.* San Francisco: Jossey-Bass.

Pinar, W. 1981. "Whole, bright, deep with understanding": Issues in autobiographical method and qualitative research. *Journal of Curriculum Studies* 13, no. 3: 173–88.

Pinar, W., and M. R. Grumet. 1976. *Toward a poor curriculum.* Dubuque, IA: Kendall/Hunt.

Polkinghorne, D. E. 1997. Reporting qualitative research as practice. In *Representation and the text: Re-framing the narrative voice*, eds. W. G. Tierney and Y. S. Lincoln, 3–21. Albany: State University of New York Press.

Richardson, L. 1990. Writing strategies: Reaching diverse audiences. *Qualitative Research Methods*. Volume 21. Newbury Park, CA: Sage.

———. 1994. Writing: A method of inquiry. In *Handbook of Qualitative Research*, eds. N. K. Denzin and Y. S. Lincoln, 516–29. Thousand Oaks, CA: Sage.

Ricoeur, P. 1984. *Time and narrative*. Vol. 2. Chicago: University of Chicago Press.

Robinson, J., and L. Hawpe. 1986. Narrative thinking as a heuristic process. In Carter, *The place of story*, 5–12.

Schlink, B. 1997. *The reader*. Trans. C. Brown Janeway. New York: Vintage Books.

Sumara, D. 1996. *Private readings in public: Schooling the literary imagination*. New York: Peter Lang.

van Manen, M. 1991. *The tact of teaching: The meaning of pedagogical thoughtfulness*. Albany: State University of New York Press.

Afterword: Envisioning Complicated Conversation at the Table

Maria Piantanida and Noreen B. Garman

We hope that the preceding chapters have provided some glimpses into the challenges and rewards associated with the struggle toward representation in interpretive dissertation writing. In closing, we want to offer a few thoughts in relation to several questions that often arise when we talk about our dissertation experiences at conferences:

- Are these dissertations anomalies?
- Can such dissertations be done without a group?
- Is your group itself an anomaly?
- What does it take to start and sustain a study group?

It would be presumptuous to assume that our small discourse community is the only one in which thoughtful interpretive dissertations are being written. Indeed, we have met faculty and students from universities in the United States, Canada, and Australia who are engaged in exciting and meritorious interpretive dissertation research. What may be unusual, however, is the study group context within which the contributing authors have grappled with the nature of interpretive research in general and the representation of their inquiries in particular.

As indicated in the preface, the study group has been meeting almost continuously for nearly twenty-five years. Although membership has changed, the two of us have been involved since the outset, and many of the current members have been involved for more than a decade. Participation in the group is by invitation, is voluntary, and occurs outside of formal academic structures. Given the professional and personal demands upon group members' time, this ongoing commitment to the group is remarkable. We often wonder what draws individuals to the group and what they find compelling enough to warrant remaining long after completing their dissertation research. While we do not presume to speak for group members, we offer some observations that we have made over the years.

Earlier, we mentioned Noreen's dining room table as both the physical and symbolic space in which we meet. Coming to the table symbolizes a *willingness to engage in complicated conversation*. Many of us spend our days in worlds of practice that are fraught with complexities—too much to do, too little time, too few resources, too much paperwork and regulation, too little celebration of the intellect—despite the fact that our worlds center around education. In response to these demands, the functionalist mantra seems to be "Keep it simple and do it fast." Merely civil conversation often seems to be a luxury; deliberately complicating a conversation may seem to be sheer lunacy. Yet those of us who are drawn to the table yearn for a community that not only acknowledges the complexities of educational practice, but also probes those complexities for meaning and insight. It is this shared inclination for deliberation that seems to attract members to the group. We speculate that those who resonate with the nature of the deliberative conversation remain.

The duration of the group, the stability of membership, and the compatibility of members give rise to the question of whether we run the risk of parochial thinking or sacrificing intellectual rigor for the sake of friendships and group congeniality. Perhaps it is because of these very risks that the notion of "complicated conversations" holds such power for us. In *The Courage to Teach*, Parker Palmer (1998) contends that "to teach is to create a space in which the community of truth is practiced" (90). Truth, he goes on to say, "is an eternal conversation about things that matter, conducted with passion and discipline" (Palmer 1998, 104). We hope that the chapters in this book have conveyed a sense of both the passion and discipline with which the authors have pursued their inquiries into issues that matter. Issues that matter are, by their very nature, complex. As professionals, as inquirers, as scholars, we can choose to acknowledge and grapple with the complexities or ignore them.

At one of our meetings, a member talked about an in-service program offered by her district. The speaker put forward a singular model of best practice for teaching reading. Troubled by such a simplistic view, our colleague felt compelled to ask if other research provided a fuller picture or a diversity of claims about best practices for reading.

"No," responded the speaker. "This model is research-based and the evidence clearly shows that this is *the* best practice for teaching reading."

"Are you saying that this one approach works for all children, with no exceptions?" our colleague asked.

"Yes."

Such singularity of vision is disturbing in its lack of historical perspective and apparent disregard for philosophical and theoretical discourses about an issue that matters very much to many committed educators. Were this an isolated incident, it might not be so troubling. Bill Pinar (2004), however, paints a rather provocative and persuasive portrait of rampant anti-intellectualism, not only within our society, but ironically within education itself. Within such a broader social and professional milieu, then, the space around Noreen's table becomes a haven, an intellectual home for those of us who want to understand the nuances of our practice in relation to the discourses of our fields of study. To this space, we bring a willingness to complicate our conversations. As Jerome Bruner (1966) suggests, "Education must, then, be not only a process that transmits culture, but also one that provides alternative views of the world and strengthens the will to explore them" (117).

Over the years, we have given some thought to the nature of this willingness to explore alternative views. Perhaps most fundamental is a *willingness to engage in shared learning* with the group members. Educators talk a lot these days about "engagement" as a critical characteristic of learning. Among other things, engagement means being present. In literal terms, being present in our group means physically sharing the same time and space with an understanding that when one is not there, even for a short period of time, the group suffers. Figuratively, being present means being connected, not merely by listening, but also by struggling to understand and extend the individual and group deliberations. We marvel at the willingness of busy practitioners to come at the end of a long day of teaching to meetings that last at least three and sometimes as much as five hours. Several individuals travel more than an hour each way to be present for one another. Equally remarkable is the way in which group members are present to each other's dissertation journeys, coming to know the substance of the study and the method.

Such willingness for engagement could not be fulfilled if there were not a reciprocal *willingness to risk*. In educational literature, risk is often associated with deliberative discourse (and knowledge-generating.) However, it is scary to share a tenuous idea that has not been well thought-out or documented. Yet some of the most powerful insights can come from the stance and counter-stance that we take as we exchange ideas.

We find it interesting to consider how the exchange of ideas takes place within the study group. It is difficult for us to recall times when ideas were debated in a classical sense of pro and con. Rather, each of us brings different perspectives and passions to the topics under discussion, and each of us has a way of adding these perspectives to the conversation. Marilyn, for example, listens so carefully with an ear for social justice issues. If she thinks that someone is overlooking that aspect of an issue, she calls attention to the oversight, but always with such gentleness and respect for the individual. Kathy's style is very different from Marilyn's, but when something is troubling her, she does not remain silent. Sometimes it takes her a while to get to the source of trouble, but the group gives her time to talk it out, because more often than not she's picked up on a very important, but subtle, point. When Wendy describes how she is visualizing an issue, she puts the topic under discussion into a very different perspective.

We could go on, describing everyone in the group, but the point is that we challenge each other's thinking from the core of who we are, what matters to us, how we think, and the bodies of literature with which we are familiar. This form of intellectual exchange is made possible because members demonstrate a *willingness to be authentic*.

Mention of authenticity risks conjuring up images of touchy-feely encounter groups, what one colleague derisively dismisses as "group gropes." This is not what we have in mind. Again, Palmer's (1998) thinking is helpful:

> The hallmark of the community of truth is not psychological intimacy or political civility or pragmatic accountability, though it does not exclude these virtues. This model of community reaches deeper, into ontology and epistemology—into assumptions about the nature of reality and how we know it—on which all education is built. The hallmark of the community of truth is in its claim that *reality is a web of communal relationships, and we can know reality only by being in community with it*. (95, emphasis in original)

If, as we contend, interpretive inquiry requires grappling with issues of epistemology and ontology, where can doctoral students turn for insight into their own worldview? Without some grounding in philosophical discourses, abstract discussions of epistemology and ontology often lack conceptual substance. We do not claim to be philosophers, nor do we claim to have mastered the complexities of epistemology and ontology. But authentic exchanges about the topic and process of our inquiries have given us glimpses into who we are and what we believe about the nature of our educational practice. Through these glimpses we have found ways in which to foster greater congruence between how we enact our practice and how we inquire into it.

Another aspect of our conversational space is a *willingness to strive for balanced participation*. Interestingly, several years ago the space around Noreen's table was becoming quite crowded. Concerned that the group was growing too large to offer adequate attention to both current and incoming members, Maria offered to form a second study group. After several meetings, the embryonic group disbanded.

In reflecting on the failure of this well-intentioned effort, we began to appreciate at a deeper level the power of the study group's culture. Part of this culture includes norms of participation. Each member is conscious of her responsibility to initiate, to give responses, to ask, to clarify and challenge, to summarize, and so on. As newcomers join the conversation, they have an opportunity to observe the nature of the conversation, to sense its rhythms, to understand its purpose, and then to find ways to ease into the deliberations. Yet as Lynn's story of crying in the closet reminds us, this entry is not without anxiety. Indeed, most study group members have stories of their early experiences with the group. These are often shared with new members, usually with good-natured kidding and much laughter. In this way, members seek to create spaces so that the group is productive for all.

The efforts to be welcoming and inclusive are augmented by a *willingness to care about the health of the group.* Through patience, curiosity, and engagement, group members develop mutual respect for each other, become interested in one another's topics and ideas, and begin to weave stories not only of individual dissertations, but also of the group. As stories of past dissertations are told and retold, group members begin to sense the legacy of scholarship being passed down from one generation of the group to the next. In the process, a commitment to the quality of work expands beyond one's own study to contributing to the work of others.

This commitment manifests in several ways. Group members devote countless hours to reviewing each other's drafts and offering comments. Individuals will come to the meeting looking wrung out from a day of teaching and announce during our initial, agenda-setting discussion that they have to leave no later than 8:30 or 9:00 at the latest. Yet they are often still at the table as the clock chimes 10:00 and then 11:00—reluctant to leave while a colleague is struggling though a conceptual impasse.

We should note that there is a dark side to this level of commitment to quality work. Several members have spoken quite painfully of their fear of not measuring up to the group's standards—whatever they imagine those standards to be. Others have become paralyzed, fearful of sharing anything less than a perfect draft. We have no easy answer to this burden of expectation. The level of deliberation emerges from the group, and the group takes pains to offer support and encouragement. But to a great extent, authentic participation in the group entails *a willingness to push intellectual reasoning to insightful and theoretic levels.* Ultimately, the purpose of the study group is to advance knowledge by drawing on the learning resources of the group. In order to carry on productive deliberations, each member is obliged to come to the discussion prepared to grapple with challenging ideas.

In closing, we want to consider the question of whether it is necessary to work in a group in order to engage in interpretive dissertation work. Clearly, we think it is an advantage to work within a community like ours. However, we also recognize that communities can take various forms. Our colleagues from Australia, for example, typically pursue their doctoral studies through distance education. At the same time, however, they often work intensively with an advisor/mentor and thus form a community for deliberation. We have also been impressed by the capacity of Australian scholars to reach across oceans to enter into cyber conversations with like-minded colleagues.

Here in the United States as well, novice scholars may choose to study at universities where they are able to work intensively with a faculty mentor. Sometimes all it takes is one or two others to form a deliberative space. What we see as problematic is the case of the student who yearns to engage in interpretive inquiries and is willing to commit the time and energy necessary to learn the craft, but has no one to guide her learning. We have met more than one doctoral student whose advisor has said in so many words, "You can do a qualitative study if you want. Let me know how you plan to do that." We are not given to many categorical pronouncements, but this situation is not likely to be productive. So we offer a final thought on willingness, one that comes from the core of Noreen's way of being with the study group. The willingness to enter into the nebulous space of complicated conversation must be *mutual* between learner and teacher, candidate and advisor, novice and mentor.

We have been enriched beyond measure and transformed beyond imagining by the conversations we share around the table. We hope in some small way, the authors in this book have offered ideas that will engender new complicated conversations among faculty and students.

References

Bruner, J.S. 1966. *On knowing: Essays for the left hand.* New York: Atheneum

Palmer, P. J. 1998. *The courage to teach: Exploring the inner landscape of a teacher's life.* San Francisco: Jossey-Bass.

Pinar, W. F. 2004. *What is curriculum theory?* Mahwah, NJ: Lawrence Erlbaum Associates.

Contributors

Kathleen M. Ceroni, Ph.D., English Teacher, Southmoreland School District, Adjunct Professor, Westmoreland County Community College

Noreen B. Garman, Ph.D., Professor, University of Pittsburgh, School of Education, Administrative and Policy Studies

Robin E. Grubs, Ph.D., C.G.C., Assistant Professor and Co-Director of the Genetic Counseling Program, Department of Human Genetics, Graduate School of Public Health, University of Pittsburgh

Pam Krakowski, Ed.D., Art Teacher, Falk Laboratory School, School of Education, University of Pittsburgh

Marilyn Llewellyn, Ph.D., Associate Professor and Director Master of Arts in Educational Praxis, Director Master of Education and Coordinator Elementary Certification, Carlow University

Marjorie Barrett Logsdon, PhD., Assistant Professor, Director of Educational Leadership Program, Carlow University

Patricia L. McMahon, Ph.D., Associate Professor and Director of Secondary Education, Carlow University

Wendy M. Milne, Ed.D. Elementary Art Teacher, Hempfield School District, Co-recipient of the 2001 Mary Catherine Ellwein Award for Outstanding Qualitative Dissertation of the American Educational Research Association

JoVictoria Nicholson-Goodman, Ph.D., Assistant Professor of Educational Foundations, Pennsylvania State University–Harrisburg

Maria Piantanida, Ph.D., Adjunct Associate Professor, University of Pittsburgh and Carlow University. Principal, Quality Learning Systems

Lynn Altman Richards, Ed.D., Elementary Educator, Mars Area Schools

Micheline Stabile, Ed.D., Special Education Coordinator of Curriculum, Assessment, Instruction, Pittsburgh Public School System; Adjunct Faculty Member Carlow University; Recipient of the 2000 Mary Catherine Ellwein Award for Outstanding Qualitative Dissertation of the American Educational Research Association; Recipient of the 1999 University of Pittsburgh School of Education Outstanding Dissertation Award

Cynthia A. Tananis, Ed.D., Assistant Professor, University of Pittsburgh, School of Education, Administrative and Policy Studies; School Leadership

Index

Abma, Tineke A., 140, 151
Acquisition, cycles of, 40–1, 43, 94
Aesthetic
    activities, 32
    aspects of pedagogy, 30
    authority to imagining, 54
    cognitive space, 53
    detachment, 21
    expression, 177
    forms of representation, 76–7
    knowing, 72, 76, 136, 190
    lens, 76
    order, 135
    satisfaction, 76
    sensibilities, 70, 72, 76
    tension, 120
    vision, 76
Agonistics of language, 51
Americans for Victory over Terrorism, 55, 61
Annells, Marilyn, 85, 95
Appadurai, Arjun, 50, 61
Aquila, R.E., 9, 13
Arrested moments of teaching, 194
Art classroom as
    haven, 72, 75
    laboratory, 72
    museum gallery, 72
    stage, 72
    studio, 72
Artist-teacher-researcher, xxiv, 127–9, 131, 134–5
Artmaking, xxiv, 127–9, 131–3, 135

Arts-based Educational Research, 133, 135
"As if" world, 164–5
Audience, 1, 130, 174–5, 179
Authorial
    Presence, 163, 171–2
    Stance, 3, 163, 183, 193–4
    Voice, 3–4
Authorship, 3, 12
Authority
    confronting, xxiii, 49, 54
    expert, 158
    figures, 159, 170–1
    inherited, 158
    -pleasing, 171
    research, 11
    textual, 158
    to imagine, x, xii–xiii, xxii, 10, 19, 22, 49, 54, 130, 135
    voices of, 10, 12
Autobiography, 51, 104
Axiology, xvii, xxiv, 57, 85, 139, 141, 151, 180
Ayers, William, 75, 78

Bakhtin, Mikhail M., 124, 144, 151
Balance, 59, 54–5, 70–2, 75–6, 78
Balancing lessons, 72, 75
Ballard, Keith, 146, 148, 152
Barnes, Julian, 156, 165
Barone, Thomas E., 46, 76, 77, 78, 120, 122, 124, 186, 197
Barrell, Barrie, 76, 78

Barrett, T., 128,129, 136
Barthes, Roland, 5, 13
Bartholomae, David, 165
Baxter Magolda, Marcia, 146, 151
Beck, Sarah W., xx, xxvi
Berthoff, Ann E., 155, 157, 158, 160, 161, 165
Bloom, Benjamin S., 33
Blumenfeld-Jones Donald S., 120, 122, 124
Bochner, Arthur P., 61, 186, 196, 197
Bollnow, Otto F., 75, 78
Broudy, Harry S., 68, 79
Bourdieu, Pierre, 52, 61, 196
Brady, Ivan, 56, 61
Bricker, Diane, 44, 46
Brodsky, C., 184, 197
Bruner, Jerome, 2, 13, 46, 72, 76, 77, 79, 136, 203, 207
Bryant, M., 13
Bumiller, Elisabeth, 56, 61
Burleigh, Nina, 56, 61

Cahn, M., 7, 14
Calder, Alexander, 68, 70, 76
Callings of
  craft, 42
  imagination, 42
  membership, 42
  memory, 42
  sacrifice, 42
Carter, K., 185, 197
Cause and effect relationship, 7
Ceroni, Kathleen M., 113, 124
Charmaz, Kathy, 56, 61, 84, 85, 86, 95
Childlike-ness, 75
Chronos, 104
Citizenship, 50–3, 56–60
Civic
  conscience, 57–8
  courage, 52, 56
  debate, 50, 56–7

engagement, 57–8
passivity, 58
responsibility, 59
Clandinin, D. Jean, 26, 33, 43, 46, 76, 77, 79, 119, 124, 197, 198
Coding, 86–8, 91, 142, 151
Coercive consensus, 59
Cognitive
  art, 53, 55
  commitments, 140
  dissonance, xxii
  domain, 165
  space, 53
Coherence, 2, 7, 13, 70, 167, 186
Coherent
  fit of method, 11
  framework, 72
  narrative, 186
  portrayal, 68
  study, 77
Colin, S.A.J., 11, 14
Complicated conversations, see conversation
Composing, 156, 158, 160, 164–5
Conceptual, xiv, xvii, xx, xxii, 5–10, 15, 28, 41, 61, 69, 84, 88, 179, 205–6
  imperative, 10
  leap, 9, 68–9, 78, 122
  mapping, 56
  meaning(s), 7, 10, 46, 142
  rigor and elegance, 9
Conceptualization, ix, xiv, 20, 25, 36, 46, 53, 69, 88, 92
Conceptualize/ing, viii, x–xi, xiii, xviii, xxiii, 35, 53, 56, 117, 149, 158, 160, 187
Connelly, F. Michael, 26, 33, 43, 46, 76, 77, 79, 118, 124, 197, 198
Conscience
  calls to, 42, 75
  civic, 57–8
  voices of, 42

Index 213

Constant comparative analysis, 86
Contemplation, 98, 105–6
　engaged, 105
　invited, 105
Conventions of
　fiction, 188
　genre, xxi, 164, 172
　inquiry, x, xx
　scientific research, 177
Conventional
　interview protocol, 118
　science report, xx, 13, 22
　wisdom, 7
Conversation
　complicated, xvii–xviii, xxii, xxiv–xxvi, 7, 202, 207
　storied, 40–1
　with scholars, 8
Corbin, Julliet, 83, 84, 86, 95, 96
Core concept, 88–89
Core portrayal, 41, 69, 72, 76
Corn, David, 56, 61
Correspond/correspondence, 2, 13, 87, 179, 183
Cottrell, June, 29, 33
Courtney, Richard, 28, 33
Craft
　a dissertation, 1
　a doctoral study, 29
　an inquiry, 11
　logic of justification, xxiii
　narrative, 77
　overview proposal, 67
　vignettes, 87, 103–4
Creative
　dramatics, 19, 21–4, 26–8, 31, 33
　latitude, xxi
　synthesis, 36, 41–3
Cresswell, John, 25, 33
Csikszentmihalyi, Mihaly, 78, 79
Cultural
　authority, 3

　contexts of schools, 123
　frames, 41, 45
　moment, 50–1, 53
　norms, xiii
　phenomenon, 49
　portrait, 55
　record, 61
　representation, 113
　repression/oppression, 54
Cultures of citizenship, 56, 58, 59–60
Currere, *50, 51, 53, 56, 195, 197*
Curriculum, 7, 21, 26, 28, 31, 33, 61, 69, 71, 75, 98, 103–4, 106–7, 167–177, 180, 195
Curriculum theorizing, 49, 51, 53, 60

Danner, Mark, 61
Data, 4, 141, 177, 176
　accumulation, xix
　collection/gathering, xix, 24, 33, 38, 86, 140
Dauenhauer, Bernard, 197
Defining moments, xviii, 103
Deliberation, vii–x, xiii, xviii, xxii, 13, 22, 24, 26, 36, 41, 87, 91, 69, 146, 157, 173, 175, 202–3, 205–6
Deliberative, xviii, xxvi, 1, 19, 42, 50, 174, 202, 204, 206
Delpit, Lisa, 76. 79
Denzin, Norman K., ix, xiii, xiv, 56, 61, 113, 124
Dewey, John, 75, 79, 133, 136
Diamond, C.T. Patrick, 136
Difference
　between data and text, 142
　between portraying results and reporting findings, xix
　embedded in concrete cases, 176
　in truth claims, 13
　responding to, 45, 50–60
Dillard, Annie, 114, 124, 156, 165
Discernment, 181

Discourse(s), xi–xii, xvii–xviii, xxii–xxiii, 3, 5, 8, 12–3, 22, 36, 38, 42–3, 49, 51, 54–5, 57–8, 60, 70, 76, 78, 102, 115, 121, 128, 132–3, 142, 162–3, 167, 173, 204, 205
    community/ies of, xxv, 2, 43, 146, 148, 201
    of field, 140–1, 149, 203
    on narrative as method, 76, 118
    reviewing, 8–10, 71
Discursive, 54, 60, 139, 164, 169
    deliberation, xxii, 146, 157, 173
    deliberator, 146, 151
    exchange, xviii, 180
    mode, 57
    moment, 56
    space/terrain, 53–4
    text, 5, 7–8, 11, 13
Dissertation
    author/authoring, xviii, 13, 128, 147
    authorities/experts, 19–20, 25–6, 78
    committee members, 11–2, 24, 77, 84–5, 120
    experience of, 19, 21, 32, 37–38, 41, 49–51, 76–7, 82–4, 92, 97–9, 113–5, 118, 123, 131–2, 139, 141, 143–4, 149, 151, 155, 170, 195–6, 201, 203, 205
    folklore, 9
    interpretive, ix, xxi, xxii, 3, 5, 9–10, 160, 206
    portrayal/representation, vii–viii, xi–xii, xix–xx, 2, 5, 9–10, 21–2, 41, 67–9, 71–2, 78, 88–89, 129–130, 134
    study group, xviii–xix
    traditional five-chapter, xix, 7, 13
    writing, ix–x, xiv, 1, 11, 29, 31, 70, 145, 157–8, 163
    writers, 2, 13, 28
Dissonance, xxi, 83–4, 114, 118, 120, 146–7, 185–6

Doctrine, 52, 57
Doll, Mary Aswell, 159, 162, 166
Douglass, Bruce G., 35, 36, 46
Dowd, Maureen, 56, 61
Downey, M., 105, 108
Doyle, W., 185
Drama of the classroom, 185
Dreams, 42, 159–160, 162
Drift
    functionalist, 144
    interpretivist, 144
Duke, Nell K., xx, xxvi

Early childhood art education/classroom, xxiii, 67, 72
Edmiston, Brian, 19, 34
Education as rhetorical practice, 7
Educational
    dictates, 36
    criticism, 121
    cultural, 61
    encounter, 180, 185–6, 195
    gatekeepers, 12
    inclusion, xxii, 35, 37–45
    journey, 27
    language, 108
    memoir, 98
    reform, 113, 132
    relationships, 103
    values, 70
Educative, 42, 183, 185
Eisner, Elliott, 1, 3, 6, 7, 9, 13, 14, 29, 33, 42, 46, 61, 62, 68, 70, 76, 77, 78, 79, 135, 136, 186, 190, 198
Elbow, Peter, 158, 166
Ellis, Carolyn, 56, 62, 196, 198
Embodied knowledge, xxiii, 69
Emig, Janet, 156, 160, 166
Emotional atmosphere, 75
Empathetic moment, 81, 91
Empathy, 41, 91, 94, 120
Encounters, 36, 39–40, 43, 82, 114, 119

Engagement
    and faith, 102
    civic, 57–8
    heuristic cycles of, 36–8, 43
    in discursive deliberation, 42–3
    in inquiry, 150
    in learning, 31, 71, 143
    in practice, 149–150, 168
    in study group, 203–5
    nodal, 59
    with literature , 106
Enunciation, 50–4, 58, 60
Epistemological, ix, xiii, xvii, 11–3, 85–6
    authority, 159
    conflicts, 52
    logics, 11–2
    perspectives, 2, 144
    purity, 144
    vacuum, 11
Epistemologically rigorous, x, 10
Epistemology, xvii, xxiv, 52, 56, 85–6, 116, 139–141, 151, 177, 180, 204–5
    of resentment, 52–3, 60
Epistemorph, 142–4, 146–7, 150
Essay
    as a dissertation, 155, 163, 164
    as a form of inquiry, 156, 160–1, 164, 167, 169–171, 175
    personal, 171, 174–8, 181
    philosophical, 176
    speculative, 160, 161, 165, 167, 169
Evaluation
    educational, 139–140, 145–6
    practice, 140, 145, 151, 180
    narrative, 146
Exegesis, 55, 98, 105, 107
Existential
    angst, xxiii, 89–90, 92–4, 185
    experience, 88–9
    nature of being at-risk, 81, 89, 91
    understanding, 178
    sense of mortality, 184

Experiential
    context, 174
    see also "text"

Faith, 93, 98–9, 101–3, 106, 108, 172
Faux, Jeff, 56, 62
Feinberg, W., 13, 14
Fictive narrative/stories, 186, 191
    mildly, 190
    wildly, 190
Field(s) of study, 10–12, 13, 203
Fine, Michelle, 56, 62
First person, writing in, 3, 149, 163
Fish, Stanley, 4, 5, 14, 62
Fishman, P.M, 116, 124
Fit
    of method, 11, 35
    ontological, 179
    rightness of, 11, 76, 78, 130
    with classroom drama, 23, 32
    with paradigm, 85
Fleckenstein, K., 187, 198
Flow, 8, 28, 35, 70, 78, 106, 170
Fontana, A., 117, 124
Ford, Richard, 56, 62
Form and meaning, xx
Forms of representation, xx, 1–2, 5, 10
    aesthetic, 76–77
Forms of understanding, 1
Foucault, Michel, 5, 14, 50, 62
Foulkes, A.P. , 121, 124
Foundational principles, 57
Fowler, L., 187, 198
Fraser, F. Clark, 90, 95
Fredericks, Marcel, 85, 95
Frey, J.H., 117, 124
Friedman, Thomas, 56, 62

Gadamer, Hans-Georg, 36, 46, 47, 109, 178, 181
Gallagher, K., 194, 198
Gardner, Howard, 1

Garman, Noreen B., 61, 46, 47, 108, 128, 129, 136, 185, 198
Genetic Counseling, see "practice –based inquiry of"
Genre, 8, 160, 163, 171, 174, 196
   conventions of, 164, 172
   of dissertation representation, 2
   essay as a genre, 174–7
   research genre, x, xx–xxi, xxiii–xxiv, 35–6, 67, 72, 76, 81, 113–4
Gergen, Kenneth J., 56, 62
Gergen, Mary, 56, 62
Ginsburg, M.B., 121, 124
Glaser, Barney G, 84, 85, 86, 95
Glatthorn, A.A., 13, 14
Goba, Bonganjalo, 102, 108
Gold-standard of research, 146
Good, Graham, 162, 166, 176, 177, 181
Goodall, H.L., 56, 62
Goodman, Nelson, 11, 14, 78, 79
Goodwin, Susan Poe, xix, xxvi
Graff, G., 124
Greene, Jennifer C, 140, 151
Green, Thomas F., 42, 47
Greene, Maxine, vii, ix, xiv, 6, 9, 12, 32, 33, 70, 71, 73, 79, 147, 151
Greenspan, Stanley I., 75, 79
Greenwood, Davvyd J., 56, 62
Grounded theory, x, xx, 81, 83–6, 88, 91–2, 139, 142, 151, 179
Grubs, Robin E., 81, 85, 86, 89–91, 95, 96, 151, 152
Grumet, Madeline R., 3, 14, 105, 108, 194, 198
Guba, Egon G., 148, 179, 181
Guzy, M.W., 56, 62

Haggerson, Nelson, L., 46, 47
Hagler, Graylan S., 56, 62
Hahn, Lewis E., 39, 47
Halpern, Jodi, 91, 94, 95
Hampl, Patricia, 158, 159, 161, 166

Harris, Wendell V., 171, 177, 181
Hawkins, Peter, 46, 47
Hawpe, Linda, 46, 47, 184, 199
Hazi, Helen M., xx, xxvi
Heaney, T., 11, 14
Helvarg, David, 56, 62
Henley, N., 116, 124, 125
Hermeneutic/hermeneutics, xix, 107, 123
   interpretations , 5, 35
   orientation, 2
   process, 106, 122
   tradition, 121
Heshusius, Lous, x, xv, 3, 15, 86, 96, 146, 148, 152, 179, 182
Heuristic
   cycles, 36–8, 40–1, 46
   inquiry, x, xx, xxii, 35–6, 39, 41
   portrayal/representation, xix, 41, 43, 46, 51, 91–2, 139, 151
Holding environment, 75
Holland, J., xi, xv
Holland, Patricia, xix, xxvi
Holquist, M., 118, 124, 151
Huebner, Dwayne, 97, 108
Huff, Anne Sigismund, 56, 62
Husserl, Edmund, 104, 195

Images, xxiv, 5, 19–26, 28–32, 38, 45, 68, 70, 77–8, 98, 101, 106, 114–5, 127–8, 131, 133–5, 145, 158–169, 162, 188, 191–2, 194–5, 197, 204
Imagic store, 68
Imaginaries, social, 50–1, 53–4, 60
Imagination, 6, 9–10, 12, 32, 36, 42, 50, 53,73, 78, 105–6, 130, 157, 159, 164–5, 186, 190, 192, 194
Imagine, xii, xii, xix, 6, 9–10, 13, 29, 32, 38, 60, 68, 69, 76, 81, 86, 98, 119, 134, 151, 189, 206,
   see also "authority to imagine"
Inclusion, see "educational"
Inner views storied, 119–121, 123

Institutional legitimacy, 10
Insulated expert, 141, 146, 151
Interpretive
    communities, 4, 36, 146
    dissertation, ix–xii, xxi–xxii, 1, 5, 9–10, 12, 143, 160, 201, 205–6
    epistemology, xxiii
    heuristic, 151
    inquiry, 12, 143
    logic of justification, xxiii, 86–7, 139
    lens/Perspective, 91, 185–6
    portrayal, 2, 75, 122
    process, 106, 121
    proclivities/sensibilities, 118, 148
    reality, 6
    research/researchers, 2, 5, 7, 12
    stance, 142, 146
    text, 142
    work, 51
    worldview, 40, 128, 139, 144
    writing, 30, 143
Interpretivists, 2, 142
Interpretivism,, tenets of, 2
Interview(s), 2, 26, 91, 116–120
Interviewer, 3, 116–7
Interviewing, xx

Janesick, Valerie J., 46, 47
Jones, Elizabeth, 75, 79
Journey, xviii, xxiii, xxiv, 8, 10, 22, 27, 29, 35, 38, 92, 97, 108, 118, 123, 134, 139, 141–2, 144–151, 169, 176, 203,
Joy, 68, 78
Judgment, 7, 11, 156, 181

Kairos, 103–4
Kairotic moments, 98
Kemmis, Stephen, 51, 61, 62
Kerdeman, Deborah, 36, 47, 178, 181
Kessels, Joseph P.A.M., 162, 166
Kilbourn, Brent, xviii, xxvi
Kincheloe, Joe L., 50, 61, 62

King, J.A., 140, 152
King, Patricia M., 146, 152
Kitchener, Karen S., 146, 152
Klein, Naomi, 56, 62
Knapp-Minick, Barbara, xix, xxvi
Knowledge, 8–13, 21–23, 27, 36, 50, 53, 57, 61, 69, 74, 76–7, 102, 114, 116, 120, 132, 139, 141, 146, 155, 160, 164, 167, 174, 176–9, 184–5, 187, 195, 197, 204, 206
Knowledge landscape, 184
Korthagen, Fred A., 162, 166
Koziol, Stephen, 29, 33
Krakowski, Pamela, 67, 73–76, 79
Kramarae, C., 116, 124, 125
Krathwohl, David R., 20, 33
Krugman, Paul, 56, 62

Labaree, David F., 83, 95, 179, 182
Language, xviii, 4, 6, 8, 24, 30–1, 37, 39, 42, 51, 55, 71, 77, 87, 97–9, 103, 107–8, 116, 118–9, 121, 128, 133, 142, 144, 156, 161, 191, 192
LaBoskey, Vicki Kubler, 76, 77, 79
LePage, 194
Laidlaw, L., 188, 194, 198
Langer, Susanne, 77, 79
Leukhardt, Joan C, xix, xxvi
Liebman, Marty, 51, 54, 61, 63
Lightman, A., 189, 198
Limits
    of expertise, understanding/vision, xi, 140, 165
    of knowledge, 146
    of studies, 86
    on discourse, 52–53
Lincoln, Bruce, 56, 62
Lincoln, Yvonna S., ix, xiii, xiv, 33, 124, 144, 152, 179, 181
Lipman J., 68, 78, 79
Lippman-Hand, Abby, 90, 95

Listening, 22, 40, 72, 76, 89, 172, 185, 203
Literature review, xx, 7–8, 23, 106–7, 163
    see also "conversation"
    see also "discourse"
Literary
    ability, 6
    avenues, 32
    critic, stance of, xxiv, 121
    criticism, 121
    figures as heuristics, xix
    imagination, 164
    narrative, 184, 186–7, 190, 195, 197
    portrayals, 120
    theorists/theory, xxiii, 5, 107, 118, 162
Lived experience, ix, 6, 50, 53–54, 145, 149–150, 167, 169, 176, 195
Llewellyn, Marilyn, 98, 108
Log of Encounters, 39
Logic of justification, x, xxiii, 3, 11–2, 82, 85–6, 139, 179
Logico-scientific
    correspondence, 2
    truth/truth claim, 2
Logsdon, Marjorie Barrett, 23, 34, 149, 152, 156, 163, 166
Lopate, Phillip, 175, 177, 182
Lopez, Gerardo R., 56, 63
Lyons, N., 76, 77, 79
Lyotard, Jean-Francois, 51, 63

Masia, Bertram B., 33
Marshall, Catherine, 25, 34
Matthews, Gareth B., 76, 79
May, Wanda T., 69, 79
Macdonald, James, 102, 103, 109
McGovern, George, 56, 63
McMahon, Patricia L., 26, 34, 67, 79, 128, 129, 136, 183, 192, 193, 198

McVikar, Polly, 136
Meaning-making, 7, 41, 114, 169, 180
Meditations, 98, 106
Meditative Writing, 98, 105–7
Membership, 42, 201–2
Memoing, 87, 91
Memoir, 98, 104–7
Memoirist, 161
Memory, 20, 32, 42, 103, 105, 155, 158–161, 165, 188, 190, 194–5
Memory texts, 160–1
Merleau-Ponty, M., 193, 198
Mertens, Donna M., 140, 152
Metaphor, xxiii, 10, 41–2, 46, 70, 75–8, 85, 105, 108, 120, 142, 144–5, 151, 159, 161, 169, 187, 191, 194,
Metaphorical telling, 194
Method, vii, viii, ix–x, xiv, xxiii, 28, 37, 82, 84, 54, 103, 107, 155, 161, 180, 184, 203,
    as technique, 2–3
    mixed, 2
    of inquiry, 7, 10–1, 98, 143, 186
    qualitative, 22, 83, 140–1
    self conscious, xvii–xviii
    see also "interpretive"
    see also "logic of justification"
    see also "writing as method"
Methodological, vii, ix, xiv, xvii, xix, 117, 118, 140
Michaels, A., 194, 198
Miller, Steven I., 85, 95
Miller, Suzanne M., 144, 152
Miller, William L., 56, 63
Milne, Wendy M., 128, 136
Mobile, 68, 70–1, 75–8
Moore, Michael T., 144, 152
Moss, Elizabeth, 33, 34
Moustakas, Clark, 35, 36, 46, 47
Mullen, Carol A., 136
Mythic, xxvi, 52, 59, 108

Index

Naiveté, 170, 172–4
Narrative, narratives
    as method of inquiry, xi, xx, xxiii, 19, 26, 32, 36, 40, 67–8, 72, 76–8, 118–9, 121, 183, 187, 196–7
    competing/conflicting, 50–3
    dominant, 50, 54–5, 57, 60
    elements/structure, 28, 119–120, 159, 161, 187
    evaluation, 145, 146
    fictive, xxiv, 186, 191–3, 197
    frame of mind, 69, 72
    hypernational, 52–3
    literary n. 184, 186, 195, 197
    and normative, xxiii, 68–72, 75, 77–8
    of nation, 52
    pedagogy, 67–8, 70, 78
    relationship with, 25–6, 183–4, 197
    representation of experience, 3, 9, 28–31, 43, 54, 67, 76, 87, 89, 120, 150, 184–7, 190, 194
    scientific, 142, 149
    triumphal, 52–54
    typology, 81, 86, 89, 91, 93
    vignettes, 81, 86–7, 91
    voice, 3
    yearnings/impulse, 3, 18, 165, 195–6
Nelson, Marie W., 144, 152
New Right, 52, 55
Newman, Jay, 93, 96
Nicholson-Goodman, J., 56, 61, 62
Novel as dissertation, 1
Nussbaum, Martha, 160, 164, 166

Oates, Joyce Carol, 56, 63
Oberg, A., 187, 198
Olesen, Virginia, xi, xiii, xv, 63
"Ologies", 139, 141
Ontology, xvii, xviv, 21, 85–6, 139–141, 151, 177, 180, 204–5
Ontological

    assumptions, 85–6
    awareness, 123
    concerns, 13
    congruence, 181
    landscape, 25, 29
    orientation, 21, 130, 183, 187
    perspective/view, 2, 22, 144
    rupture, 181
    sensibilities, 10
    stance, 1, 140
    stutterings, 118
    understandings, 3
    vacuum, 11
Orthodoxy, *53, 57–9*
"Other", 139, 178
Overview proposal, 25, 67
Ozga, J., 122, 124

Palermo, Joseph A., 56, 63
Paley, Vivian Gussin, 76, 79
Pallas, Aaron M., xvii, xxvi, 148, 152
Palmer, Parker J, 136, 187, 198, 202, 207
Palmer, Richard, 107, 109
Parsons, M J., 128, 129
Participants in
    education, 33, 43, 185, 190
    study, ix, 3, 33, 38–9, 82–3, 86–7, 89, 91–2, 116–120, 123
Paulston, Roland G., 51, 54, 55, 61, 62, 63
Perceptual codes, 56
Pedagogy, xxiii, 19, 27, 29–30, 33, 67–8, 70, 77–8, 98, 104–8, 130, 133, 159, 162, 183, 188, 193–4,
Pedagogical, 21, 30, 69, 71, 92, 98, 106, 135, 197
    image, 30–2
    life, 77, 104
    moment(s), 174, 177, 181, 184
    practice, xxiv, 133
    time, 174, 177, 181, 193–4
Pence, Penny, 29, 33

Pennsylvania Depart. of Ed., 115, 124
Perl, Sondra, 158, 166
Permission to
　author, 12
　create, 12
　generate truth claims, 7
　imagine, 67
Perry, L., 136
Personal essay, see essay
Petrosky, Anthony, 165
Phenomenology, xix
Phenomenon, 54, 87, 91, 142
　under study, 2, 68, 70, 72
Piantanida, Maria, 9, 46, 47, 85, 96, 128, 136, 160, 167, 182
Piantanida, Maria & Garman, Noreen B., xviii, 9, 41, 68, 69, 72
Pinar, William F., 4, 8, 11, 14, 50, 51, 63, 186, 198, 203. 307
Piscolish, M.A., 121, 124
Pitts, Leonard, 56, 63
Polanyi, Michael, 36, 47
Polkinghorne, Donald E., 3, 14, 46, 47, 186, 196, 197, 199
Portrayal(s), ix, 2, 4–5, 40–1, 43, 72, 76–7, 103, 120, 145, 187
Post-formal thinking, 50
Postpositivist, viii, 2–3, 83, 85, 139, 143, 146–7
Poststructuralists, 8
Practice, study of, xviii, 3–4, 6
Practice-based inquiry of
　administrative practice, 35–46
　curriculum practice, 167–181
　evaluation practice, 139–151
　genetic counseling practice, 81–95
　teaching practice, 3, 19–33, 67–78, 97–108, 113–123, 127–135, 155–165, 183–197
Prenatal testing, 81–82, 88–90, 93
Problematics, 6, 37, 40–43
Problematize/problematizing, 35, 41, 57

Process drama, 28, 30, 32
Professorial privilege, 10, 12
Public
　discourse , 55
　knowing/thinking/writing, 3, 4, 42, 77, 143, 162
　officials, 51
　space, 8, 175–6
　trauma, 50

Qualitative, 86, 143
　interpretive, 2–3, 42
　research/inquiry, vii–xi, xiii–xiv, xvii, xx, 2–3, 7, 22, 25, 83, 90, 113–4, 206
Qualitative-quantitative, 4, 13, 25, 140

Randall, Rosemary, 46, 47
Reality, 2, 6, 9, 11, 37, 44, 50–1, 71, 76, 87, 102, 106, 116, 123, 141, 180, 183, 187, 189, 193–4, 204
Realization, cycles of, see "heuristic"
Reason, Peter, 40, 46, 47
Re-engagement, 38
Reflection, 26–7, 36, 39–41, 43, 45, 55, 79, 73, 122, 133, 162, 164, 167, 169, 174, 177, 186, 188–9, 194,
Reflective Artmaking, 127–9, 131, 133, 135
Reid, Louis A., 132, 137
Reliability, 5, 178
Rennie, David L., 85, 96
Representation, xii, 29, 57–9, 104, 113
　crisis of, ix
　fictive, xxiv. 183, 186, 192–3
　forms of, viii, ix, xx, 2, 5, 76–7, 119, 190
　of dissertation/inquiry, viii, 1–2, 5, 9–10, 13, 201
　of knowledge, 12
　of relationship with narrative , 184

struggle toward/grappling with, vii, ix, xi, xxi–xii, 201
Representational practices, xii
Research
    authority, 11, 25
    dissertation, vii–x, xii, xviii–xix, 11–2, 201–2
    genre, x, xx, xxiii, 35–6, 67, 72, 76, 81
    legitimate/legitimacy, xvii–xviii, xxi, 1, 10, 12, 22, 84, 169, 179
    proposal/overview, 7, 24–5, 32, 67, 74, 83
    tradition, x, xix–xx, xxii, 3–4, 7–8, 11–2, 21, 37, 83, 85–6, 98, 121, 134, 139–140, 148–9, 167
    see also "dissertation"
    see also "interpretive"
    see also "qualitative, science/scientific"
Researcher ix–xiv, xvii, xxiv, 2, 5, 7, 9, 11, 21–2, 24–5, 35–6, 43–4, 54, 68–70, 83, 85–6, 113–4, 116–7, 120, 122, 129–130, 134, 165, 168, 186, 196–7
    artist-teacher-researcher xxiv, 127–8, 132, 133, 135
    as artist-citizen-scholar xxiii, 54
    as Protagonist 196
    functionalist 141–2
Reynolds, Gretchen, 79
Reynolds, W., 1
Rhetorical, 155
Rich, Adrienne, 106, 109
Rich, Frank, 6, 63
Richards, Lynn A., 9 33, 34, 67, 80,
Richardson, Laurel, 46, 47, 63, 87, 90, 91, 96, 104, 109, 120, 123, 124, 155, 158, 160, 166, 184, 191, 195, 199
Ricoeur, Paul, 2, 5, 14, 184, 189, 197, 199
Rieger, John, 56, 63
Roberts, C.M., 13, 14

Roberts, H., 14
Robinson, John A., 46, 47, 184, 199
Role, xvii, 3, 25, 30–1, 33, 38, 55, 59, 82, 116, 121–2, 128, 133–5, 140, 147
Rossman, Gretchen, 34
Rupture, 36, 38, 43, 50, 181
Ryan, K., 151, 152
Ryan, Michael, 56, 63

Safire, William, 56, 63
Sanida, Kathryn V., xx, xxvi
Sartre, Jean Paul, 68, 78
Scheurich, James, 5
Schlink, B., 183, 199
Scholar(s), vii, xiii, xiv, xviii, xxi, xxiii, 5, 8, 23, 30, 32–3, 36, 40, 51, 53–4, 55, 121, 140, 149, 158, 163, 167, 202, 206
Scholar-practitioner(s), x, xix, xxiii, 37, 42, 55, 143, 148, 151, 168
Scholarly, x, xiii, xix, 1, 8, 19, 20–1, 25, 29, 32, 53–4, 67, 77, 106–7, 165, 168, 170, 173
Scholarship, 11–3, 37–8, 42, 53, 55, 118, 140, 144, 148, 205
Schon, Donald A., 46, 133, 137, 181, 182, 186
Schubert, William H., 69. 80. 160, 161, 163, 164, 166–170, 170, 172–3, 175–6, 182, 198
Schwab, Joseph, 176, 182
Schwandt, Thomas A., 140, 148, 151, 152, 178, 180, 181, 182
Science/Scientific, 2–3, 7, 11, 13, 40, 83, 98, 139–140, 148–9, 176–9
Segev, Tom, 56, 63
Self
    as an instrument, 3
    authentic, 4
    -conscious method, xvii–xviii
    in dissertation writing, xxii
    in social context, 6
    -knowledge, 53

-portrait, 75, 114, 127–9, 131–3, 135, 192
Sensibilities, xx, 6, 10, 54, 66, 69–73, 75–6, 118, 172–3, 184
Sidorkin, A., 4, 14
Silverman, D., 117, 124
Slattery, Patrick, 14, 137
Smith, Dorothy E., 28, 34
Smith, John K., x, xv, 3, 15, 86, 96, 179, 182
Smith, S., xii, xv
Smyth, John, 42, 47
Social
 cartography, 53–6, 61
 constructs, 54
Socially constructed knowledge, 8, 114
Solipsism/solipsistic, 4, 8, 170, 174
Soltis, J.F., 13, 14
Sontag, Susan, 160, 162, 166
Southgate, J., 46, 47
Space
 alternatives, claims to, 54
 ambiguity of, 9, 207
 contemplative, 104–5
 dark, 9, 98, 105
 deliberative/conversational, viii, xxvi, xviii, xx, xxiii 72, 116, 123, 202–3, 205–6
 of civic debate/discourse, 49–51, 53–4, 60
 open, 130
 public, 8, 175–6
 research, 4
 sacred, 106
 shared space of author-reader, 6, 165
 symbolic/imaginative/figurative, ix, xxvi, 53, 60, 190, 202
 teaching-learning, 68–9, 75, 78, 101, 184–5, 187, 193, 195–6, 197
 theoretical, 3, 49
Spanos, W., 119, 124
Spatial relations, 49, 60

Speculation, xiv, 161, 165, 167–170, 173, 176, 179
Speculative essay, see "essay"
Spiritual/spirituality, xxiii, 97–8, 103–8
Stabile, Micheline, 35, 47
Stafford, William, 163, 166
Stake, Robert E., 145, 152
Stance, 33, 167–8, 204
 authorial/researcher, 3, 7, 38–9, 54, 116, 120, 128, 161, 163, 183, 193–4
 interpretive, 82, 85, 142
 ontological, 140–1, 142, 146, 149
Starratt, Robert J., 42, 47
Statistical correlations, 7
Stern, Phyllis Noerager, 84, 96
Stevahn, Laurie, 140, 152
Stewards of academic traditions, 11–2
Stinson, Susan W., 70, 80
Storied conversations, see "conversation(s)"
Story, xxi, 2, 6, 38–41, 44, 53, 67, 89–90, 107, 116, 119–123, 155, 161, 165, 183–192, 194–6, 205
 telling, 11, 164, 196
 teller, 3, 185
Storying, 40, 43
Stout, Candace, 133, 137
Strauss, Anselm L., 83, 84, 85, 86, 95, 96
Struggle, x–xi, xviii, xxi, xiii, xxv, 1, 8, 13, 19, 37,49, 52, 53, 60, 67–9, 86–7, 97, 99–100, 102–3, 113, 115, 120, 122, 132, 139, 141–2, 145–151, 156–7, 160
 see also "representation"
Study Group, see "dissertation"
Subjects, xi–xii, 3, 117, 159, 196
Sullivan, Anne, 76, 80
Sumara, Dennis, xxiv, 84, 85, 86, 91, 96, 188, 194, 195, 198, 199
Systems of intelligibility, 4

Index

Tananis, Cynthia A., 84, 85, 86, 91, 96, 139, 152
Taubman, Peter, 14
Taylor, Betsy, 56, 63
Teacher as artist, 70, 72, 76
Tension, 12, 51, 54, 69–70, 72, 77, 120, 170, 192, 195–6
Teodosijevic-Ryan, Jasmina, 56, 63
Text/texts
    discursive, 7–8, 11
    experiential, 6–7, 9
    of talk, 115, 117–8, 120, 123
    social text, ix
    theoretic, 6–8
    theory of , 5
Thorne, B., 116, 124, 125
Tierney, W.G., 3, 56, 63, 199
Time
    contemplative, 105–6
    cosmic, 184
    pedagogical, 193–4
    school time, 188
    vertical time, 194
    see also "kairos"
Tompkins, Jane, 159, 166
Transitional object, 75
Tripp, D.H., 116, 125
Trustworthiness, 5
Truth, 11, 55, 102, 144, 173–4, 177, 180, 192, 202, 204,
    claims, x, 2, 5, 7, 11, 13, 40, 54, 56, 177
    modernist notion of, 11
Typology, 61, 81, 86, 89, 91, 93
    as rhetorical device, 90

Ueland, Brenda, 172, 173, 182
Understanding
    nature/forms of, 1–4, 128–9, 178
    ontological, 3
    sympathetic understanding, 73
    through reflection, 186–7

    writing toward, 160–1, 163, 169

Validity, 5, 179
van Manen, Max, 80, 84, 96, 174, 182, 184, 197, 199
Vellenga, Tom, 56, 63
Verisimilitude, 6, 26, 40, 77, 193
Vignette, 5, 40, 81. 69, 72–5, 86–9, 91, 98, 103–4, 142
Visual portrayal, 49
Voice/voices
    authentic , 4
    authorial , xxii
    conflicted research, 144
    dominant , 11
    first person, 3
    "hybrid construction" of, 144
    interpretive, 149
    multiple/many, 10, 165
    of advocacy, 55
    of authority/expert, 12, 21, 78
    of conscience, 42
    of other(s), 11, 115, 116, 118, 120, 148, 158, 162, 171
    of storyteller, 3
    three different voice identities, 3
    women's, xii

Warrants/warranting, 7–8, 173
Weis, Lois, 56, 63
Welty, Eudora, 161, 166
Wide-awakeness, 73
Wilhelm, Jeffrey, 19, 34
Winner, Ellen, 132, 1137
Winnicott, Donald, 75, 80
Worldview, viii, xxii, 2–3, 52, 85, 116, 139–142, 144, 146, 148–9, 151, 180, 205
Writing as
    method/mode of inquiry, 158, 160, 162–3
    recursive/iterative, 29, 173

Young, Lauren Jones, xvii, xxvii

Zeichner, K.M., 122, 125
Zinn, Howard, 56, 63
Zinsser, William, 104, 109
Zwicky, J., 187

COMPLICATED CONVERSATION

A BOOK SERIES OF CURRICULUM STUDIES

This series employs research completed in various disciplines to construct textbooks that will enable public school teachers to reoccupy a vacated public domain—not simply as "consumers" of knowledge, but as active participants in a "complicated conversation" that they themselves will lead. In drawing promiscuously but critically from various academic disciplines and from popular culture, this series will attempt to create a conceptual montage for the teacher who understands that positionality as aspiring to reconstruct a "public" space. *Complicated Conversation* works to resuscitate the progressive project—an educational project in which self-realization and democratization are inevitably intertwined; its task as the new century begins is nothing less than the intellectual formation of a public sphere in education.

The series editor is:

>Dr. William F. Pinar
>Department of Curriculum and Instruction
>223 Peabody Hall
>Louisiana State University
>Baton Rouge, LA 70803-4728

To order other books in this series, please contact our Customer Service Department:

>(800) 770-LANG (within the U.S.)
>(212) 647-7706 (outside the U.S.)
>(212) 647-7707 FAX

Or browse online by series:

>www.peterlangusa.com